PREPARE TO WIN

"We're all a bunch of mugs! We work twenty-four hours a day, don't eat; we don't sleep and we spend all of our money just so we can go out again next Sunday and break the damned car."

Horst Kwech, Circa 1970

"There's no such thing as luck—you make your own."

Carroll Shelby, Circa 1968

PREPARE TO WIN

by Carroll Smith

AERO PUBLISHERS, INC.

329 Aviation Road Fallbrook, Cal. 92028

Library of Congress Catalog Card Number: 75-1565

Smith, Carroll
   Prepare to Win.
California   Aero Publishers, Inc.
1975   1-10-75

ISBN 0-9651600-3-3

Printed and Published in the United States by Aero Publishers, Inc.

FOREWORD

Carroll has been racing for a long time. When he started the only change you could make in most cars was the driver, and real race cars had the motor where it belonged (in front). He has been racing, as a paid professional, ever since. Bear that in mind as you read this book.

Carroll, Scat to his friends, is best known for the contribution he made to the Ford Le Mans effort. He was Project Engineer and Team Manager for Carroll Shelby who was prime contractor to Ford. Suffice to say they won Le Mans—and the World Championship. All of this is of very little import to you because, unless you are overburdened with top executives who keep meddling with your racing department, much of the knowledge which Carroll picked up there will be of little use.

More relevant, perhaps, is his experience in getting people out of the shit. He has worked for teams with considerably fewer resources than Shelby/Ford and it is his achievements with these teams that are, to my mind, most significant. All that he seems to require is the same desire to win on the part of the driver and the mechanics (if any) as he has himself. To say that this desire is single minded would be gross understatement. It is fanatic.

His techniques are simple, logical and thus reasonable—both in terms of feasibility and cost. It goes without saying that, particularly in professional racing, a car which finishes almost always takes less money to keep it going. His cars finish.

Carroll accepts the necessity for motors in his cars with a certain amount of reluctance. He regards them as fallible links in an otherwise controllable system. At best they are power units . . . change when necessary. Don't expect him to tell you that a killer motor is the only way to win.

If Carroll accepts motors with reluctance, his attitude toward drivers is ambivalent. One side of this attitude borders downright resentment. Not only are drivers fallible but they prevent proper triangulation of the central bay of the chassis. They require constant tuning and they are subject to unpredictable occurrences of brain fade. On the other hand, Scat was a driver for a long time. He knows what it is that drivers do; he knows how it should be done, and he knows what goes on inside the driver's head. Deep down I think that he likes us. All of this makes Carroll remarkably skillful, if not benevolent, at pumping up a driver who is lagging about and/or calming one down when he has lost control. It also gets the car sorted out in a hurry.

Jon Woodner
Berkeley, California
December 18, 1974

PREFACE

I have been informed that, in order to be respectable, a book of this nature should have an Author's Preface. I certainly want the book to achieve respectability. As nearly as I can tell—from reading the Prefaces to all of the technical books that I own—Prefaces exist so that the Author can explain his motivation and tell the reader why he feels that he was qualified to write the thing.

With respect to motivation I could follow the common trend and state that, since Motor Racing has been good to me, I want to put the sum of my experience back into the Sport. Motor Racing has been good to me because I have worked hard to be successful. I do not consider Motor Racing a Sport—It is a Way of Life and a Business. Anyway, I am not an altruistic person. For many years I have given away a lot of piecemeal advice. This book is an attempt to organize all of the information that I have on the subject of preparation in one place and to sell it—for the technical benefit of the reader and the financial benefit of the Author. If the attempt is successful, PREPARE TO WIN will be followed by TUNE TO WIN.

My qualifications are simple. I have been in Professional Road Racing for a long time. Valid experience is the sum of what we learn—from others or by ourselves. I have been privileged to work with a great many intelligent, talented and dedicated men—Engineers, Drivers, Mechanics and Managers. I have learned something from each of them and a great deal from some of them. I tried listing these men but gave up when the numbers became unmanageable. I thank each of them.

Carroll Smith

TABLE OF CONTENTS

CHAPTER ONE

THREADED FASTENERS

There now exist, on this side of the Atlantic, a large number of sophisticated racing cars. Unfortunately there is no matching abundance of personnel with the experience and know-how to properly set up and maintain the equipment. This sweeping generalization is well supported by the large percentage of non-finishers at all levels of motor racing. Most of these DNFs are caused by parts breaking, coming adrift, bursting asunder or just plain falling off.

There is no shortage of well written and well researched books and articles explaining why various theories having to do with chassis and suspension design, aerodynamics, tire development and other aspects of vehicle dynamics do or do not work. However I have not seen anything in print that offers the beginning racer (or the more experienced racer, for that matter) specific advice about how to prepare his car in such a way that all of the various gubbins will remain in place so that he can concentrate on driving the thing. Nor have there been any offerings to help him obtain all of the performance that the designer put into his car.

We will now attempt to do just that. We will keep theory to an absolute minimum and concentrate on what to use, how to use it and where to obtain it. I make no pretense of objectivity. There are satisfactory alternate ways to do anything. The hardware, methods and approaches that follow are those that I have found most effective and practical.

We will begin by destroying a few illusions:

It is not necessarily true that a decision to start out in a so called lower class of racing will lead to less complex and sensitive equipment. Except for the engine and the wings a Formula Ford is comprised of the same number of parts as a Formula One Car. Further, the arrangement, function and inter-dependence of these parts is virtually identical as is the necessity for careful and knowledgeable assembly if the thing is going to work.

There are only two reasons why your shiny new (or not so shiny old) racer was shipped to you in one piece—if it was. First, it is cheaper to ship that way and, second, it is the only way that the seller could be sure that at least a majority of the parts did indeed reach you. The odds are 100 to 1 that whoever screwed it together knew that HE wasn't going to race it or be responsible for it. Trust him not! Strip the vehicle to its last nut and bolt and start from zero. At worst you will end up with an intimate familiarity with its nethermost regions and any faults that develop in the future will be your own. At best you will discover and rectify, at moderate cost, all of the errors and shortcomings of your predecessor.

THERE IS NO MAGIC! The one basic truth of successful race car preparation bears repeating. THERE IS NO MAGIC! There is only logic, common sense,

forethought, vast amounts of hard work and a fanatic dedication to the task at hand.

TOOLS

If you will twist nuts, then you must have nut twisters. I have seen cars well prepared with the most fantastic assortments of junk tools, but the right ones do make it easier, quicker and more enjoyable. A fortune need not be invested (at least not in the beginning), especially if a discount can be wheedled from a cooperative dealer. With no discount the best value per dollar is Sears' Craftsman line. If you live in Los Angeles pay a visit to Vogel Tool Company and Sam's Tool Mart (Table 2) before going to Sears. With a discount, Proto, S-K and Mac are good. Top of the line is, of course, Snap-On and, while no discount will be obtained, if aesthetics are your bag, it is almost worth the exorbitant price just to look at the tools. What with the price and the number of tools that walk away in the natural course of a season, I don't buy Snap-On.

Besides the odd-ball tools you may require for your particular little beast you will need:

> A set of short pattern combination open end and box end wrenches from 5/16" to 15/16". Make sure that the box ends are twelve pointed.
> A set of open end wrenches, 5/16" to 15/16". Angle offset wrenches are preferable.
> Adjustable (Crescent) wrenches, 6", 8" and 12". May the aircraft industry forgive me, but they *are* the cheapest way to do many things. Please be careful not to ruin the part.
> A set of Allen keys from 3/32" to 3/8". Funds permitting, get a set of Allen sockets (3/8" drive) as well.
> A good set of screwdrivers.
> A 3/8" drive socket set including ratchet handle, speed handle, 3", 8" and 18" extensions, 12 point sockets from 5/16" to 7/8", and a spark plug socket with rubber retaining sleeve.
> Pliers—needle nose, duckbill, diagonal cutters, blacksmith's nippers, vice grips (curved jaw) and, if possible, a pair of Robinson safety wire twisters.
> Gasket scraper and a triangular bearing scraper.
> Small brass hammer and small ball pein hammer.
> Large brass hammer.
> A set of drifts and punches.
> Two or three assorted cold chisels.
> A good pop rivet gun.
> Electric drill motor. Preferably with 3/8" chuck and vari-speed drive.
> High speed steel drill bits from 1/16" to 1/2" in 1/16" increments (with shanks turned to 1/4" or 3/8" so they will fit in the drill motor), plus an assortment of number 21, 29 and 30 drill bits for rivets.
> An 18" machinist's scale and a good 10 foot tape measure.
> A pair of 6" dividers and a 6" inside caliper.
> Left and right handed Wiss aviation sheet metal snips.
> A good 3/8" drive torque wrench.

These are the tools you *need*. Some of the most useful "nice to have" items are:

A set of Bonney wrenches, 11/16", 7/8", 15/16", 1", 1 1/16", 1 1/8", 1 3/16", 1 1/4", 1 3/8", 1 7/16" and 1 1/2" for AN and Aeroquip plumbing fittings.
A pair of dial reading micrometer calipers.
1/8" and 5/32" cleco pins and pliers.
An assortment of "C" clamps and spring clamps.
1/4" drive socket set.
Tap and Die set.
Whitney #5 junior punch set.
A one inch dial indicator.
A couple of finishing hammers, a hide mallet and an assortment of dollies.

It is also necessary to have some convenient method of storing and transporting your tools. I've tried everything from fishing tackle boxes to roll away cabinets. At present I take two small Kennedy machinist's chests to the race track. One contains wrenches and twisting tools for mechanical work and the other contains fabricating and measuring tools along with the usual assortment of bits and pieces which come in handy. Either can be lifted with one hand and carried anywhere.

Remember from the beginning that you will be buying tools and equipment for as long as you are fiddling with race cars— no one ever has enough—and that you may be able to deduct at least a portion of their cost from your income tax. So save the receipts and keep records.

THREADED FASTENERS

Now that we have nut twisters, it is appropriate to attack the most basic parts of the vehicle—nuts and bolts which we will lump under the generic term "threaded fasteners." There is more misinformation in circulation concerning nuts and bolts—particularly bolts—than all the other parts combined. Claims and counterclaims of Grade 6, Grade 8, superior to Grade 8, etc. stare smoothly from the printed page to seduce the unwary. Don't be deceived—use no SAE grade bolts, of whatever specification, in a stressed application. They were never designed for our applications. Their quality control is minimal or non-existent. Furthermore, you will pay more for a so called "grade 8" bolt than you will for a good aircraft bolt and then you are going to have to saw off half the thread, finish the sawed off end and maybe drill a safety wire hole in the head. The F.A.A. doesn't allow the use of SAE graded bolts on aircraft and that should be some sort of a clue.

Many years ago the powers that be, concerned with the frequency with which aircraft parts were coming unbolted and falling out of the sky, sat down and devised a set of standards for aircraft hardware known as the AN (Air Force, Navy) specifications. This has now become MS (Military Specification) and is augmented by NAS (National Aerospace Standard). The full set looks like ten encyclopediae and is not available to the public. Van Deusen Aircraft Supply Company's Hardware Catalog, usually out of print, lists everything we are interested in and is a gem. Failing that, Stanley Dzik's book, available at your local aircraft supply house, runs it a distant second. Standard Pressed Steel Company's catalog, "Bolts For The Aerospace Industry," is a comprehensive list of just about

every available good bolt plus a vast compilation of fastener data.

Basically, the AN, MS and NAS hardware offers us a range of fasteners designed to do a job very similar to ours and manufactured to very stringent standards. Dimensions are closely controlled, surfaces are true, strength and hardness are consistent and dependable, they will bend before they break and every size and configuration is available. All this should cost a fortune—and it would—except that they have been manufactured by the million under pre MacNamara cost plus contracts and are more or less readily available on the surplus market.

For our purposes we need to consider only five series of bolts, two of nuts and three of washers.

BOLTS

For most fine threaded bolt applications use the AN 3 through AN 20 series of airframe bolts illustrated in Figure (6). These are hexagon headed tension bolts available in all UNF sizes. Length of thread is consistent in each diameter and is calculated to accept a washer under the head, a washer under the nut, a full-height tension nut and leave 3 1/2 threads exposed after the nut. Unthreaded (shank or grip) lengths are available from 1/16" to 6" in increments of 1/8", thus providing the proper length bolt for any installation. They come in carbon steel, stainless steel and aluminum. For the steel series which is of interest to us, minimum ultimate tensile strength is 125,000 p.s.i. and shear strength is 75,000 p.s.i. which means that a 3/8" x 24 bolt, properly installed and torqued, has an ultimate strength of 10,000 lb. in tension, 8,200 lb. in single shear and 16,400 lb. in double shear. If you or I ever approach that kind of load without hitting something very solid, we had better buy a new drawing board. The bolts have true bearing surfaces under the heads and, by a simple alteration in part number, are available with the heads and/or shanks drilled for safety wire or cotter pins, thus saving many tedious hours of labor and innumerable broken drill bits. Always buy the bolts with drilled head, if you have the option. They don't cost more, the hole doesn't weaken the bolt and you never know when it is going to come in handy.

For coarse threaded applications use the AN 73A through AN 81A series—sometimes referred to as "engine bolts." Same general specification as AN 3 through AN 20 airframe bolts but with slightly thicker heads and available in both fine and coarse thread. With the notable exceptions of cylinder head bolts and main bearing cap bolts most coarse threaded applications are lightly loaded so that SAE grade 6 or any commercial socket head cap screw can be safely used. The trouble here is that a certain amount of modification of the commercial bolt is going to be necessary to make it work correctly. Stay away from SAE grade 8 bolts as they tend to be brittle.

If you want to go wild on the weight saving bit without spending the bucks for titanium (which tends to gall on steel anyway) you can use the NAS 464 series of shear bolt which have thinner heads (don't use them in tension applications) and shorter thread lengths to suit shear stop (one half height) nuts. They are also made from a stronger alloy than the standard AN airframe bolts with an ultimate tensile strength of 160.000 p.s.i. A very closely equivalent bolt is the NAS 1103 through NAS 1120 series.

English construction tends more and more to demand the use of internal wrenching (Allen) bolts. The NAS 144 through NAS 158 series or the MS 20004 through MS 20024 series come in standard grip lengths and UNF thread configurations and are vastly superior to the standard commercial Allen bolt. They do require the use of NAS 1430 or MS 20002 series countersunk washers under their radiused heads. Commercial Allen bolts are very hard indeed and require a lot of hand work to make them fit the individual application.

If the designer has erred and you are bending a bolt due to overload, use the NAS 624 through NAS 644 series Hi Strength bolts. These twelve point external wrenching bolts are expensive, but you will only buy them once. Again the large radius between the head and the shank requires the use of a countersunk washer.

Standard AN, MS and NAS head markings are illustrated in Figure (1).

WASHERS

Use AN 960 series (.062" thick) and AN 960L series (.031" thick) washers. Surfaces are flat and true and they also make good shims. They are dirt cheap. They are available in both steel and aluminum. When I can get them surplus (rarely) I use the aluminum washers for most applications, although overtightening will ruin them.

NUTS

Use only elastic stop nuts with the full nylon locking ring (MS 20045 or AN 365 for full height and MS 20064 or AN 364 for sheer stop nuts). They are reusable almost indefinitely. The rule of thumb is that if the steel thread is not visibly damaged and you cannot turn the nylon locking ring onto the bolt with your fingers, it is OK. Unlike the various all-metal lock nuts these do not harm the male threads. If the temperature of the installation will exceed 250°F. Use an MS 21045 flex-loc nut plus red loc-tite or use one of the oval section high temperature nuts—"jet nuts" from Earl's Supply are best. An alternate solution for any lock nut is, of course, a castle nut and cotter pin but they are seldom used today—too much work!

Figure (2) shows some of the possible nut, bolt and washer combinations.

HARDWARE

Finding a reasonable source for this hardware will require some detective work. Nation-wide firms that stock mil-spec items are Van Deusen Aircraft Supply and Albany Products but they don't like selling in small quantities, the price is high and the firms generally uncooperative. Earl's Supply has a good line of AN and NAS fasteners by mail order. Your local airport is almost guaranteed to have a good stock and a little snivelling may get you a friendly price. The best bets, however, are the surplus houses—should you be so fortunate as to live near one. Start with the yellow pages under the headings of Aircraft Parts and Supplies. Industrial Fasteners and Government Surplus. Going the surplus route

means learning to identify the parts yourself. It also means doing a lot of looking which can be rewarding if you have the time and enjoy sorting through interesting bits. Take a list of what you need by diameter, thread pitch, grip length and head configuration as well as by part number. Bring a micrometer caliper and be prepared to spend some time digging through bins and boxes. At least you'll get inside some unusual places and meet some interesting people. You will also buy a collection of fascinating gadgets you didn't know that you needed and which will come in handy if you never use them. Buy enough so that you don't have to go back very often. Carefully measure all surplus bolt diameters, particularly the shanks, as many special purpose oversize bolts get surplused. These bolts look standard to the naked eye and are absolutely useless to us.

Every bolt *should* have a washer under the head. Every nut *must* have a washer under it. This prevents galling the part while tightening and minimizes the chance of false torque readings. It also looks nice and shows that you care.

TORQUE

It is perfectly true that every threaded fastener should be installed to a predetermined torque with an accurate torque wrench. The proper torque is usually 90% of the yield strength of the bolt or stud. It is equally true that this is hopelessly impractical. Obviously all engine and transmission bolts and studs must be torqued as must all critical suspension bolts in tension. For the rest, let your conscience be your guide. Remember that over-tightening is responsible for more failures than under-tightening. If in doubt use a torque wrench and the values in Figure (3). These values are for AN 3 through AN 20 airframe bolts and should be increased accordingly for Hi Strength bolts. They are for cadmium plated bolts with no lubricant. Consult your engine builder for critical engine fastener torque values.

SAFETY WIRE

Do not trust lock washers! If it doesn't have some sort of a self locking nut, safety wire it. Always install safety wire so that it tends to tighten rather than to loosen the bolt. Use stainless steel wire of .032" diameter. .020" is handy for #10-32 screws and the like. Do not twist the wire too tightly or it will break—either now or later. Practice makes perfect. Good safety wiring is a fine outlet for one's artistic yearnings. The best $20 you can spend is for a pair of Robinson safety wire twisters. All other brands are vastly inferior. If you cannot afford the twisters use duckbill pliers and time. After cutting off the end of the wire, double it back on itself tightly to prevent .063" holes in your body when next you come near the part. Figure (4) illustrates the do's and don'ts of safety wiring.

PRACTICAL PROCEDURE

One of the least appreciated factors in bolt use is the fact that the threaded portion of a bolt should never be loaded in shear. This not only decreases the strength of the installation by decreasing the cross sectional area of the loaded portion of the bolt, but a thread inside a sized hole is liable to act as a low speed mill, doing unthinkable things to the hole.

11

Figure (1): Specification of Common Surplus Bolts

X = NON CORROSION RESISTANT STEEL ▭ = ALUMINUM
▭ = CORROSION RESISTANT STEEL △ = CLOSE TOLERANCE BOLT
 E = OVERSIZE SHANK

HEAD MARKING	DESIGNATION	ULTIMATE TENSILE STRENGTH	NOTES
(hex head marked X)	BOLT, MACHINE AIRCRAFT AN 3 THRU AN 20	125,000 p.s.i.	MOST COMMON SURPLUS BOLT FINE THREAD ONLY SUITABLE FOR ALL CHASSIS APPLICATIONS DRILLED HEAD AVAILABLE
(hex head, drilled, marked X)	BOLT, MACHINE AIRCRAFT DRILLED HEAD AN 73 THRU AN 81	125,000 p.s.i.	AVAILABLE BOTH FINE AND COARSE THREAD INTERCHANGEABLE WITH AN 3 THRU AN 20
(round head with triangle)	BOLT, MACHINE AIRCRAFT, CLOSE TOLERANCE AN 173 THRU AN 186	125,000 p.s.i.	SHANK DIAMETER SLIGHTLY OVERSIZE TO PRECISION FIT REAMED HOLE
(hex head marked NAS 1107, triangle, X)	BOLT, HEX HEAD, CLOSE TOLERANCE, SHORT THREAD NAS 1103 THRU NAS 1120	160,000 p.s.i.	SHORT THREAD FOR USE WITH SHEAR STOP NUT ONLY. CLOSE TOLERANCE FIT THIN HEAD FOR SHEAR APPLICATIONS.
(hex head marked NAS 464, triangle, X)	BOLT, SHEAR, CLOSE TOLERANCE NAS 464	160,000 p.s.i.	NOT SUITABLE FOR TENSION APPLICATIONS. USE SHEAR STOP NUT ONLY. SAVES SOME WEIGHT.
(hex head marked NAS 1307, triangle, X)	BOLT, HEX HEAD, CLOSE TOLERANCE NAS 1303 THRU NAS 1320	160,000 p.s.i.	SIMILAR TO AN 3 THRU AN 20. MUCH STRONGER BOLT.
(hex head marked NAS 2907, X, triangle, E)	BOLT, .0156" OVERSIZE SHANK, CLOSE TOLERANCE NAS 2903 THRU NAS 2920	160,000 p.s.i.	DO NOT BUY! WILL NOT FIT STANDARD HOLE
(hex head marked NAS 3007, X, triangle, E)	BOLT, .0156" OVERSIZE SHANK, CLOSE TOLERANCE NAS 3003 THRU NAS 3020	160,000 p.s.i.	DO NOT BUY! WILL NOT FIT STANDARD HOLE
(internal hex head, and NAS 147 side view)	BOLT, INTERNAL WRENCHING, STEEL NAS 144 THRU NAS 158	160,000 to 180,000 p.s.i.	SAME AS MS 20004 THRU MS 20024. INTERNAL HEX MAY STRIP WITH CONTINUED USE
(12 point external wrenching head)	BOLT, 12 POINT EXTERNAL WRENCHING NAS 624 THRU 644	180,000 p.s.i.	SUPER BOLT!

BOLT TYPE:
ULT TENS:
SINGLE SHEAR:
DOUBLE SHEAR:

SAE GRADE 5
14,200 lb.
10,300 lb.
20,600 lb.

AN 7-21 A
13,600 lb.
11,250 lb.
22,500 lb.

NAS 464-7A-25
16,800 lb.
14,300 lb.
28,600 lb.

NAS 627-25
23,175 lb.
16,250 lb.
32,500 lb.

1.50"

WASHER AN 960-716

WASHER AN 960L-716

WASHER MS 20002-716 (COUNTERSUNK)

START OF THREAD

AN 365—7/16 x 20 ELASTIC STOP NUT

AN 364—7/16 x 20 SHEAR STOP NUT

Figure (2): Nut and Bolt Combinations for 1.50" Work Thickness

13

Figure (3): Recommended Nut Torques for AN 3 Thru AN 8 Bolts

BOLT DIAMETER THREAD PITCH	FULL HEIGHT ELASTIC STOP NUT	1/2 HEIGHT ELASTIC STOP NUT
10 x 32	3 to 4 lb/ft	2 to 3 lb/ft
1/4 x 28	8 to 10 lb/ft	5 to 6 lb/ft
5/16 x 24	18 to 20 lb/ft	10 to 12 lb/ft
3/8 x 24	32 to 34 lb/ft	20 to 22 lb/ft
7/16 x 20	68 to 72 lb/ft	40 to 42 lb/ft
1/2 x 20	78 to 82 lb/ft	50 to 54 lb/ft
10 x 24	3 to 4 lb/ft	2 lb/ft
1/4 x 20	6 to 8 lb/ft	3 to 4 lb/ft
5/16 x 18	12 to 14 lb/ft	8 to 10 lb/ft
3/8 x 16	22 to 24 lb/ft	13 to 15 lb/ft
7/16 x 14	38 to 40 lb/ft	22 to 24 lb/ft

Also the major diameter of the thread is slightly smaller than the shank of the bolt which results in either a loose fit or a stepped diameter within the bore. Whenever the correct grip length bolt is available, use it. If it is not, use the next size longer and more washers. Never die-cut more threads onto a bolt. All good bolts have rolled threads. A die leaves a sharp "vee" section at the thread root and a jagged transition from thread to shank, both of which are certified stress raisers and a clear invitation to failure. Lathe-cut threads are acceptable if necessary so long as a slightly radiused tool is used and attention is paid to the thread run out to avoid the creation of a stress raiser. All this is especially true of tension and single shear applications.

If a bolt doesn't want to go into its hole there is usually a perfectly reasonable explanation. It is unlikely that a large hammer is going to help and serious harm may result from its use. The cause is almost always misalignment of one or more parts. A tapered alignment pin and a little patience will usually solve the problem. In extreme cases I use a dummy bolt with a gradual taper at the threaded end. The dummy bolt is tapped and turned (not beaten) through from the backside to align the parts. The proper bolt is then tapped through from the front side leaving everything in its place and the dummy bolt on the floor. I carry a whole series of tapered dummy bolts around with me. If space doesn't allow this procedure and time is of the essence, grind a 45° tapered flat on one side of the bolt to be used and tap it through.

While on the subject of holes for pins and fasteners it should be pointed out that drill bits, particularly with hand held drill motors, tend to cut oversize. The best procedure is to drill the hole to the next undersize letter or number drill and ream to finished size. If possible the operation should be done on a lathe or a drill press. This is never practical in the field but a set of fractional sized reamers is a practical addition to the tool kit. Close attention to the physical condition of one's drill bits pays large dividends in the quality of the holes one produces.

INSERTS

Another side of the fastener question has to do with inserts. It is often necessary to attach something (a clamp, a stop, a bracket, an access panel) to a tube, sheet metal panel or casting where you can't use a nut and a bolt and don't want to use rivets. Usually you will want the item to be attached to be quickly and easily detachable. You have several choices. Figure (5) illustrates some of the alternatives for sheet metal.

Figure (4): Safety Wire Application

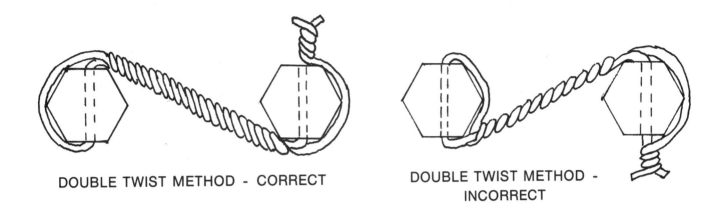

DOUBLE TWIST METHOD - CORRECT

DOUBLE TWIST METHOD - INCORRECT

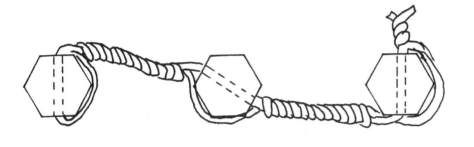

DOUBLE TWIST METHOD - MULTIPLE FASTENER

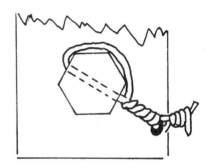

DOUBLE TWIST - SINGLE FASTENER

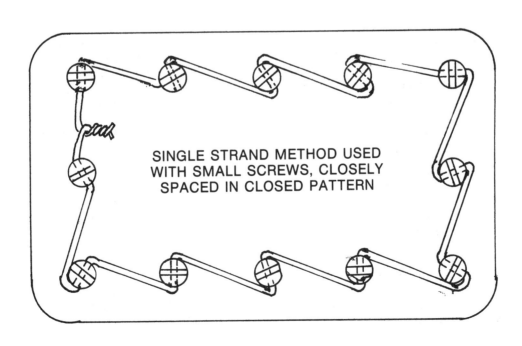

SINGLE STRAND METHOD USED WITH SMALL SCREWS, CLOSELY SPACED IN CLOSED PATTERN

Figure (5): Methods of Attaching Auxiliaries to Sheet Metal Panels

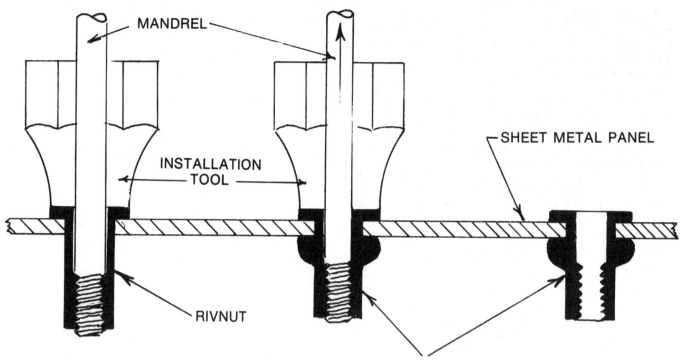

MANDREL

INSTALLATION TOOL

SHEET METAL PANEL

RIVNUT

RIVNUT BY B. F. GOODRICH - ALSO AVAILABLE AS COUNTERSINK UNIT
THE NUTSERT BY AVDELL IS SIMILAR BUT LESS POSITIVE (AND LESS BULKY)

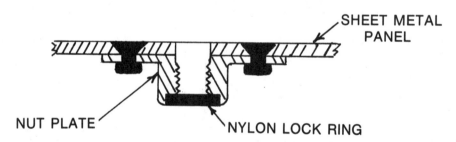

SHEET METAL PANEL

NUT PLATE

NYLON LOCK RING

NUTPLATE - AVAILABLE IN MANY CONFIGURATIONS IN BOTH STEEL AND ALUMINUM

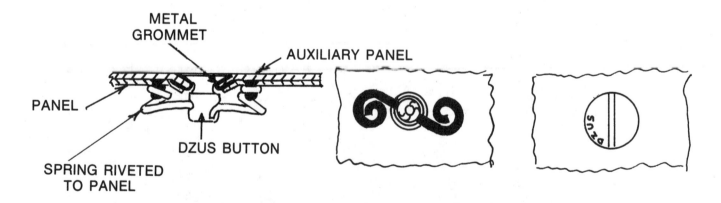

METAL GROMMET

AUXILIARY PANEL

PANEL

DZUS BUTTON

SPRING RIVETED TO PANEL

DZUS FASTENER - 1/4 TURN TO LOCK
AVAILABLE IN MANY CONFIGURATIONS AND SIZES

NUT PLATES

The nut plate provides a quick and inexpensive way to end up with a captive self locking nut on the inside of a sheet metal panel. They are available in a wide variety of shapes and configurations to suit almost any application. The only drawback is that they cannot be used in blind applications. Some care is necessary in laying out the location of nut plates and in their installation to ensure that everything lines up and fits when the job is done. Nut plate drill guides are available at nominal cost from your aircraft supply house, but no one ever has or uses them. The usual method is to drill and deburr the holes in the item to be mounted and then to transfer the holes carefully onto the panel. Attach the required nut plates temporarily to the panel with machine screws and then drill the rivet holes in the panel using the factory supplied holes in the nut plates for drill guides. Before installing the nut plates for real it is necessary to deburr (and probably countersink) the holes in the panel. During the deburring process it is wise to drill the machine screw holes in the panel 1/32" oversize. It is also wise to perform this operation one nut plate at a time. If all of the nut plates are removed at once, and not put back in their original locations, any dimensional errors in the position of the rivet holes will result in one or more nut plates ending up off location. Nut plates are also available with the nut part floating in a cage allowing some alignment to take place after assembly.

RIV—NUTS

B. F. Goodrich markets a marvelous device called the Riv-Nut which is the answer for blind applications. This is an internally threaded blind rivet easily installed with fairly expensive tooling. The installed unit provides a stable female-threaded anchor in thin sheet metal at reasonable cost. Avdel and others make similar widgets but I have found the Riv-Nut to be superior because it is not particularly fussy about exact hole size and, if properly installed, it is almost impossible to twist out. It is available in both steel and aluminum. For our purposes the aluminum is best—besides, it is easier to drill out when the time comes.

Nothing is more frustrating than having a threaded anchor twist when you are trying to remove an access panel or whatever. I strongly suggest removing all of the idiot devices found on English racing cars and replacing them either with nut plates or with Riv-Nuts.

DZUS FASTENERS

For attaching body panels, either metal or fibreglass, and non-structural access panels nothing beats the ubiquitous Dzus fastener. Again a multitude of types, sizes and materials is available—often on the surplus market. Easiest to use is the EHF series which is flange mounted and requires no tooling. All of the other types require special tools. However, the EHF series seldom appears on the surplus market and the tools are very easy to make. The standard series also looks neater. Speaking of looks, don't paint the actual head of a Dzus button as the paint will flake off the second time you unfasten the Dzus. It is also best to use something other than the usual small screwdriver when operating the device to avoid damaging the slot. Both the buttons and the spring wires come in different lengths to accomodate varying thicknesses of material.

THREADED INSERTS

Murphy's well known laws apply particularly to threaded holes in aluminum and magnesium castings. Consequently a threaded hole in either material from which the stud or bolt will be removed with any frequency requires a threaded insert. Otherwise it can be guaranteed that the threads will strip and that they will strip at the most inopportune time. A variety of suitable inserts is on the market. To my knowledge all of them are good. I use Helicoils because I happen to own all of the taps and inserters to use them and because the Helicoils themselves are very cheap (the tooling is not). Long-Lok Corporation has a device called the T-Sert which features a nylon self locking element and which installs with standard taps and drills. The same is true of Newton Corporation's Keen Sert. I consider Rosans to be the best, but they require a lot of tooling.

LOC-TITE

We'll close the threaded fastener discussion with a few words about Loc-Tite, the racer's salvation. Loc-Tite, in its various grades, is a series of liquid self hardening resins which means simply that IF the right grade is PROPERLY applied to a threaded fastener, it will take the same amount of torque to undo the thing that it took to tighten it and, further, that it WILL NOT vibrate loose. This does not mean that a drop of any old kind of Loc-Tite on a dirty, oil covered bolt will keep the bolt from coming undone. It also does not mean that Loc-Tite is a substitute for safety wire, self locking nuts or sound engineering practice.

For our purposes there are two grades of Loc-Tite locking resins, one sealant, two cleaners and a gap-filler. To lock a stud in place use Stud Lock (red). To lock a bolt into a blind hole or a non-locking nut onto a bolt use Nut Lock (blue). To seal a joint from leaking use Hydraulic Seal. To clean any and all surfaces prior to the application of any grade of Loc-Tite use lacquer thinner, acetone or MEK. Loc-Tite cleaner is too expensive. Do not use gasoline which leaves an oily film. Loc-Tite applied to a dirty or oily surface achieves only one result—a false sense of confidence which can only lead to your (or at least the part's) undoing.

My last words on Loc-Tite concern Loc-Tite Bearing Mount. Despite your best efforts and intentions, you will occasionally come across a loose bearing housing or a loose bush with no replacement available and no time or facility for remachining. Bearing Mount, used according to directions, will save the day. Carry it with you; use it when you must. But replace or re-machine the offending item as soon as possible. Do not use it indiscriminately. In the presence of a proper mechanical fit it is just not necessary and makes disassembly difficult (heat helps). The same is true of the use of Loc-Tite compounds in conjunction with self locking fasteners.

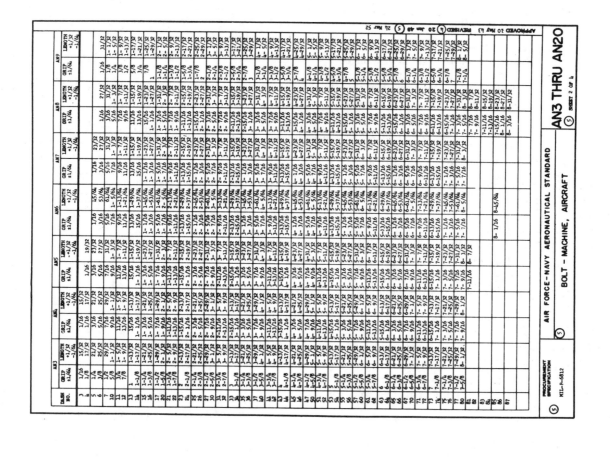

Figure (6): Airforce-Navy Aeronautical Standards for Aircraft Machine Bolts

18

CHAPTER TWO

PLUMBING AND PLUMBING STUFF

If I were asked what single category of failure (other than brain) is the most common cause of race car retirements, my answer would be "plumbing failure." Give a thought to the number of cars, within the scope of your personal knowledge, that DNF'd last season because of water, oil or hydraulic line failure. It is incredible!

The rather inelegant generic term "plumbing" includes all of the lines, tubes, hoses, fittings, clamps and holding brackets which transport fluids from one part of the car to another as well as the tanks and reservoirs in which the fluids are stored. We will discuss the reservoirs later as component parts of their individual systems. For our present purposes we will divide the lines, hoses and fittings into four convenient groups: water, oil and fuel, hydraulic fluid and, finally, vent and breather. For now we will confine the discussion to the mechanics of plumbing, leaving the design of the systems to their own chapters.

WATER SYSTEM

Water lines are about as simple as you can get. Maximum pressure involved is 22 p.s.i. Maximum temperature is 256°F. (for a very short time). The lines exist only to carry hot water from the engine to the water radiator or radiators and cooled water back to the engine. With these requirements it should be impossible to go wrong. Not so! Water line failures are distressingly common and are almost always caused by use of the wrong materials, improper procedures or by scraping the water line on the race track. The rules are short and simple, but crucial:

(1) Throw away all of the present rubber water lines.

(2) Throw away all of the "Made in England" hose clamps and any other hose clamps which are not stainless steel and which do not feature worm gear construction with the slots in the band section of the clamp extending all the way through the band.

(3) Bead the ends of all metal lines. Earl's Supply sells a very good Parker tube beading kit at a nominal price. Leave a minimum 1/2" gap between adjacent ends of metal lines to be connected by rubber hose. This will put some compliance into the system and allow the various pieces to align themselves without stretching or straining anything. Maximum gap should be two diameters.

(4) Use only Gates "Green Stripe" rubber water hose. No doubt there are equally good hoses available from other manufacturers. I have not found them. As "Green Stripe" is difficult to locate, I should point out that all moulded hoses are abominable. To be considered, a water hose must have a fabric core and must be spiral wound. Dayco is a good quality easily obtainable brand. The use of a silicon based lubricant on the hose I.D. makes installation much easier and will come in very handy when the time comes to remove the hose. Hoses should be discarded after six months of use.

(5) Use only good quality worm gear hose clamps in which the slots go all the way through the band. Stainless is much to be preferred. Ideal is a good, readily available brand. If possible get the type which are operable by both a screwdriver and a 5/16" wrench.

Make very sure that the clamp is installed on the tubing side of the bead on the metal line and leave a minimum of one clamp width of hose beyond the clamp. If in doubt, or if the clamp is going to be particularly inaccessible, double clamping costs and weighs nothing and is good insurance. Install the clamps so that you can get a screwdriver or wrench onto each one without dismantling the car. Tighten all clamps with the system hot and safety wire the clamps. If nothing else, the wire will tell you that the clamp has been tightened.

(6) Make damned sure that no part of the water system, rubber or metal, is the lowest point of the car, can rub against anything at all, is going to cook a portion of the driver or is immediately adjacent to fuel, brake or clutch lines.

(7) For rigid tubing use a weldable aluminum alloy. 3003 is cheapest. 5052 bends easiest. For straight lengths .049" wall is sufficient. If the tube is to be bent buy the tubing in the annealed condition with .063" wall. Pressure check all welds prior to installation of the tube. Support rigid tubing with a clamp or cradle at least every 36" and at each end. Tape the inside of all cradles and clamps to prevent chafing the tube. Particularly if the tube is to run outside the car where it will be exposed to the abrasive effects of sand and rocks, it pays to cover it with vinyl heat shrink tubing (but only after the tube has been pressure checked). Some sort of chafing strip between the tube and the chassis is a must.

(8) An 18 or 22 p.s.i. pressure cap costs no more than a 12 p.s.i. unit and is excellent insurance. The aluminum Corvette header tank is as good as anything you can make, certainly lighter and probably cheaper. It is also large enough. Safety wire the pressure cap. I run a total recovery closed water system so that I don't have to worry about replacing the overflow from the header tank when things get really hot—as in during a pit stop. Make sure that the header tank is above top water level in the engine and that all circulating lines are below it.

(9) Pressure check the entire system frequently. Some engines must have the cylinder heads hot torqued prior to pressure testing. The Stant Corporation makes a very good pressure test kit at a nominal price.

(10) Install a small diameter bleed from the top of the water radiator (outlet side) to the header tank. Depending on the engine and the water pump you may also have to bleed the cylinder head top water points and/or the eye of the water pump to the header tank. The use of a "swirl pot" in the water outlet line or lines from the engine will cure almost all steam pocket and aeration problems. The top of the swirl pot must be bled back to the header tank.

(11) Use some sort of water soluble oil (in very small quantity) in the coolant. If you are using an aluminum radiator, block or heads or if you have water in contact with magnesium (as in the engine plate) use one of the standard corrosion inhibitors. Do not use any of the leak fixers as they will clog the radiator cores. If you insist on using a leak fixer, do not use the pellet type and don't keep adding to it. All of the proprietary coolant additives which claim to increase cooling efficiency are useless as is ethylene glycol which merely increases the boiling point and is a very efficient leak seeker.

(12) A stout 1/4" mesh by .062" wire diameter stainless steel screen placed at least two inches in front of the radiator will stop almost any rock. If this seems excessive, imagine the impact force exerted by a 1/4 lb. rock when hit by a car at 150 mph. If no rock screen is installed, sooner or later you will lose a radiator.

(13) Inspect lines very frequently for cuts, chafes, dings, etc. Temporary repairs can be effected by epoxy resins or by clamping a

piece of rubber water hose over the offending portion. Permanent repairs should be welded. Weldco's aluminum solder is invaluable in emergencies.

(14) Radiator cores fill up with rubber dust, dirt and track grime very quickly. The fins get bent by the little chips that pass through the rock screens. It is essential to keep the cores clean and the fins straight. It is also essential to have the radiator backflushed and boiled out every couple of months. Painting it black will do no good at all, will probably impair cooling efficiency and will make it difficult to repair.

(15) So much for the water lines!

OIL LINES AND FITTINGS

The most frequently asked question regarding oil and fuel lines is, "Is all of that lovely and expensive red and blue and silver Aeroquip stuff really necessary?". No, it isn't necessary, but if you can afford it it does offer some very real advantages over anything else that will do the job:

(1) It doesn't leak.
(2) It doesn't come undone.
(3) It doesn't burst, collapse, wear through or wear out. The stainless steel protective braid will, however, abrade through just about anything that it comes in contact with.
(4) It is virtually heat and flame proof.
(5) It is the lightest stuff that will do the job well.
(6) It is versatile and indefinitely re-usable.
(7) If not idiot proof it is at least fool proof.
(8) It looks nice.

Luckily, a little forethought planning and scrounging can save a lot of money. Step one is to obtain Aeroquip's Catalog #105 and the Earl's Supply Catalog. You are interested in Aeroquip 601 lightweight engine hose and the "Little Gem" aluminum hose ends. Familiarize yourself with the catalogs and hit the surplus trail again. Aircraft salvage operations, if you can find one, are an excellent source for both Aeroquip stuff and AN fittings. Some remarkable bargains can still be found. Any bargain means a lot of dis-assembling and cleaning but this is no big thing. If you can't find what you need locally, order it from Earl's. Be very specific and order it all at one time. Make up your own lines rather than paying someone else to do it for you. Earl and Joe Factor both feature bargains in made up lines with hose ends as does Cal Aero Supply. United Parcel Service is the best delivery method.

Since Aeroquip is both bullet proof and reusable, a few well chosen spares will be sufficient. Remember, however, that you are not likely to find much of a stock available at the East Nowhere Grand Prix. The Aeroquip catalog will tell you all that you need to know about assembling and running the line and fittings. Do it their way and remember that too long is a lot better than too short. When re-using fittings make very sure that you get any residual bits of neoprene out of the recess in the sleeve—an old hacksaw blade ground into a very thin hook does the job nicely. Cut the line square and clean—a beverly shear does an excellent job as does a very sharp, very wide chisel with a BIG hammer and a hard backing surface. If none of the above is available, wrap the line with masking tape and cut it with a 32 teeth per inch hacksaw blade.

Obtain an assortment of plastic caps and plugs for sealing hose ends and AN fittings when they are apart. With respect to oil and fuel systems cleanliness is a good bit ahead of Godliness. Never discard any Aeroquip fitting or part of a

fitting unless it is either bent or broken. Never discard a piece of line longer than 4". You'll find a use for it someday.

Since the bulk surplus supply of Aeroquip has dried up, Earl's Supply has recently introduced their very own hose ends. They are comparable in every way and directly interchangeable with Aeroquip. They are also available in a bunch of useful configurations for racers that Aeroquip never thought of—including a line of swiveling fittings. Clever people! They are also slightly less expensive.

Another excellent substitute is the Speedflex line available from Weaver Brothers. This is a push-on type fitting which is slightly lighter, considerably less bulky and much more difficult to remove than Aeroquip.

A set of "Bonney" wrenches makes working on Aeroquip and such much more pleasant and vastly reduces the possibility of overtightening. They are expensive at retail but some surplus houses, notably Vogel Tool Co., stock them at reasonable prices.

Work clean, keep lines to minimal length and bend radii large enough to prevent kinking. Keep hot fluid lines away from fuel, hydraulic and cooled fluid lines as well as away from the driver. Support lines by means of clamps or ti-wraps to convenient tubes, panels, or bulkheads. Make very sure that all lines and fittings are well above the bottom of the chassis and that they clear all suspension links during the full range of travel. Also make sure that no line is going to be pinched or crushed when the car is jacked.

AN FITTINGS

To go with the Aeroquip fittings and lines you will need a supply of aluminum AN fittings. These are available from the same sources in a variety of configurations. Order by part number to avoid disappointment. Figure (7) lists about every fitting you will ever use. You need not concern yourself with any material except aluminum.

Tapered pipe threads should be avoided when at all possible. Sometimes it is not possible—or practical—to avoid them. Do not overtighten tapered pipe threads—especially into light alloy castings. Always use an anti-sieze compound on tapered pipe threads. To convert English parallel pipe threads to American tapered pipe (or, better, to straight threads) either drill out the offending hole and tap it American or silver solder BSP threads to steel AN fittings. To convert the ubiquitous Coventry Pressings oil coolers to AN ports, saw off the stock BSP ports (plugging the thing with a rag coated with heavy grease will keep the swarf out of the cooler) and heliarc the appropriate AN fitting in place.

If you have a choice always use an "O" ring and a straight thread with the AN 815 union in preference to a tapered pipe thread. You will seldom have this choice except when designing new parts.

"O" RINGS

"O" ring seals should be used in preference to any other kind. Parker Seal Company's "O" Ring Handbook (Catalog #5700) is the bible and should be adhered to in detail. It must be stressed that the "O" ring is not a gasket and cannot be treated as such. Groove design varies with the application and particularly with the direction of pressure. It is all in the handbook—in the "Military Seals" section.

Figure (7): Aircraft AN and MS Tube Fittings

AN 807 — ADAPTER-- HOSE TO BULKHEAD

AN807 NO. BRASS	ALUM.	HOSE I.D.	TUBE O.D.
4	4D	1/4	1/4
6	6D	3/8	3/8
8	8D	1/2	1/2
10	10D	5/8	5/8
12	12D	3/4	3/4
16	16D	1	1
20	20D	1-1/4	1-1/4
24	24D	1-1/2	1-1/2

AN 838 — HOSE TO BULKHEAD

AN838 NO. BRASS	ALUM.	HOSE I.D.	TUBE O.D.
4	4D	1/4	1/4
6	6D	3/8	3/8
8	8D	1/2	1/2
10	10D	5/8	5/8
12	12D	3/4	3/4
16	16D	1	1
20	20D	1-1/4	1-1/4
24	24D	1-1/2	1-1/2

AN 840 — ADAPTER— HOSE TO PIPE THREAD

AN840 NO. COPPER ALLOY	ALUM.	HOSE I.D.	PIPE SIZE
4	4D	1/4	1/8
6	6D	3/8	1/4
8	8D	1/2	3/8
10	10D	5/8	1/2
12	12D	3/4	3/4
16	16D	3/4	3/4

AN 842 — ELBOW—PIPE THREAD AND HOSE 90°

AN842 NO. COPPER ALLOY	ALUM.	HOSE I.D.	PIPE SIZE
4	4D	1/4	1/8
6	6D	3/8	1/4
8	8D	1/2	3/8
10	10D	5/8	1/2
12	12D	3/4	3/4
16	16D	1	3/4

AN 844 — ELBOW—PIPE THREAD AND HOSE 45°

AN844 COPPER ALLOY	ALUM.	HOSE I.D.	PIPE SIZE
4	4D	1/4	1/8
6	6D	3/8	1/4
8	8D	1/2	3/8
10	10D	5/8	1/2
12	12D	3/4	3/4
16	16D	1	3/4

PIPE FITTINGS

Produced to all applicable Government specs and drawings. Manufactured in aluminum alloy, brass, and steel as shown in the tables. Available in larger sizes than shown. (All prices and delivery information upon request, on fittings not shown in price list.)
Use AN or MS number plus dash number when ordering. Example: AN 911-4 (Nipple, pipe thread ½'', Brass.) Prices on request.

AN 910 — COUPLING—PIPE THREAD

AN910 NO. COPPER ALLOY	ALUM.	PIPE THREAD
1	1D	1/8
2	2D	1/4
3	3D	3/8
4	4D	1/2
6	6D	3/4
8	8D	1
10	10D	1-1/4

AN 911 — NIPPLE—PIPE THREAD

AN911 NO. COPPER ALLOY	ALUM.	PIPE THREAD
1	1D	1/8
2	2D	1/4
3	3D	3/8
4	4D	1/2
6	6D	3/4
8	8D	1
10	10D	1-1/4

AN 912 — BUSHING—REDUCER PIPE

AN912 NO. COPPER ALLOY	ALUM.	PIPE SIZES
1	1D	1/4-1/8
2	2D	3/8-1/4
3	3D	3/8-1/8
4	4D	1/2-3/8
5	5D	1/2-1/4
6	6D	1/2-1/8
7	7D	3/4-1/2
8	8D	3/4-3/8
9	9D	3/4-1/4
10	10D	1-3/4
11	11D	1-1/2
12	12D	1-3/8
13	13D	1-1/4-3/4

AN 913   MS 20913 — PLUG— SQUARE HEAD PIPE THREAD

AN913 NO. COPPER ALLOY	ALUM.	STEEL	PIPE THREAD
1	1D	1S	1/8
2	2D	2S	1/4
3	3D	3S	3/8
4	4D	4S	1/2
6	6D	6S	3/4
8	8D	8S	1
10	10D	10S	1-1/4

AN 914 — ELBOW—INTERNAL AND EXTERNAL PIPE THREAD 90°

AN914 NO. COPPER ALLOY	ALUM.	PIPE THREAD
1	1D	1/8
2	2D	1/4
3	3D	3/8
4	4D	1/2
6	6D	3/4
8	8D	1
10	10D	1-1/4

AN 915 — ELBOW—INTERNAL AND EXTERNAL PIPE 45°

AN915 NO. COPPER ALLOY	ALUM.	PIPE THREAD
1	1D	1/8
2	2D	1/4
3	3D	3/8
4	4D	1/2
6	6D	3/4
8	8D	1
10	10D	1-1/4

AN 916 — ELBOW—INTERNAL PIPE THREAD 90°

AN916 NO. COPPER ALLOY	ALUM.	PIPE THREAD
1	1D	1/8
2	2D	1/4
3	3D	3/8
4	4D	1/2
6	6D	3/4
8	8D	1
10	10D	1-1/4

AN 917 — TEE—INTERNAL PIPE THREAD

AN917 NO. COPPER ALLOY	ALUM.	PIPE THREAD
1	1D	1/8
2	2D	1/4
3	3D	3/8
4	4D	1/2
6	6D	3/4
8	8D	1
10	10D	1-1/4

AN 918 — CROSS—INTERNAL PIPE THREAD

AN918 NO. COPPER ALLOY	ALUM.	PIPE THREAD
1	1D	1/8
2	2D	1/4
3	3D	3/8
4	4D	1/2
6	6D	3/4
8	8D	1
10	10D	1-1/4

AN 775 — BOLT—UNIVERSAL FITTING

AN775 NO. STEEL	ALUM.	TUBE O.D.	THREAD SIZE
4	4D	1/4	7/16–20
5	5D	5/16	1/2–20
6	6D	3/8	9/16–18
8	8D	1/2	3/4–16
10	10D	5/8	7/8–14

AN 776 — ELBOW—UNIVERSAL 90

AN776 NO. STEEL	ALUM.	TUBE O.D.	THREAD SIZE
4	4D	1/4	7/16–20
5	5D	5/16	1/2–20
6	6D	3/8	9/16–18
8	8D	1/2	3/4–16
10	10D	5/8	7/8–14

AN 777 — ELBOW—UNIVERSAL 75°

AN777 NO. STEEL	ALUM.	TUBE O.D.	THREAD SIZE
4	4D	1/4	7/16–20
5	5D	5/16	1/2–20
6	6D	3/8	9/16–18
8	8D	1/2	3/4–16
10	10D	5/8	7/8–14

AN 778 — ELBOW—UNIVERSAL 45°

AN778 NO. STEEL	ALUM.	TUBE O.D.	THREAD SIZE
4	4D	1/4	7/16–20
5	5D	5/16	1/2–20
6	6D	3/8	9/16–18
8	8D	1/2	3/4–16
10	10D	5/8	7/8–14

AN 804 — TEE—FLARED TUBE WITH BULKHEAD ON RUN

AN804 NO. STEEL	ALUM.	TUBE O.D.	THREAD SIZE
2	2D	1/8	5/16–24
3	3D	3/16	3/8–24
4	4D	1/4	7/16–20
5	5D	5/16	1/2–20
6	6D	3/8	9/16–18
8	8D	1/2	3/4–16
10	10D	5/8	7/8–14
12	12D	3/4	1-1/16–12
16	16D	1	1-5/16–12

AN 806 — PLUG—FLARED TUBE

AN806 NO. STEEL	ALUM.	TUBE O.D.
2	2D	1/8
3	3D	3/16
4	4D	1/4
5	5D	5/16
6	6D	3/8
8	8D	1/2
10	10D	5/8
12	12D	3/4
16	16D	1

AN 814   AN 814-L (SHOWN) — PLUG AND BLEEDER SCREW THREAD

AN814 NO. STEEL	ALUM.	TUBE O.D.	THREAD SIZE
2	2D	1/8	5/16–24
3	3D	3/16	3/8–24
4	4D	1/4	7/16–20
5	5D	5/16	1/2–20
6	6D	3/8	9/16–18
8	8D	1/2	3/4–16
10	10D	5/8	7/8–14
12	12D	3/4	1-1/16–12
16	16D	1	1-5/16–12

AN 815 — UNION—FLARED TUBE

AN815 NO. STEEL	ALUM.	TUBE O.D.	THREAD SIZE
2	2D	1/8	5/16–24
3	3D	3/16	3/8–24
4	4D	1/4	7/16–20
5	5D	5/16	1/2–20
6	6D	3/8	9/16–18
8	8D	1/2	3/4–16
10	10D	5/8	7/8–14
12	12D	3/4	1-1/16–12
16	16D	1	1-5/16–12

AN 816 — NIPPLE—FLARED TUBE AND PIPE THREAD

AN816 NO. STEEL	ALUM.	TUBE O.D.	PIPE SIZE
2	2D	1/8	1/8
3	3D	3/16	1/8
4	4D	1/4	1/8
5	5D	5/16	1/8
6	6D	3/8	1/4
7	7D	1/2	1/4
8	8D	1/2	3/8
10	10D	5/8	1/2
12	12D	3/4	3/4
16	16D	1	1

AN 817 — NUT—SLEEVE COUPLING

AN817 NO. STEEL	ALUM.	TUBE O.D.	THREAD SIZE
2	2D	1/8	5/16–24
3	3D	3/16	3/8–24
4	4D	1/4	7/16–20
5	5D	5/16	1/2–20
6	6D	3/8	9/16–18
8	8D	1/2	3/4–16
10	10D	5/8	7/8–14
12	12D	3/4	1-1/16–12
16	16D	1	1-5/16–12

AN 818 — NUT—COUPLING

AN818 NO. STEEL	ALUM.	TUBE O.D.	THREAD SIZE
2	2D	1/8	5/16–24
3	3D	3/16	7/16–20
4	4D	1/4	7/16–20
5	5D	5/16	1/2–20
6	6D	3/8	9/16–18
8	8D	1/2	3/4–16
10	10D	5/8	7/8–14
12	12D	3/4	1-1/16–12
16	16D	1	1-5/16–12

AN 819   MS 20819 — SLEEVE—COUPLING

AN819 OR MS20819 NO. STEEL	ALUM.	TUBE O.D.
2	2D	1/8
3	3D	3/16
4	4D	1/4
5	5D	5/16
6	6D	3/8
8	8D	1/2
10	10D	5/8
12	12D	3/4
16	16D	1

AN 820 — CAP—FLARED TUBE FITTING

AN820 NO.	TUBE O.D.	THREAD SIZE
2	1/8	5/16–24
3	3/16	3/8–24
4	1/4	7/16–20
5	5/16	1/2–20
6	3/8	9/16–18
8	1/2	3/4–16
10	5/8	7/8–14
12	3/4	1-1/16–12
16	1	1-5/16–12

AN 821 — ELBOW—FLARED TUBE 90°

AN821 NO. STEEL	ALUM.	TUBE O.D.	THREAD SIZE
2	2D	1/8	5/16–24
3	3D	3/16	3/8–24
4	4D	1/4	7/16–20
5	5D	5/16	1/2–20
6	6D	3/8	9/16–18
8	8D	1/2	3/4–16
10	10D	5/8	7/8–14
12	12D	3/4	1-1/16–12
16	16D	1	1-5/16–12

AN 822   MS 20822 — ELBOW—FLARED TUBE AND PIPE THREAD 90°

AN OR MS NO. STEEL	ALUM.	TUBE O.D.	PIPE THREAD
2	2D	1/8	1/8
3	3D	3/16	1/8
4	4D	1/4	1/8
5	5D	5/16	1/8
6	6D	3/8	1/4
8	8D	1/2	3/8
10	10D	5/8	1/2
12	12D	3/4	3/4
16	16D	1	1

AEROQUIP SUBSTITUTES

If you decide that you cannot afford the Aeroquip route, the AN 840 series of beaded tube fittings and a good grade of fabric cored neoprene or Buna N hose that will hold the pressures and temperatures involved will do. In this case, previous remarks concerning hose clamps apply.

HYDRAULIC SYSTEMS

I have yet to see a new race car delivered with brake and clutch plumbing that is unsafe. A noticeable functional improvement can and should be made by substituting Aeroquip 66000 series Teflon and stainless steel flexible pressure lines for the often supplied fabric and neoprene units. This eliminates line swelling under pressure, resulting in a firmer brake pedal, which in turn improves the driver's feel and hence his control of the vehicle under braking. Earl's will supply complete conversion kits if you specify line length and type of fitting required. It is more economical to make up your own.

Although other companies manufacture hose and fittings and line that look like Aeroquip 66000, in this case there is no acceptable substitute. Installation is simple and straightforward but make sure that your lines are long enough to that full steering lock, full bump, full droop and any combination thereof cannot tighten the lines. Also be very sure that the lines cannot get caught on anything during suspension movement. Where a line passes through a panel or bulkhead it is essential to provide chafe protection by means of some sort of grommet. This holds true for all lines, hard or soft.

I either substitute the Aeroquip 66000 series line for all hydraulic tubing or convert the stock idiot hard line fittings to AN fittings and double flared bundy tubing with AN 818 compression fittings and AN 819 coupling sleeves throughout. This is probably a complete waste of time and effort but I just don't like pipe fittings.

When replacing hydraulic hard lines use only genuine Bundyweld steel tubing (3/16" O.D. x .031" wall for the brakes and 1/4" O.D. x .031" wall for the clutch—clutch actuation displaces a lot more fluid than does brake application). The equivalent Aeroquip sizes are 66000-3 and 66000-4. Since the English double flare is difficult to form and prone to leak, it is convenient when replacing lines to convert to AN fittings as mentioned above. American double flares are easily formed with any of the proprietary flaring tools. When running hydraulic lines, look ahead, and make sure that changing an engine isn't going to make it possible to bump, squeeze, crimp or otherwise damage the lines. Thoughtful location of the rear brake "tee" can work wonders in this direction. While on the subject of the rear brake tee I should mention that this little item should be placed below the rear calipers and that the rear brakes should be plumbed in such a way that the fluid passes from the tee to each caliper separately. If the tee is placed at one of the calipers, you will have hell bleeding the system.

VENT, OVERFLOW AND BREATHER LINES

So far as vent, overflow and breather lines are concerned, since temperature and pressure are usually not considerations, Aeroquip is a waste of money and weight. This is not necessarily true of water bleed lines. Tygon tubing, provided that it is kept away from exhaust pipes and the like and is not collapsed by tight bends, is adequate. Make sure that overflow lines cannot discharge their contents onto exhaust pipes (black flag) or rear tires (spin out).

Many racers use plastic hose and compression fittings for oil and fuel pressure lines (to the gauges), hydraulic reservoir to master cylinder hoses, radiator vent lines (to the header tank) and the like. I used to. After considerable thought, I no longer do. I use armored Teflon from Earl's or Aeroquip, with proper hose ends and adaptor fittings, for all of the above. It costs more; it weighs more—and I don't care. When I used plastic I always had niggling little doubts, "what if the raditor bleed line chafes through—or gets cut/crushed in a minor accident that would not by itself stop the car?"—that sort of thing. I no longer have those doubts. This may be one more example of "over Carroll"—but I sleep nights. In fact my whole system of racing car preparation is designed to allow me to do just that—sleep nights.

Thoughtful grouping and routing of the various lines and support by means of Adell clamps and cable ties will do wonders for the appearance of the vehicle.

One last word concerning plumbing has to do with the high pressure plastic hose commonly used to supply fuel from the Lucas metering unit to the injector nozzles. This line must be protected from chafing and must be frequently inspected for signs of axial cracking where it is pushed on to the barbed end fittings. The cracks will always be axial and will not be very noticeable. The lean cylinder and/or merry little fire that will result if the crack is not detected will be both noticeable and expensive. The standard English tubing is excellent but doesn't last forever. Some of the American substitutes are awful. Be very careful.

CHAPTER THREE

RIVETS, RIVETING AND WELDING

If we could be certain that repairs and/or modifications to our racer would never enter into our program and if we were going to buy, instead of make, all of the replacement parts, then we could skip this chapter entirely. Since such certainties do not exist in the real world in which we race, we had best investigate the rest of the fastening and joining picture.

The increasing popularity of the so called "monocoque" chassis (technically, due to acess problems, they are not of monocoque but "stressed skin" construction) has increased the scope and complexity of riveting on race cars. Gone are the days when a fist full of hardware store pop rivets and a 1/8" drill would get you by. It is worth it. Chassis are now both lighter and stronger as well as a damn sight safer to be in when they hit something.

RIVETS AND RIVET JOINT DESIGN

Basically rivets can be divided into two broad groups; blind rivets, installed from one side only of the work and solid or hard rivets which require access to both sides of the work. Popular opinion has it that hard rivets are stronger than blind rivets. As we will see this is not necessarily true (Figure 8). Books could be and have been devoted to the selection and use of rivets. We will discuss only those types of rivets and those aspects of riveting which are commonly used in race car construction.

The strength of a rivet installed in tension is determined by the tensile and shear strength of the rivet material, the diameter of the shank, the upsetting of the "shop formed" head and the resistance of this head to being broken off or pulled through the hole. In most applications we will not be interested in the strength of rivets in tension as we will avoid such applications like the plague. Rivets, like welds, are terrible in tension. Figure (9) illustrates the easy way to convert riveted brackets from tension to shear.

We are, however, vitally interested in rivet strength in shear. Shear strength of a riveted joint is dependent upon a multitude of factors including: rivet material and design, fit of the rivet in the hole (it should be slightly loose—almost line to line), upset (expansion) of the shop formed head, thickness and tensile strength of the material to be joined, alignment and deburring of the rivet holes, rivet pattern selected, rivet spacing and, with blind rivets, whether or not the mandrel or stem is going to remain in place, at what point relative to the work thickness the stem will break, stem material and how tightly the stem is gripped by the rivet itself. Obviously a hollow rivet with no stem is nowhere near as strong as the same rivet with a solid mandrel. Equally obviously a rivet stem not tightly gripped by the rivet, or a

rivet which is loose in its hole will allow undesirable relative motion to develop. A rivet mandrel which has broken between the work surfaces will not lend any shear strength to the joint.

Standard aircraft practice calls for placing rivets in shear and for designing all riveted joints so that any failure will be a rivet failure rather than a material failure. This last is desirable in aircraft because they are vastly overdesigned and the chance of the failure of a few isolated rivets leading to catastrophe is remote due to the "fail safe" design of aircraft structures and components. Isolated rivet failure is much easier to detect and remedy than incipient failure of metal.

This philosophy is also valid when applied to the main structure of the racing car—except that all of us are too lazy to make the required calculations and too conservative to believe them anyway. There are, however, exceptions. It is common (and perfectly acceptable) procedure to attach trailing arms (radius rods) and the like to the chassis by means of sheet metal brackets riveted to the skin. These brackets, and the rivets which secure them, must accept very high loadings under braking and acceleration. Failure of the bracket leads to instant and utter disaster. Four times during a recent season I witnessed riveted radius rod bracket failure. In each case the offending bracket was attached by a single row of 1/8" solid rivets direct to chassis skin with no provision for spreading the loads. While this was a case of bad mechanical design (all suspension and chassis loads should be fed into corners and the loads spread over a large area by the use of gussets), the failure was a rivet failure and was easily prevented by the few crews with foresight by the simple expedient of welding a sheet of .049" mild steel onto the bracket, doubling the rivet pattern, increasing the rivet diameter to 5/32" and installing a doubler plate on the inside of the skin Figure (10).

Anyway, in this instance (and others, depending upon the design of the vehicle, where no back-up or fail-safe provision exists) it is best to make the riveted joint so strong that overloading will be evidenced by distortion of the skin rather than by failure of the rivets. See Figure (11). This can be accomplished by increasing the density and/or area of the rivet pattern and by the use of doubler plates and/or gussets. It is best to seek experienced advice in such situations. It is also best to cast a very jaundiced eye over your new racer before venturing onto the race track. Even the best of designers make mistakes in this area, and some of the less than best seem to specialize in it.

Fortunately people have been riveting aircraft together for some years now, and the same gents who devised the AN

Figure (8): Cross Sectional View of Various Rivet Types

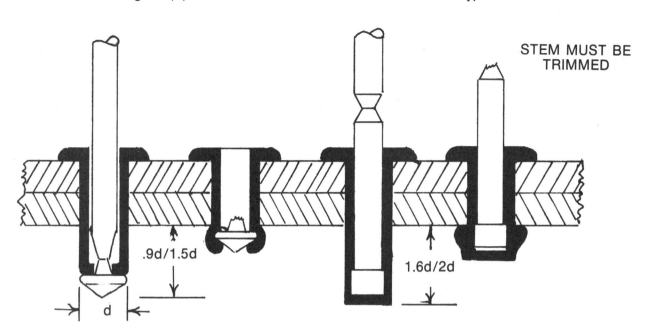

STEM MUST BE TRIMMED

.9d/1.5d

d

1.6d/2d

Hollow core "pop" rivet. Stem not retained in shear plane. Shear strength (1/8" diam.) 305 lb. Not for structural use.

Solid core, closed end. Solid core, closed end, "pop" rivet. Stem positively locked in shear plane. Shear strength (1/8" diam) 480 lb. Suited for Structure.

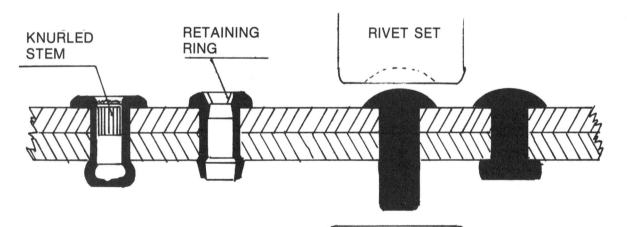

KNURLED STEM

RETAINING RING

RIVET SET

BUCKING BAR

Flush-break "pop" rivet. Stem locked in shear plane. Shear Strength (1/8" diam.) 440 lb. No stem trimming required. Suitable for structure.

Cherrylock structural rivet. Stem locked in shear plane. Shear Strength (1/8" diam.) 388 to 615 lb. No stem trimming required. Suitable for structure.

Solid "AD" Rivet. Shear strength (1/8" diam.) 388 lb. Suitable for structure.

Figure (8a): Relative Ultimate Shear Strength of Various Rivet Types

MANUFACTURER	USM "pop"	USM "pop"	USM "pop"	Avdel	Cherry	Cherry	Various
RIVET TYPE	Hollow Core	Solid Core	Flush-break	Avex	CR2263	CR2249	Solid "AD"
RIVET MATERIAL	5056 Alum.	5056 Alum.	5056 Alum.	5056 Alum.	5056 Alum.	5056 Alum.	A17ST Alum.
STEM MATERIAL	Carbon Steel	Carbon Steel	Carbon Steel	Carbon Steel	7075 Alum.	4130 Steel	None
RIVET DIAMETER (in.)	1/8 5/32	1/8 5/32	1/8 5/32	1/8 5/32	1/8 5/32	1/8 5/32	1/8 5/32
ULTIMATE SHEAR (lbs.)	305 430	480 650	440 570	210 305	388 596	615 976	388 593

standards for threaded fasteners have learned all about rivets and rivet patterns. Figures (12) and (12a) give recommended rivet diameters in terms of work thickness and pattern spacing in terms of rivet diameter. I personally tend to regard single row rivet patterns in main structure as a crime against nature. I also use only 1/8" and 5/32" rivets and fairly wide patterns.

POP RIVETS

For non-structural uses the garden variety aluminum hollow-core "pop" rivets from your local hardware store are adequate. Bought in lots of 50 or 100 from the hardware store they are also damned expensive. You are going to use a lot of them! Buy them in lots of 1000 or more from your local friendly United Shoe Machinery or Avdel distributor (yellow pages). Buy a good pair of hand pop rivet pliers (best I have found is Marston Corporation's HD-2 Hand Riveter which comes with noses for 4 mandrel diameters) and use the proper length rivet for the work. Rule of thumb is that the rivet (under the head) should be .9 to 1.4 diameters longer than the work thickness. If the rivet is too short it won't upset (expand) sufficiently to form a good head. If the rivet is too long it won't upset properly either and will look messy to boot. The critical nature of rivet length combined with the varying thickness of the joints to be riveted means carrying around a bunch of different length rivets which tends to be a pain. The Avdel Corporation has a neat little device called the AVEX rivet which does away with this problem. Some genius designed this rivet so that the upsetting process begins at the work face rather than at the end of the rivet. Consequently one length of rivet covers a very wide range of work thicknesses. It is a strong, efficient, good looking and convenient rivet. It is also cheap. I use nothing else.

When riveting to fibreglass use a washer under the shop formed head. Otherwise the rivet will eventually pull through the fibreglass. Steel and monel pop rivets are ridiculous and should not be used. Besides, they are difficult to remove. Pop rivets are available with countersunk heads. The appearance of a car is improved all out of proportion to the labor involved in their use. You have to de-burr the hole anyway and it only takes another second to countersink it. If strength is a major consideration (as in wings) dimple the countersink rather than cutting it.

Use aluminum rivets with steel mandrels of the "break stem" type. (The pull through type has very limited strength.) Use sharp drill bits (#30 for 1/8" diameter and #20 for 5/32")—except for Avex rivets which require #29 and #19 respectively—and take the time to deburr the holes after you drill them—the burrs prevent proper upsetting of the rivet and also prevent the two work pieces from touching.

RIVET HOLES

It is normally best to pre-drill (or punch—the Whitney Jr. #5 punch is the riveter's best friend) the holes in the smaller of the two pieces to be joined. Use even spacing laid out with a pair of dividers, pencil compass or a ruler. An automatic center punch for about $4.00 is a big help, but regardless of method, center punch the holes. Hold or clamp the pieces in place and start drilling your through holes in the center of the hole pattern. Drill only two holes and install cleco clamps. Proceeding from the center outward, drill and clamp as you go. This method ensures a proper fit and does away with the embarrassing possibility of predrilling all the holes and then redrilling because of errors in measurement or distortion because the two pieces weren't mated when the holes were drilled. After the holes are deburred, finish all edges before riveting. Theoretically the parts should be given a light coat of zinc-chromate before installation. In practice this is usually restricted to structure (in which case one of the commercial structural adhesives should be used at the joint itself) and ferrous parts. Three M's 2216A and 2216B "Structural Adhesive" is my favorite.

The trouble with the garden variety pop rivet is that you get less than you pay for. The mandrel is not particularly well retained and invariably breaks off well below the work surface. For scoops, spoilers, trim, clamps, etc., this is acceptable, always assuming that enough rivets are used. For structure, forget it!

STRUCTURAL BLIND RIVETS

Full structural blind rivets, offering strength equal to or surpassing that of solid rivets, are available from, among others, Cherry Rivet Division of The Townsend Corporation and The Huck Corporation. They are beautiful, certified, not very expensive but require expensive tools for installation. Fortunately there are blind rivets available which, while not aircraft certified, offer sufficient strength for our applications combined with reasonable ease of installation and nominal cost. In my experience the best of these "semi-structural" blind rivets is United Shoe

Figure (9): Welded and Riveted Brackets With Welds and Rivets in Tension and Shear

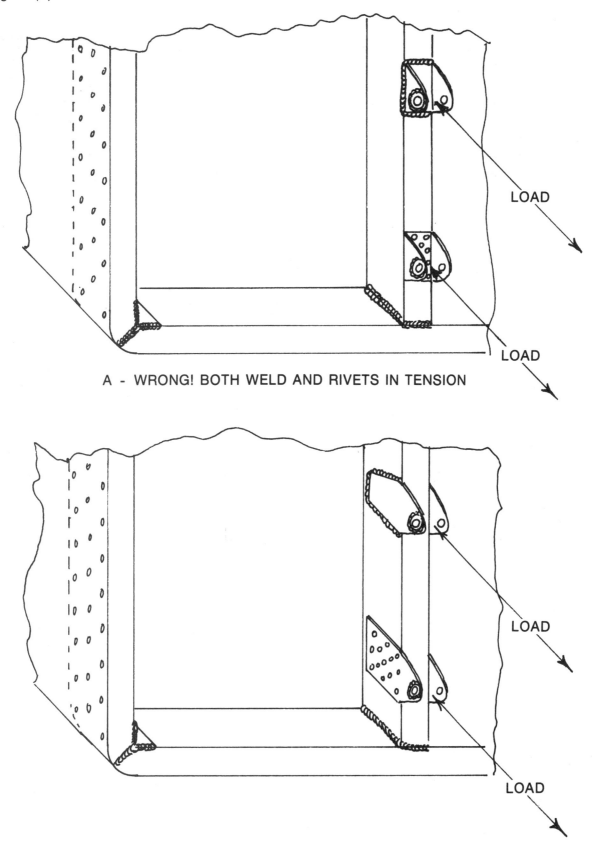

A - WRONG! BOTH WELD AND RIVETS IN TENSION

B - RIGHT! BOTH WELDS AND RIVETS IN SHEAR. MORE WELD AREA AND MORE RIVETS

Figure (10): Overkill Field Modification to Underdesigned Radius Rod Bracket Attachment

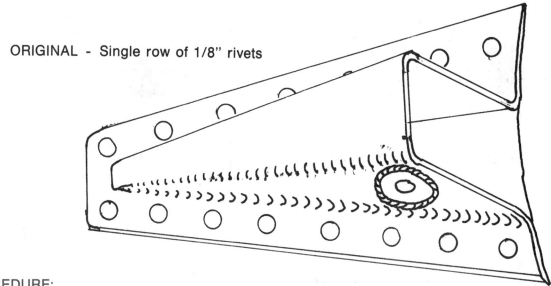

ORIGINAL - Single row of 1/8" rivets

PROCEDURE:
(1) Remove bracket; shape .049" mild steel extension plate; weld plate to bracket; reform after welding; trim and finish edges.

(2) Drill every other original rivet hole in bracket to 5/32"; drill new series of 5/32" hole in extension plate; deburr holes.
(3) Attach modified bracket to tub with cleco clamps through original 1/8" holes left in bracket.
(4) Drill 5/32" holes in tub using bracket as drill jib. Cleco each hole as it is drilled. Remove 1/8" clecos and enlarge 1/8" holes to 5/32".
(5) Remove bracket, deburr all holes and rivet bracket in place.

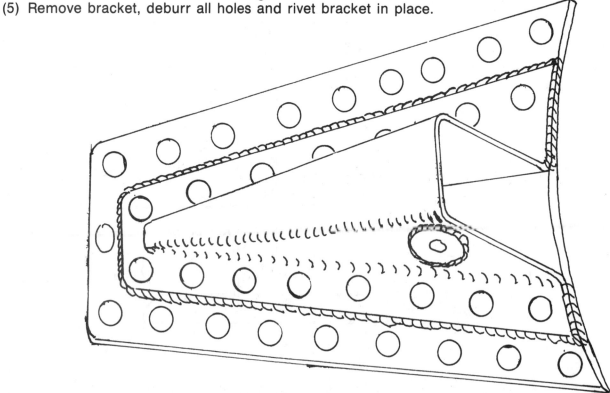

IF DESIRED A DOUBLER PLATE CAN BE ADDED INSIDE THE TUB.

28

Figure (11): Possible Types of Improper Riveting and Examples of Overstressed Skin

HOLE TOO SMALL   HOLE TOO LARGE

RIVET TOO   RIVET TOO   SHEETS NOT PULLED TOGETHER
LONG   SHORT   WHEN RIVET BUCKED

SINGLE ROW RIVET JOINT AFTER BENDING AND TENSION STRESS IN
SHEETS HAS EXCEEDED ELASTIC LIMIT OF MATERIAL

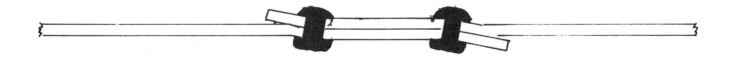

DOUBLE ROW RIVET JOINT AFTER BENDING AND TENSION STRESS IN
SHEETS HAS EXCEEDED ELASTIC LIMIT OF MATERIAL

Figure (12): Suggested Structural Rivet Patterns

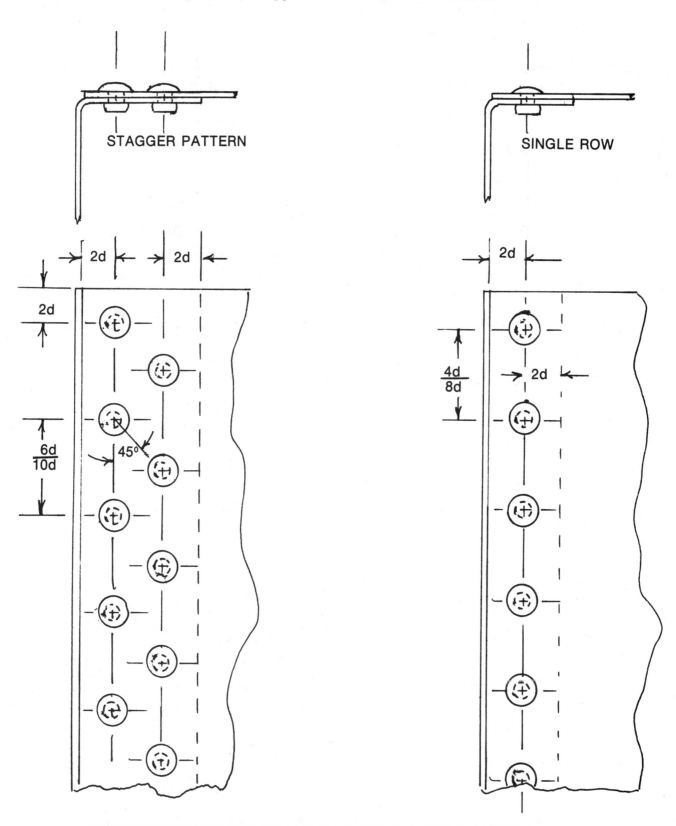

ADJUST RIVET SPACING TO MAKE PATTERN COME OUT EVEN.
IN BOTH CASES RIVET DIAMETER SHOULD BE 1-1/2 to 2 TIMES WORK
THICKNESS or 2-1/2 TO 3 TIMES THICKNESS OF THICKEST SHEET.

30

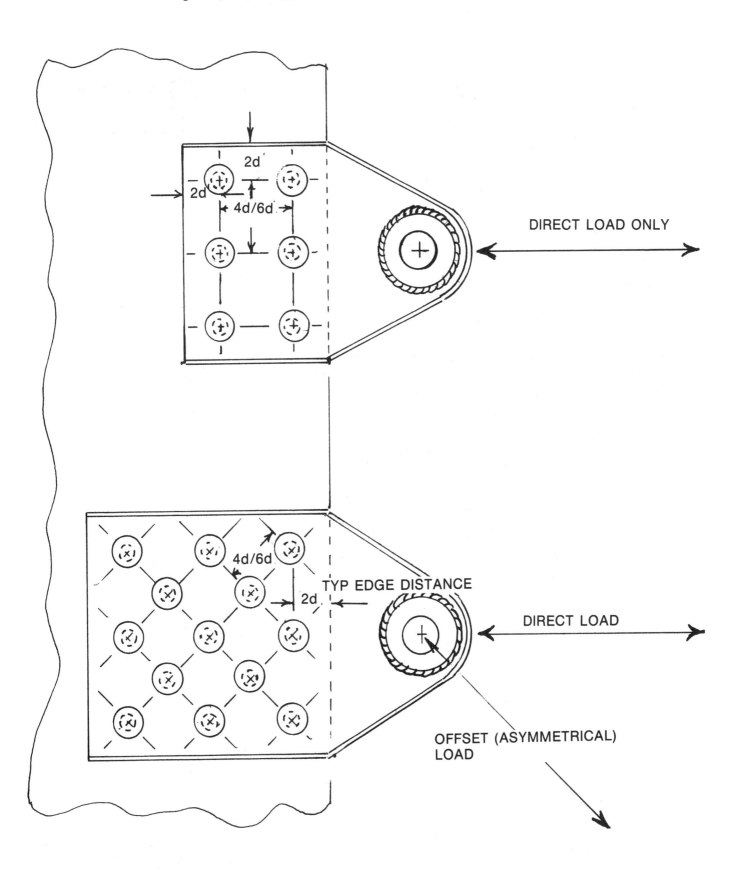

Figure (12a): Suggested Rivet Patterns For Brackets

31

Figure (12b): Riveting Sequence in Order to Minimize Possibility of Distortion in Long Patterns

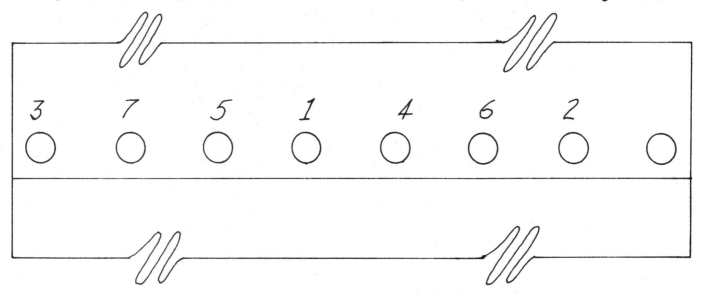

Machinery's closed end, solid core line. These offer positive mandrel location, the stem breaks well above the work surface (and must therefore be trimmed) and can be pulled by a hand gun . . . by a very strong man. If you are going to use very many of them either a compound lever hand tool or a pneumatic tool is a good investment. For mandrel trimming, a flat jawed pair of diagonal cutting pliers is available from your local aircraft supply house, or use normal "dykes" ("Blacksmith's Nippers" are very good) and grind to finish with any kind of a stone or abrasive wheel in a drill motor or die grinder.

A possible alternative is USM's "flush-break" line in which, assuming that the correct length rivet is used, the mandrel breaks just below the surface of the manufactured head. The stem is well retained by the rivet material which squeezes a knurl on the mandrel. This particular rivet is hard to find, but I have used it successfully in some semi-critical applications. The published data looks good.

SOLID RIVETS

The traditional rivet is the "hard" or "solid" or "bucked" rivet. It is stronger than most blind rivets, dirt cheap (surplus) and looks good. It is also a good bit more work to install, requires access to both sides of the work and necessitates the use of a pneumatic riveting hammer with the correct rivet sets. Most race cars are hard riveted. This is because the extra labor involved is offset by the skill and expertise of the very experienced people who do the riveting. They are FAST! This makes bucking rivets a pretty cheap operation in production. Hole drilling and hole preparation is the same regardless of the type of rivet used. If you are building race cars or doing much chassis repairing you will just about be forced to invest in pneumatic riveting equipment. For the occasional repair, it is probably cheaper to farm the job out or to borrow or rent the equipment.

Many types of solid rivets are available. Only the "AD" rivet of A17ST aluminum alloy should be used. This rivet is easily identified by a small indentation in the center of the

manufactured head. The alloy 1100 dead soft rivet head has no marking at all. This is a very popular rivet for tanks because it can be welded after it has been bucked. It is not intended for structural use, although many constructors use it because it is very easy to buck—you can do a satisfactory job with a small ball-pien hammer. All other head identifications are cause to discard the rivet. These other rivets are of different alloys and cannot be properly upset with normal equipment at room temperature. Be careful when buying surplus!

RIVETING TECHNIQUE

Practice bucking rivets on scrap material before attacking a tub. Two people do it a lot better than one. Use the correct rivet length. Long rivets can be cut to length with diagonal pliers but it is better to use a rivet cutter (local aircraft supply house again) as a pair of "dykes" leaves the end of the rivet in a vee shape which makes it difficult to hold the bucking bar true to the rivet. A pressure regulating valve on the rivet gun is a necessity. Make sure that the manufactured head of the rivet is tight against the sheet and true to the surface. The correct rivet set for the rivet used must be tight against the manufactured head and the bucking bar must be tight against the end of the rivet and true to the surface. Hold the bucking bar firmly against the rivet and pull the trigger. Adjust air pressure until a short burst of 10 or 12 blows will upset the rivet properly. See Figure (13). A fair amount of practice is necessary to achieve proficiency. Once proficiency is achieved, however, the speed with which rivets can be bucked is astounding. It is necessary to inspect both sides of each rivet after bucking. If the upset is insufficient, re-buck it. Most other deficiencies require removal of the rivet. The common deficiencies are also described in Figure (13).

Some tips are:

(1) When drilling around fuel cells, water tubes, fluid lines, etc., and removal is not practical or desirable, install a piece of tubing over the drill bit to serve as a stop. This will

Figure (13): Formed Rivet Head Dimensions and Configurations

A — FORMED HEAD DIMENSIONS

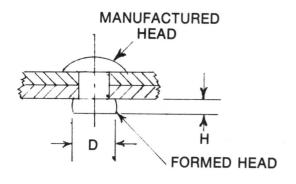

FORMED HEAD DIMENSIONS

RIVET SHANK DIAMETER	DIAMETER (D)	HEIGHT (H)
3/32"	.125"	.031"
1/8"	.165"	.047"
5/32"	.205	.055"

B — RIVET LENGTH AND HOLE DIAMETER

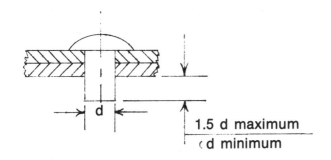

1.5 d maximum
d minimum

RIVET SHANK DIAMETER	HOLE DIAMETER	DRILL BIT
3/32"	.098"	#40
1/8"	.128"	#30
5/32"	.161"	#20

C — FORMED HEAD CONFIGURATION

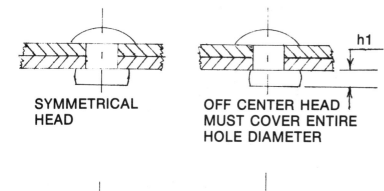

SYMMETRICAL HEAD

OFF CENTER HEAD MUST COVER ENTIRE HOLE DIAMETER

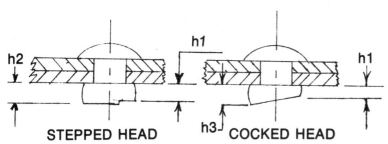

STEPPED HEAD

COCKED HEAD

FORMED HEAD CONFIGURATION

RIVET SHANK DIAMETER	3/32	1/8	5/32
h1 min.	.031	.047	.055
h2 max.	none	trim to fit	
h3 max.	.075	.088	.120

prevent drilling a neat round hole in the fuel cell or whatever. Or go crazy—buy real drill stops from the Aircraft Supply House.

(2) All shop formed heads inside of fuel cell cavities must be covered with tape to prevent chafing the cell. It is lighter and easier (where it is possible to get the rivet gun inside the cavity) to place the manufactured head inside the cavity and form a shop head outside. Make damn sure that all of the swarf is cleaned out of the fuel cavity prior to installing the cell.

(3) Masking tape over the manufactured head will hold the rivet in place and go a long way toward preventing skin damage when the rivet set slips. In this way a whole line of rivets can be pre-installed and then bucked in sequence. Make very sure, however, that the operator of the bucking bar is backing up the same rivet that the rivet gun operator is about to shoot.

RIVET REMOVAL

Things being what they are, anything installed on a race car will sooner or later have to be removed. This is just as true of rivets as anything else. As usual there is one right and several wrong ways to do it.

With blind rivets, an attempt to just drill them out will result in a very dull drill bit in short order and may result in some nasty little spiral marks on the skin from the bit skidding off the mandrel. These are known in the trade as "drill tracks." If the mandrel is punched out with the appropriate drift punch (watch the fuel cells and back up the work with something solid to prevent deforming the sheet metal), the rivet head can be drilled off with the next size smaller drill bit. The rivet can then be drilled out with the same bit and the hole cleaned with the original size drill bit. This procedure doesn't take any longer than the usual straightforward attack with a drill and it sure saves drill bits. It also makes a much neater job. Figure (14) illustrates.

The procedure for solid rivets is similar (Figure (15)). The major difference is that the rivet is punched out instead of drilled out. Again the work must be solidly backed up to avoid deforming metal. If you must use a chisel to chip off the manufactured heads after drilling through most of them, round the corners of the chisel and grind a one-sided point on the damn thing so that it can get under the head. In all probability you will still scratch or gouge the skin. If you do screw up the hole, the next size larger rivet must be installed. Cherry rivets are available in 1/32 oversized diameters.

WELDING

In addition to being bolted or riveted, metal is also joined by welding. Welding is without doubt the most critical of all joining processes. It is also the most difficult. We are not going to attempt any sort of a comprehensive discussion of welding. The only way to learn good welding is by study and practice. Any of the welding supply houses have good texts, as do the public libraries. The best way to learn is to attend a good welding school or to have a certified welder teach you. This is particularly true of heliarc welding.

FUSION WELDING

The most common form of welding is gas fusion welding in which the parts to be joined are heated to the melting point with an oxyacetylene torch and fused together with or without a suitable filler rod. This method has the distinct advantage of being easy to do but, due to the fact that the metal at and near the weld has been necessarily heated beyond its crystallization point, the grain structure in the weld area becomes similar to that of cast iron and so is considerably less able to resist shock and vibration than is the original metal. Hammering or normalizing (heating the local area to cherry red and allowing to cool in still air) will help, but you had better be an expert. This local chrystalization can be considerably reduced by using an inert gas tungsten arc welder (heli-arc or argon-arc) in which heat is produced by electric current passing from a tungsten arc to the grounded work surface to produce a controlled puddle. Filler material is added from a rod as in gas fusion welding. The work area is shielded by a flow of inert gas (helium or argon) which prevents local oxidation and contamination of the weld. The other important benefit of tungsten arc welding is that heating of the parent metal is confined to the area of the join, vastly reducing crystalization. It is extremely important to avoid undercutting the weld and to still achieve full penetration. While crystalization is reduced to a minimum, it still exists and vital welds should be stress relieved by normalizing. Filing a weld bead is a giant NO NO! There is nothing wrong with the appearance of a good bead and filing it cuts across stress lines and removes metal.

As we are working with comparatively thin sections, it is difficult when fusion welding to avoid weakening the joint either by undercutting or by local crystalization. For this reason it is common practice on both race cars (required by USAC) and aircraft to use E 4130 steel in the normalized condition for all highly stressed members such as suspension links and to regain the original grain structure and strength after welding by stress relieving and normalization. This can be done in the shop with a torch, or it can be farmed out to a heat treating shop.

HEAT TREATING

Component strength can be increased about 30% by heat treating the 4130 parts. Do not heat treat higher than Rockwell C Scale 24 to 26, or the resultant loss in ductility will offset the strength gained. All of this tends to get rather expensive, requiring the use of a heliarc and access to heat treating facilities. Heat treaters charge by the batch, so it is as well to wait until you have a number of parts ready. A heat treated part cannot be repaired to original strength in the field. Consequently I don't do much heat treating of fabricated parts—except for suspension links. Until quite recently I didn't use much 4130 chrome-moly steel, preferring good old cold drawn 1015 mild steel and 1010 cold rolled mild sheet. After some bad experiences with poor quality mild steel (blamed by the suppliers on the advent of "inferior foreign steel" into the U.S. market and the introduction of Cor-ten and Core-forty steels into the remelting process), I have switched to commercial grade E 4130 in the normalized condition. I did so more for reasons of consistent quality than for the extra strength and toughness of the material, but the extras are a no cost bonus. 4130 is a little tougher to work with, but not much, and, in the commercial grade, the difference in cost is not great. If I am going to heat treat, however, I still use aircraft quality stock and get certification papers (which don't cost

Figure (14): Rivet Removal

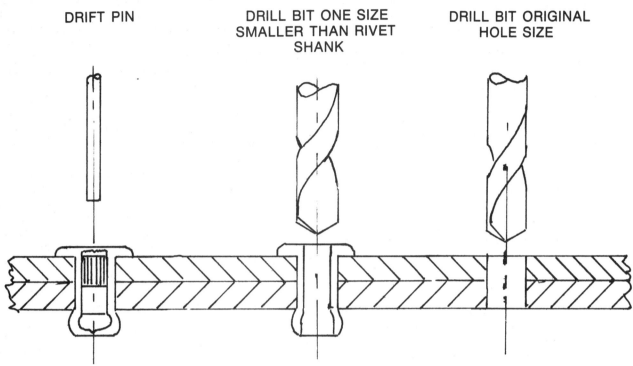

DRIFT PIN   DRILL BIT ONE SIZE   DRILL BIT ORIGINAL
                 SMALLER THAN RIVET   HOLE SIZE
                       SHANK

B - Blind Rivet:
  (1) Punch mandrel out of rivet with sharp hammer blow.
  (2) Using next size smaller drill bit, remove rivet head. Stop at this point and remove head from drill bit.
  (3) Drill through with undersize bit.
  (4) Clean hole with same size bit used to drill original hole.

extra). I also get certification on all high alloy steels and all structural aluminum. That way I am sure what I'm getting.

4130

While we're on the subject, lets digress long enough to put down the 4130 myth. E 4130 chrome-moly steel is not some sort of super material. It came into popularity in the days of welded tubular aircraft fuselages because it is slightly stronger and a good bit tougher than mild steel, can be very successfully stress relieved with a torch after welding and is eminently weldable. Unless the part is to be heat treated the gain in strength is not spectacular. Shelby seamless steel mechanical tubing, which is readily available almost anywhere, has, in the half-hard condition, an ultimate tensile strength of 75.000 p.s.i. and a yield point of 55,000 p.s.i. E 4130 has, in the normalized condition, an ultimate of 92,-000 with a yield of 75,000. While 4130 is excellent for tubular structures and sheet fabrication, it does not make good shafts, axles, gears, etc., as it is not suitable for parts with varying cross sections. It is also difficult to machine, has poor deep hardening properties and poor fatigue resistance at high heat treats. A great many racers firmly believe that anything made from 4130 represents some sort of ultimate—it just ain't so. Forgings—axles, gears and such—should be made from 4340, or one of the newer, stronger and trickier maraging steels.

NICKEL BRONZE WELDING

Our English friends have led the way in solving most of the problems associated with welding the ferrous components on race cars. Virtually all of the steel welding on English cars is of the low-temperature, nickel-bronze variety, using an oxyacetylene torch with a nickel-bronze alloy filler rod. In this method, also called fillet-brazing, a large fillet or bead of low melting point filler alloy is deposited on the metals to be joined at a temperature well below that at which crystalization occurs. The work surface must be absolutely clean and a flux must be employed to allow the welding alloy to properly adhere to the parent metal. The result is a joint as strong or stronger than a fusion weld with no undercutting and no crystalization of the parent metal. The disadvantages are that the part cannot be heat treated and that the welding and preparation are a bit touchy. In this country welding alloys, flux and descriptive literature are available from Eutectic, Allstate, Amaco and Weldco. Your local welding supply house can supply information and descriptive literature. Eutectic's handbooks are particularly good.

Figure (15): Rivet Removal

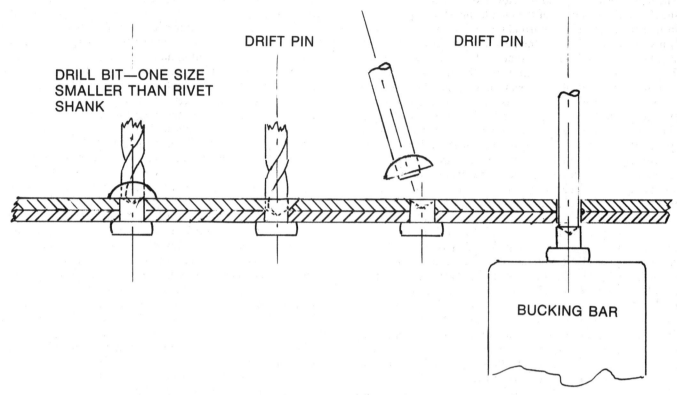

DRILL BIT—ONE SIZE SMALLER THAN RIVET SHANK

DRIFT PIN

DRIFT PIN

BUCKING BAR

A - Solid Rivet:
   (1) Drill into center of manufactured head. In order not to enlarge hole stop at intersection of head with shank.
   (2) Manufactured head will probably fall off while drilling. If not, insert drift pin in head and snap off. Do not use chisel!
   (3) Place bucking bar against formed head to prevent skin distortion and tap rivet out with drift pin and hammer.

Two actual methods are available, flux coated rod and the "jet fluxer." With the coated rod, the flux is melted by the torch and deposited on the work. Disadvantages include the difficulty of seeing what you are doing, imperfect fluxing, difficulty of removing the glassy flux residue after welding and limited storage life of the rod. With the jet fluxer, available from Allstate for about $80.00, a container of liquid flux is connected to the acetylene line, and the flux is then carried in the gas and issues from the torch—automatically fluxing the work and acting as a partial contamination shield. You can see exactly what is happening, and a much neater and stronger job results. The fluxer is well worth the nominal purchase price. It should be pointed out that once a set of lines and torch have been used with a jet fluxer, they are perfectly O.K. for ferrous fuxion welding but must be cleaned before an attempt is made to gas weld aluminum. In practice the best solution is to have two sets of welding lines with Tee connections at the regulators. One set of lines is used with the fluxer and one is kept sacred for aluminum. The torch and tips will clean themselves very rapidly so that two sets of these expensive components are not necessary. Speaking of torches (proper-

ly called mixing chambers) lets enter a plea for sanity. We don't need the huge "shipyard" torches normally found in automotive shops. They are awkward, difficult to use, nasty and expensive. Trying to weld two pieces of .035" steel with a torch that is two feet long and weighs four pounds is like attempting brain surgery with a hatchet. The best torch I have found at a reasonable price is the Victor "J" torch.

Anyway, back to Nickel Bronze welding (see Figure (19)). Extreme care is called for. Surfaces to be welded must be free of scale and absolutely clean because the alloy will not adhere to an unclean, scaly oily surface. This means emery cloth followed by MEK (not gasoline). Temperature must be closely controlled. If the work goes beyond a "dull cherry red" intermolecular penetration of the parent metal grain structure by the nickel in the welding alloy will result in a brittle joint. Mechanical fit of the parts must be very good indeed (this is true of all welding, brazing and soldering—gap rod is a NO NO!). A neutral or slightly "soft" flame should be used with a one size smaller tip than usual (0 and 00 pretty well covers the normal range). Blue cobalt lenses make the "black heat" at which welding should take place visible. Fluxing of the surface is visible and should proceed about 1/8" ahead of the weld puddle. The nickel-bronze should not flow like brazing material but should "tin" just ahead of the puddle and should puddle and form a bead similar to a normal fusion rod. As this is actually a surface tension weld, the bead must be larger than a fusion bead. Rule of thumb is that the bead or fillet should be 2 to 4 times the minimum work thickness—if you are welding two pieces of .063" wall tubing, the fillet should be 3/16" to 1/4" wide with 1/8" as a minimum. Use a rod big enough to do the job—3/32" and 1/8" are the most useful diameters and keep the flame moving in a spiral motion to spread the heat over the entire area of the fillet.

Properly done, nickel-bronze welds are as strong or stronger than fusion welds. Due to the low temperature used no crystalization occurs and undercutting is not possible. However, the only person who knows whether or not it is a good weld is the welder. Too little heat means that adhesion will not occur. Too much heat leads to a brittle joint. Both can result in a normal appearing joint. Practice a lot! Do not use silicon-bronze rod. It looks the same, is easier to use and is much weaker than nickel bronze. The best rod that I have found is Bronzecraft #3 from Weldcraft Ltd., Slough, Bucks, England. I have 5 or 10 lb. each of 3/32" and 1/8" included with a parts order from England once a year. It flows and puddles better than any of the domestic products, is equally strong, and much cheaper. The best domestic alloy that I have found is Eutectic's EutecRod 16 (bare) or EutecRod 16 FC (flux coated). Eutectic's MAINTENANCE WELDING DATA BOOK is the best source of printed information. Allstate equivalents are ALLSTATE 16 and ALLSTATE 11.

ARC WELDING

A few words on arc welding: The stick welder is very useful when the truck or trailer breaks. It is also useful on stock cars. It has no place at all on race cars.

ALUMINUM WELDING

There is no way to escape welding aluminum sheet. So long as race cars have oil tanks, scoops, etc., we will be welding sheet aluminum—thin sheet aluminum. It is not as difficult as people would have you believe. Aluminum possesses five characteristics which make it tricky to weld:

(1) It does not change color under heat so that the welder has no visual indication from color of the approach of the melting point.

(2) It has a low melting point—approximately 1,215 degrees F.

(3) When the melting point is reached, aluminum collapses suddenly and without warning, producing a neat hole in the work.

(4) The surface of aluminum oxidizes very rapidly under heat, and the aluminum oxide formed has a higher melting point than the aluminum itself. This oxide forms a shield underneath which the work is liable to melt.

(5) Aluminum is very weak when heated, tends to distort greatly and so must be very well supported during welding operations.

First make sure that the alloy with which you are playing is weldable. Tanks and things are normally fabricated from Alloy 3003-H 14 which is aminently weldable. Of the structural alloys, 7075 and 2024 are not weldable, 6061 and 5052 are. It should be remembered, however, that welding a structural alloy removes its temper and returns the sheet (or casting) to the dead soft condition in the area of the weld.

Next, make sure that you have suitable filler rod for the alloy being welded. The best method is to shear off a thin strip from the same sheet. It is important that the rod thickness be very close to the work thickness. Use a tip one size larger than you would for fusion welding of the same thickness of mild steel. Use a slight excess of acetylene (carburizing flame) and adjust gas velocity to achieve a very soft flame.

Use only fresh aluminum welding flux mixed into a thin paste with water. Clean both the rod and the surface to be welded and coat both with flux by brushing on a thin layer.

Preheat the work surface. As the metal is being heated, note what happens to the flux. The water boils off at 212°F. At about 400°F., the flux turns into a flaky solid substance and takes on a chalky appearance. At about 900° to 1000°, the flux will turn grey and watery. This indicates that the flux is chemically reacting with the aluminum oxide and you are just about ready to weld. Now is the time to apply the flux coated rod to the joint. When fusion does take place, it will happen very fast, and you had best be prepared to move flame and filler rod along the joint rapidly. It takes a lot of practice to consistently achieve penetration without blow holes and with good looking beads.

Welding of sheet aluminum is made considerably easier by thoughtful selection of the type of joint to be used. Flange welds, either corner flanges or edge flanges, are considerably easier than butt welds Figure (16). If a butt weld must be done, it is best to arrange the joint so that it occurs very soon after a flange or edge has been formed Figure (17). In this way distortion will be minimized. Any sheet aluminum to be welded should be tack welded at about 1" intervals before the seam is welded. This is also true of sheet metal. This is particularly essential when butt welding. Sheets must be well supported while welding to avoid distortion Figure (18). You must be careful, however, to make sure that the supports do not form a heat sink to remove the heat from the work area making control more difficult than it should be. The torch should be held at an angle of 30 degrees from the plane of the weld to avoid blow holes. For the same reason the tip should never approach closer than 1/8" to the work surface and must constantly be kept in motion.

SILVER SOLDERING

Silver soldering, often called "hard soldering," is a low temperature brazing process using an alloy of silver and copper. Silver solder melts at about 1100°F. as opposed to about 1700°F. for the normal brass spelter used in brazing. The process is particularly useful in making special or trick AN fittings from brass or steel components and for making home made nut rings. A special flux in paste form is required and should be kept separate from the rest of the welding kit, preferably with the silver solder itself. Parts to be joined must be absolutely clean and should have a gap of

Figure (16): Types of Sheet Metal Welded Joints

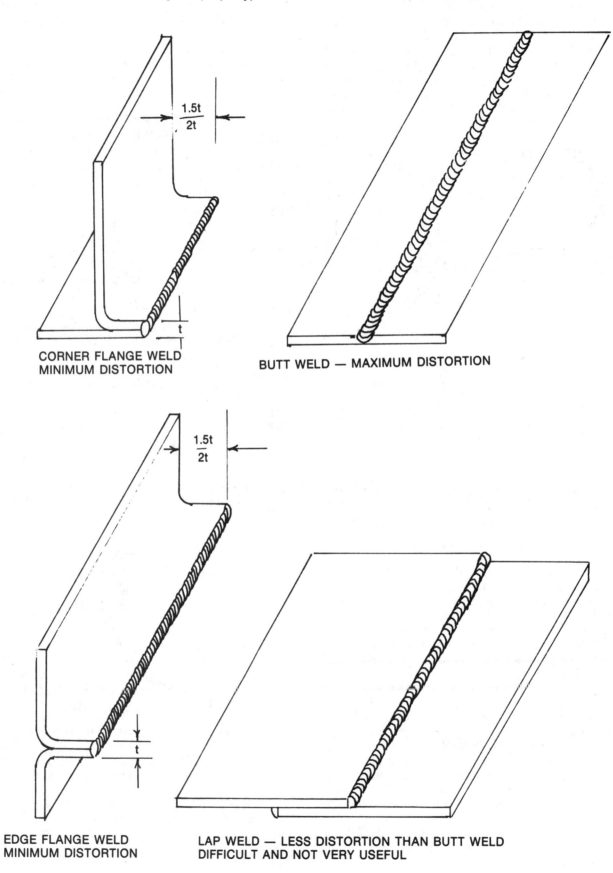

CORNER FLANGE WELD
MINIMUM DISTORTION

BUTT WELD — MAXIMUM DISTORTION

EDGE FLANGE WELD
MINIMUM DISTORTION

LAP WELD — LESS DISTORTION THAN BUTT WELD
DIFFICULT AND NOT VERY USEFUL

Figure (17): Various Types of Welds Illustrated on an Aluminum Oil Tank

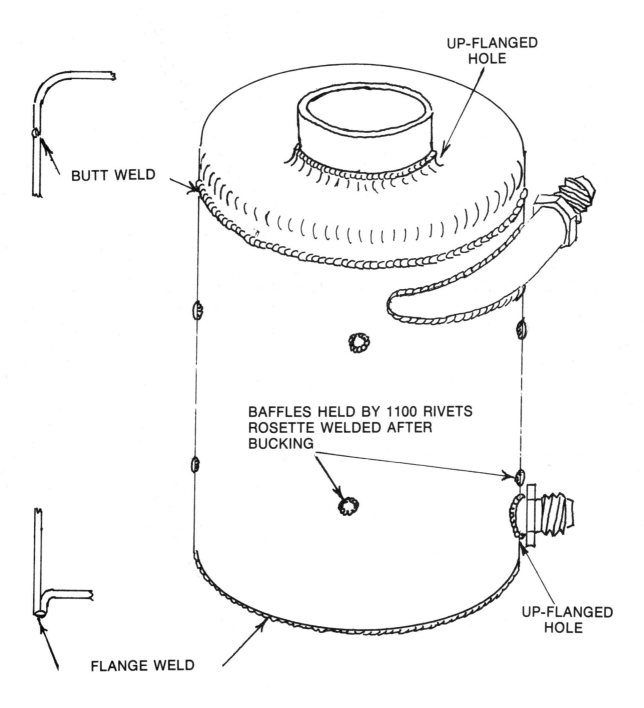

UP-FLANGED
HOLE

BUTT WELD

BAFFLES HELD BY 1100 RIVETS
ROSETTE WELDED AFTER
BUCKING

UP-FLANGED
HOLE

FLANGE WELD

Figure (18): Jig for Butt or Flange Welding Sheet Aluminum or Sheet Steel

ALUMINUM
SHEET

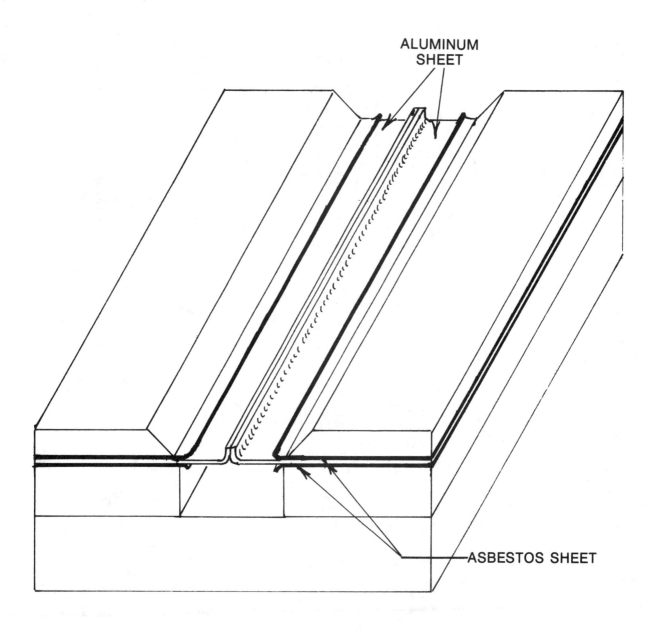

ASBESTOS SHEET

It is unlikely that anything this elaborate will be seen in a racing shop. The function can easily be duplicated with scrap bits of metal, wood or masonite.

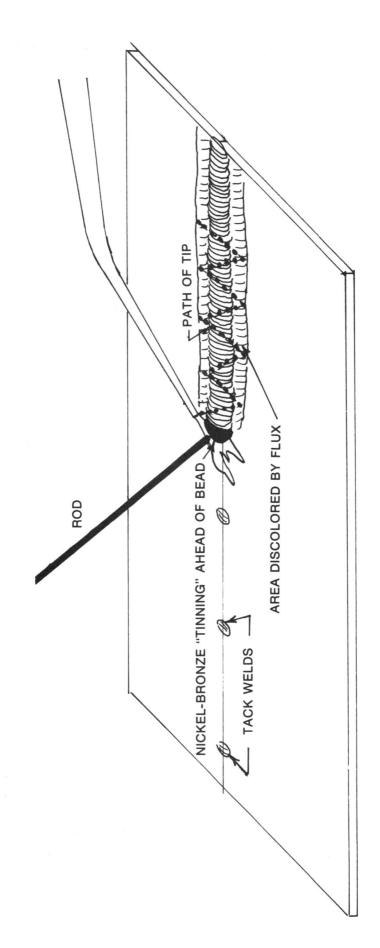

PROCESS FOR ALUMINUM IS SIMILAR BUT FLAME IS "SOFTER", BEAD IS MUCH NARROWER. PENETRATION IS ACHIEVED AND FLUX IS BRUSHED ON TO WORK AND ROD. MUCH LESS FILLER ROD IS USED WITH ALUMINUM.

ROD

PATH OF TIP

NICKEL-BRONZE "TINNING" AHEAD OF BEAD

TACK WELDS

AREA DISCOLORED BY FLUX

Blowpipe held at 30° angle to work—advanced with zig-zag (or spiral) motion to insure adequate and even heating of weld area. Bead formed by dipping rod into "puddle". If sheet is more than 1/16" thick, edges of joint should be beveled.

Figure (19): Butt Weld Formed by Nickel-Bronze Low Temperature Process Using "Jet Fluxer".

.002" to .005". Parts are flux coated, clamped together and heated to a dull red. Solder is then applied to the joint and will be "wicked" into the gap forming a permanent join. If the temperature is not sufficient, the solder will form balls and run everywhere but into the joint. Silver solder does not work on aluminum. It does, however, join stainless steel both to itself and to ferrous metals. It is about the only method we have of joining dis-similar metals and of joining brass.

WELDING NON-FERROUS CASTINGS

Every so often it becomes necessary to weld on an aluminum or magnesium alloy casting. Unless you are really good don't try to do it yourself. Take it to a certified aircraft welder, tell him what the alloy is, and hope for the best. It is absolutely necessary to preheat such castings and to cool them slowly after welding, otherwise cracks are guaranteed. It is also necessary to realize that welding removes whatever heat treat the part had and locally reduces the weld area to the annealed condition.

BONDING

We will close our discussion of joining with a brief description of bonding. Structural bonding, used without mechanical fasteners, is becoming very popular in the aerospace industry. It is not for us! Bonding is the process of joining structural members by surface attachment. Surface attachment is the term applied to molecules adhering to each other. Surfaces must be absolutely clean in order for the parent metal to mate with the adhesive (not glue!). A full structural bond requires either heat or pressure (or both) and so is beyond our scope. On the other hand, the use of a bonding agent in conjunction with a riveted joint will prevent chafing, prevent corrosion, increase strength and improve fatigue resistance. There is no reason why we shouldn't use it and lots of reasons why we should. All of the structural adhesives are two part epoxies and all must be used according to directions. I use 3M structural adhesive because it is available at a reasonable price and seems to do the job well. Three things are critical:

(1) The surfaces to be joined must be clean. They don't have to be rough—just clean. I use Tide and a scrub brush, rinse with lots of water and finally rinse with MEK.

(2) Once the adhesive is applied you don't have time to fit parts; they must be prefitted.

(3) The most common error is using too much adhesive. The optimum adhesive layer thickness is like one molecule. Tongue depressors, kitchen knives and spatulas make good applicators. Don't leave any voids.

When the riveting is complete, you will find that a fillet of adhesive has been squeezed out of the joint. Wipe it off with a rag and MEK before the adhesive sets. You'll have hell afterwards. Some adhesives require that the metal be primed with a very light coat of zinc chromate prior to application of the adhesive. Read directions!

CHAPTER FOUR

BASIC METAL WORK

Having investigated the various methods of joining two pieces of metal, it is time to face the inevitable fact that before we can rivet, bolt or weld bits together, it will be necessary to manufacture at least one of the bits. You are going to spend a lot of time making pieces—both simple and complex—from metal. Once again it is not practical to write a treatise on metal work—the book stores and libraries are full of excellent texts. We will discuss only the basic techniques which are in common use in racing.

HOLE DRILLING

Probably the most frequent act of violence performed on metal is the simple operation of drilling holes in the stuff. On the face of it one merely grabs a drill bit, crams it into a convenient drill motor and has at it. This approach will indeed lead to the manufacture of a hole in the metal, in you or in both. If the hole is in the metal it should be round, of the desired diameter (and depth, if it is not a through hole), in the desired direction, free of burrs and in the required location. The consistent achievement of all of these ends requires some forethought. Let's start with the drill bit itself.

DRILL BITS

Figure (20) illustrates the basic nomenclature of the drill bit. In order to drill true holes it is essential that the point angle and the lip angle be correct and that the cutting edges be of equal length and angle. As shown in the drawing the ideal point angle varies with the nature of the material being drilled. High speed steel drill bits (the only kind we are interested in) are normally supplied with a 59° point angle and a 12° lip angle. This configuration is suitable, if not ideal, for just about anything that we will be doing. The trick is to keep it that way!

Sooner or later, through normal wear or (more commonly) through abuse, every drill bit will be damaged or become dull. Since they are expensive we do not throw them away—we sharpen them. A great many people sincerely feel that they can do an excellent job of sharpening drill bits by hand. I cannot, and I know damned few people who can. For a very nominal sum your friendly machine supply house will sell you a simple holding device which clamps on to your bench grinder and which holds the drill bit at the angle you have selected while you grind it. With a reasonable amount of care, a very good job can be done—if the grindstone has been dressed. Black and Decker has an automatic electric drill bit sharpener which I have never been able to make work at all.

STARTING THE HOLE

It is not reasonable to expect a drill bit to start a hole all by itself. If you apply enough pressure to start a hole in virgin steel, the bit will inevitably wander, the hole will end up where you didn't want it, wear will be accelerated and the surface of the work will have some intriguing little spiral marks called "drill tracks" leading from the point where you started trying to drill to the point where the hole ended up. This is what center punches are made for. The idea of the center punch is to form a large enough crater at the desired center of the hole-to-be so that the chisel point of the drill will center in the crater and the cutting edges of the drill bit can do the cutting. The chisel point is not meant to, and won't cut. Since the center punch, with its 90° point, is not exactly a precision instrument, the prick punch, with a 30° point, should be used for locating the hole. Enlarge the prick punch mark with a center punch to form a crater large enough to start the drill bit. The transfer punch is another kettle of fish. It is used to transfer, more or less accurately, the center of an existing hole in one piece of material to the desired location of a matching hole in another piece. Some care is necessary in the use of any punch to insure that the punch is held normal to the work surface and struck squarely with the hammer. Otherwise the punch crater will wander off location. Figure (21) illustrates the three types of punches and the simple solution to the old problem of how to start a drill on a skewed surface. If really accurate hole location is required, start the hole with a center drill, either in a drill press or a lathe.

DRILL MOTORS

Most holes are drilled with the ubiquitous 1/4" electric drill motor. These devices normally operate at about 2000 rpm which is fine for a 1/8" drill bit but not too good for 3/16" and larger. The larger the drill bit, the slower it must be turned. Overspeeding is guaranteed to burn the outer edges of the cutting lips to the lasting detriment of both hole and bit. Any decent drill press is speed adjustable and a vari-speed electric drill motor is a good investment. Pneumatic drill motors are the way to go in sheet metal work as the drill speed is infinitely adjustable by the operator as he works. You won't find any electric drill motors in aircraft sheet metal shops! Although exact drill speeds are a function of material hardness, toughness and thickness as well as drill bit diameter and cutting angles, making comprehensive tables impractical, the basic guide is shown in Figure (22). More detailed tables are found in MACHINERY'S HANDBOOK and the like. The bigger the drill, the slower the rpm.

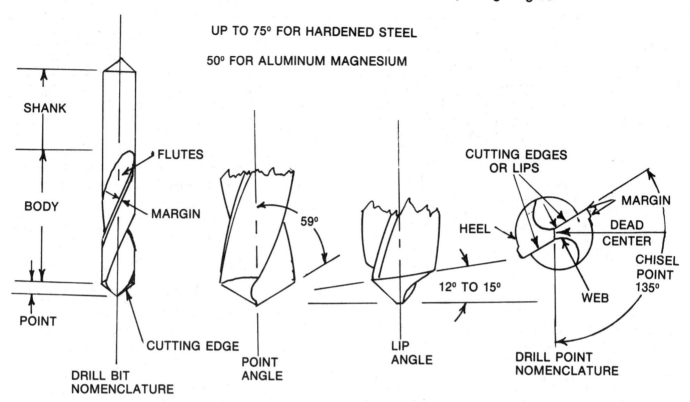

Figure (20): Drill Bit Nomenclature and Sharpening Angles

UP TO 75° FOR HARDENED STEEL

50° FOR ALUMINUM MAGNESIUM

DRILL LUBRICANTS

Holes in steel should be drilled with a lubricant. This will result in both a better hole and longer drill bit life. Any soluble oil will do nicely. Most of us use engine oil because it is always available. Aluminum should be drilled dry or with Kerosene or Lard Oil. Stainless requires Lard Oil. Magnesium is usually drilled dry.

LARGE DIAMETER HOLES

It is foolish to attempt to drill a large diameter hole in one operation. You will end up with a triangular lobed hole of varying dimensions. If the hole is to end up larger than 3/16" in diameter, start it with a smaller drill and enlarge it gradually. In sheet metal, if the hole is to be larger than 1/4", use a punch, a hole saw or a tapered reamer. For sheet metal holes larger than 1.0", if you don't have the correct punch or hole saw, use many cuts with a smaller punch or drill bit and finish with a file. At some point, depending on your assortment of snips, you will be able to do it with snips or a nibbler. If the material is too thick to punch go to the ancient method illustrated by Figure (23). Spot weld cutters make excellent hole saws in the smaller sizes.

As the drill bit is about to break through the material, drilling pressure must be reduced. Otherwise the material will climb the bit which is bothersome and can result in nasty scars on your hands. Additionally the far side of the hole will be buggered.

DEEP HOLES

When drilling deep holes remove the bit frequently to clear the chips and lubricate generously as the lubricant also serves as a coolant. Deep holes should be drilled in a drill press or on a lathe as it is almost impossible to drill them straight by hand. When using the drill press, take the time to securely clamp the work (and the drill vise, if you are using one). We all have scars from the "It'll be all right just this once" attitude.

DEBURRING

Once you have succeeded in drilling the hole, debur both sides of the work. If it is a critical hole, drill it a few thousandths undersize and ream to finish size (don't expect a hand reamer to cut more than .002" or .003"). Safety wire holes should be countersunk at both ends to prevent the sharp edge from cutting the wire. Deburring can be accomplished with a variety of tools. The most common is a large drill bit held in and twisted by the hand. This is slow, uncomfortable and does a nasty job. A "dog leg" deburring tool costs like nothing and does a neat and quick job. For deburring a large number of holes—as in sheet metal work—a piloted countersink in a drill motor is the hot set up when used with discretion. For holes which must be countersunk, a drill motor operated adjustable positive stop countersink of the proper angle can be had surplus for about $4.00. Make damned sure that countersinks (and counterbores) are held in line with the hole.

Figure (21): Drilling Offset Holes and Illustration of Punches

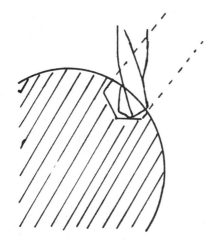

To start a drill on an inclined surface first start a hole with a larger drill bit normal to the part. Center punch desired hole location and start drill.

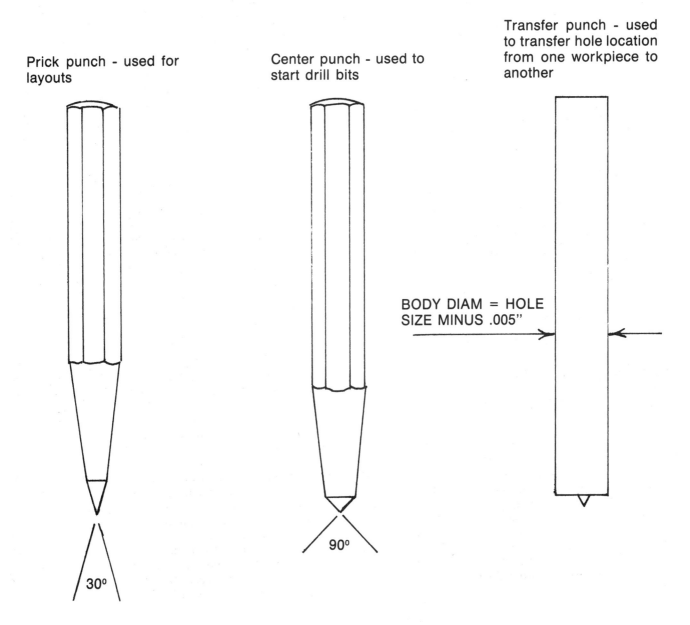

Prick punch - used for layouts

Center punch - used to start drill bits

Transfer punch - used to transfer hole location from one workpiece to another

BODY DIAM = HOLE SIZE MINUS .005"

30°

90°

Figure (22): Cutting Speed (in rpm) For High Speed Steel Drill Bits

DRILL DIAM. IN INCHES	CAST IRON AND HARD STEEL	MILD STEEL	ALUMINUM AND MAGNESIUM
1/16	6000	4800	FASTEST SPEED
1/8	3000	2400	8000
3/16	2000	1800	5000
1/4	1500	1200	3800
5/16	1300	900	3000
3/8	1000	800	2500
7/16	800	700	2000
1/2	750	600	1800

METAL CUTTING

Next to drilling the most common operation in metal work is cutting. Sheet metal is cut with various types of hand snips, nibblers, and shears. Tubing is cut with tubing cutters and hacksaws while the ends are shaped with snips and files.

HACKSAWS

The faithful hacksaw just has to be the most mis-used tool in the world. First off, good hacksaw blades are expensive. They are, however, more than worth the price as cheap ones just don't work. Good ones improperly used also don't work. High speed steel flexible backed blades are what you want. You will need 18 teeth per inch, and 24 teeth per inch blades and should have a few at 32 teeth per inch for thin wall tubing and hard stuff. The idea is to keep a minimum of 2 teeth cutting at all times (yes, that does mean that you shouldn't saw thin sheet metal directly across its edge— slant the saw to get some teeth in contact). The thinner the cross section of the work, the finer the blade you should use. Also the harder the work, the finer the blade. For mild steel bar stock and the like use 18 tooth pitch. For tubing use 24. For very thin wall tube, etc., use 32. Hacksaw frames are cheap, and you should have at least two so you are not forever changing blades. The blade must be installed with the teeth pointing away from the handle.

HACKSAW TECHNIQUE

Make very sure that the work is firmly held in the vise or whatever. Always start the cut with a light forward stoke.

ALL cutting is done on the forward stroke. The back stroke serves only to return the blade to the starting point and to clear the chips. Use no pressure at all on the back stroke and bring the saw STRAIGHT BACK. Hold the saw firmly with BOTH hands and use the full length of the blade on each stroke. Saw at a steady rate of 40 to 50 strokes per minute and use only enough pressure to make sure that each tooth cuts a little metal. The man who saws furiously with heavy (and usually short) strokes is slow and breaks a lot of blades. Those that he doesn't break he burns up. His cuts look bad and so does he.

SNIPS

At least three pair of snips are required—left hand cutting, right hand cutting and straight. The left and right handed snips should be WISS compound aviation snips; all other brands are inferior. The straight snips should be "Standard Tinsmith's Snips" in as large a size as you feel is practical. The compound snips have the disadvantage of leaving a slightly serrated edge, but since all cut edges must be finished anyway, this is no big thing and the effort saved by their use is enormous. To avoid ragged edges never cut to the full depth of the blades—cut to about two thirds blade depth—and make sure that the blades are tracking in the cut as you go.

When cutting a piece from a large sheet with snips (necessary only when a squaring shear, power snips or power nibbler are not available), use the standard tinsmith's snips and always cut from the left side of the work which allows the piece being cut to curl up. It is almost impossible for a large sheet to curl down—particularly if you are

46

Figure (23): Use of Drill, Chisel and File to Obtain Large Area Holes in Metal Too Heavy to be Cut With Snips

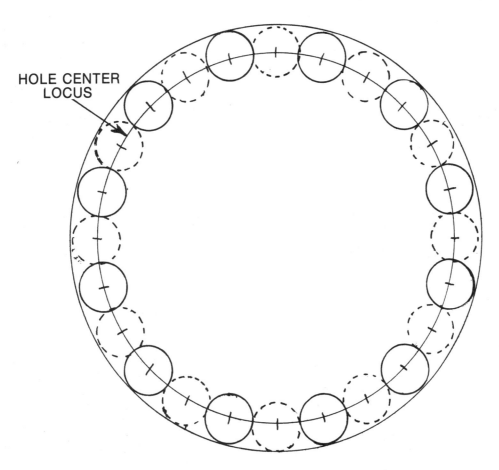

HOLE CENTER
LOCUS

CENTER PUNCH ALL HOLE CENTERS
DRILL ALTERNATE HOLES FIRST
CUT ANY METAL REMAINING BETWEEN HOLES WITH COLD CHISEL
FINISH WITH FILE

wrestling with it on the floor or a bench.

Never cut to the intersection of an inside corner with snips. The cuts will overlap onto the part and leave a beautiful built in stress raiser. Drill or punch a small hole at the corner and cut to the hole. The hole also marks the corner for you. About $5.00 will buy you a pair of hand nibblers by the Adel Tool Company. They are invaluable for cutting inside shapes in thin sheet metal—particularly when the sheet metal is already installed on the car. A vast number of deburring and dressing tools are marketed. I prefer the BurrQuik Set Model 500 by UMPCO Inc. It is small, cheap and will do holes, edges and tubing I.D.s. All edges should be finally finished with a folded piece of fine emery cloth.

FILES

Another severely abused tool is the file. At least 1000 different types are made. We don't need very many of them. Most of our filing will be to finish a part rather than to remove large amounts of metal (which closely resembles very hard work). The single cut file in the second bastard grade will do nicely for almost everything. You should have a couple of different sizes of flat and half round files, a few rat tails and a set of "Swiss Pattern" files for fine work. A curved tooth or "vixen" is handy for aluminum work and maybe a couple of large double cut bastards for roughing will complete the set.

Files seldom get dull—the teeth get clogged. Buy a file card and use it every time you use a file. Brush with the angle on which the teeth are cut.

Points to remember in filing are:

(1) Always use a file handle and make sure that it is tight on the tang. Not only does this prevent you from punching a hole in your hand, but it gives you much better control over the file.

(2) File teeth face forward. Like the hacksaw, the file cuts only on the forward stroke. On steel, lift the file from the work on the return stroke to avoid dulling it.

47

With aluminum let it ride on the work with zero pressure to clean the teeth.

(3) The work must be held firmly and positively to prevent slipping of the work and tooth chatter.

(4) Use both hands. File with a steady even stroke using just enough pressure to keep the teeth engaged in the cut. Use the full length of the file on each stroke. With a round or half-round file the cut will be smoother if the file is rotated slightly during the forward stroke. A slicing motion during the cutting stroke will go a long way toward eliminating hollows in the work.

(5) The file is a specialized cutting tool. It is brittle. It is not a hammer; it is not a chisel; it is not a pry bar. It should not be thrown in loose with other tools and it should not be allowed to become rusty.

(6) If there is another way available to do the job it is almost bound to be less work than filing. Frequently there is no other way.

That's pretty much it for the tools used in drilling and cutting sheet metal and tubing. We won't discuss chisels except to say that you should have a couple of cold chisels and that they should be kept sharpened.

The actual manufacture of parts can be grouped into three overlapping classifications—tubular work, sheet metal work and machining.

TUBULAR WORK

I personally feel that tubular work is the easiest of the lot. The fit of tube intersections is critical, but it is also easy, if somewhat time consuming. Figure (24) shows the easy way to lay out junctions of one tube with another. Cutting is done with a hacksaw and the tube end is shaped to fit with left and right handed snips and various files. Heavy wall tubing is both roughed and finished with files which is laborious. We shouldn't be using any heavy wall tubing on a race car anyway. If a run of identical parts is to be made and a milling machine is available, it may well be worthwhile making a fixture and forming all of the tube ends on the mill. Tubing should not be clamped directly in a vise. The use of wooden vee blocks Figure (25) will prevent crushing and/or marring the tube.

Figure (24): Method of Laying Out Tube Junctions

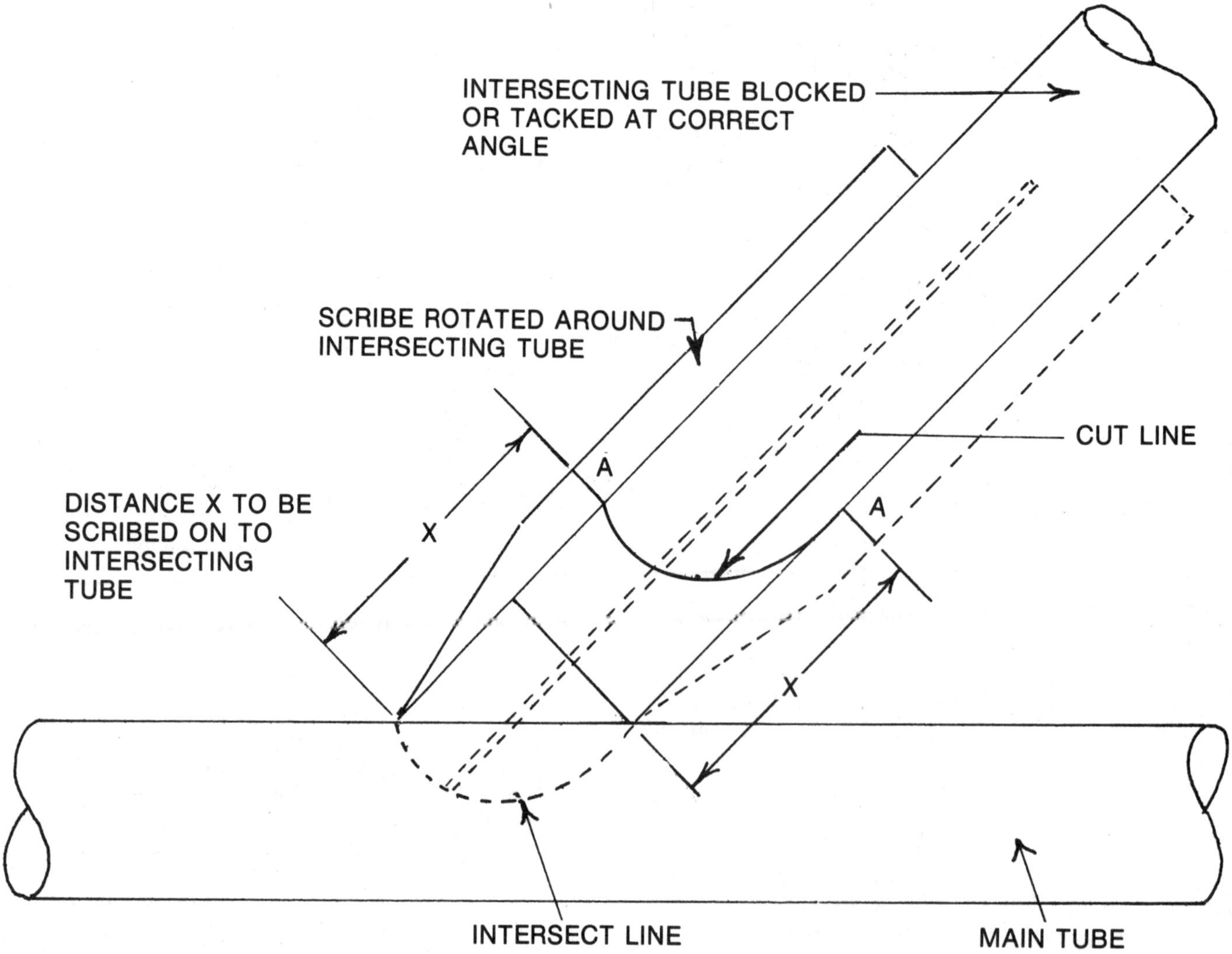

INTERSECTING TUBE BLOCKED OR TACKED AT CORRECT ANGLE

SCRIBE ROTATED AROUND INTERSECTING TUBE

CUT LINE

DISTANCE X TO BE SCRIBED ON TO INTERSECTING TUBE

INTERSECT LINE

MAIN TUBE

48

Figure (25): Use of Wooden Vee Blocks to Hold Tubing in Vise

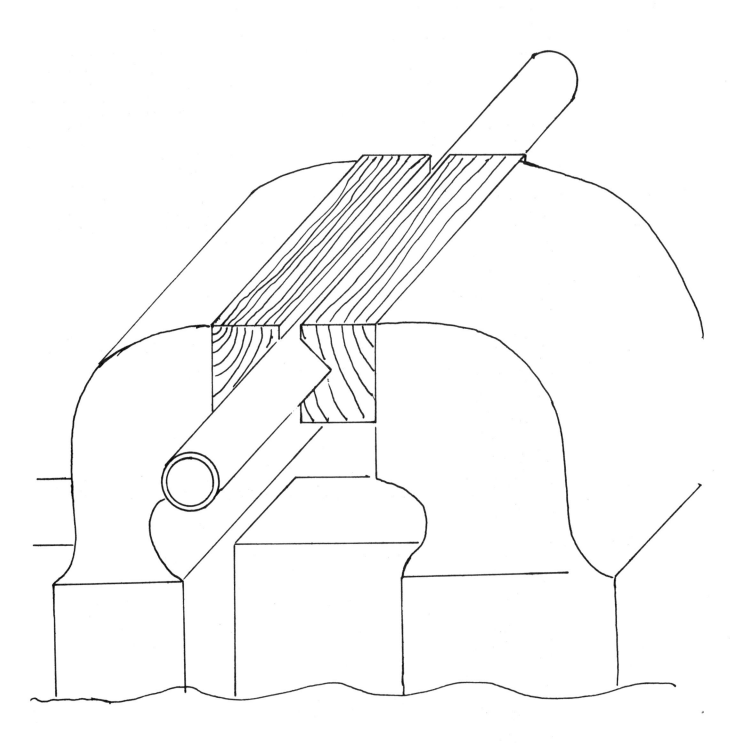

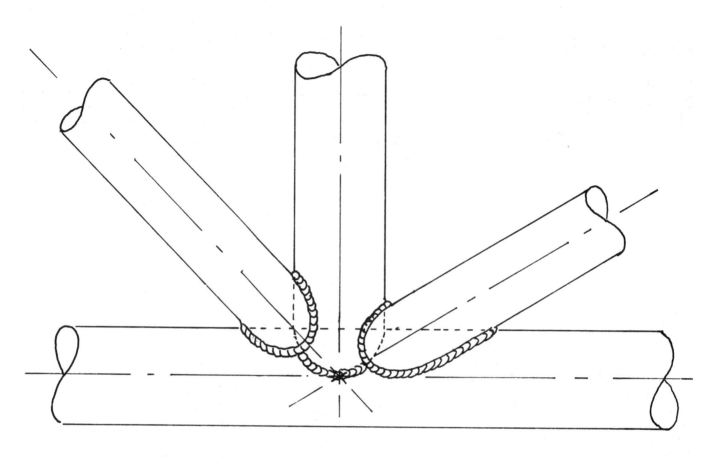

Figure (26): Multiple Tube Junction. Note That All Tube Centerlines Converge at Centerline of Main Tube.

TUBULAR JOINTS

When constructing multi-tube joints it is very important to lay out the tubes so that the axes of all the tubes in the joint meet at a common intersection at the axis of the major tube. Figure (26) illustrates this point. It is also critical that all welds be placed in shear rather than in tension. This can be accomplished by chamfering or fishmouthing the joint. Figure (28) If a butt weld must be used (and it very often must), then the joint should be reinforced by a finger plate Figure (29) Plain butt welds should be avoided.

Repair of damaged tubular structures can be accomplished by inside sleeves Figure (30), outside sleeves Figure (31), finger plates Figure (32), gussets Figure (33), or a combination of methods. The repaired structure will invariably be heavier than the original but it should be equally strong.

Suspension links, mounts and braces require some sort of end fitting to allow attachment and/or adjustment. Figures (34), (35) and (36) illustrate some of the usual methods. Figure (37) shows the construction of a split type tubular clamp used in many applications.

When using split outside sleeves or any type of inside sleeve it is essential to leave sufficient gap so that the sleeve can be welded to the tube, as shown in Figures (27) and (30). Rosette welds should be 1/4 tube diameter with a minimum of 3/16". They should be liberally used.

FIXTURES FOR TUBULAR WORK

When making or repairing tubular parts some sort of holding fixture will normally be necessary in order to keep the parts in their proper alignment while welding. The fixture requirement can vary from a couple of C clamps and a plate to a full chassis fixture. Necessity is the mother of invention! Don't spend time and money building a fixture that is more elaborate than necessary. When tempted (and you will be) to start cutting and welding without taking the time and trouble to rig a fixture, remember the Racer's motto, "We didn't have time to do it right; but we found time to do it twice."

SHEET METAL

So much for tubes. Sheet metal can be vexing—particularly when you don't have much equipment to work with. Most of us don't—and that includes some very successful car builders who do beautiful work. If you are so fortunate as to have a squaring shear, a leaf brake, a box and pan brake, slip rollers, a rotex punch, a Do-All band saw and a combination beading and rolling machine, then you undoubtedly know how to use them, and you are looking good—until you arrive at the East Oshkosh Grand Prix and are reduced to a pair of 2x4s and a hammer. It is very true that fine results are a damn sight easier to achieve with good equipment, but it is equally true that the racer had

Figure (27): Split Sleeve Reinforcement

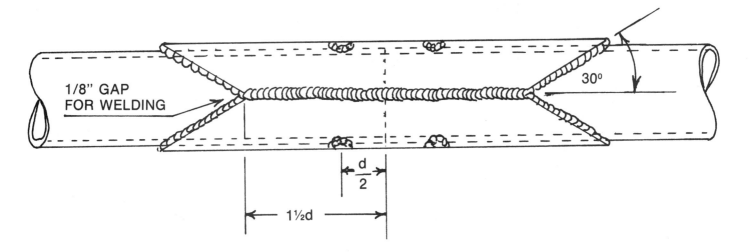

better learn how to achieve virtually the same results without it, because that's the way he is going to do most of his work. While there is only one Phil Remington, you can learn to do a decent job in the field—and you had better!

TOOLS

The obvious tools that you are going to need—rawhide and wooden mallets, planishing hammers, dollies, etc., should be augmented by some lengths of straight angle iron, 2 1/2" x 2 1/2" x 1/4" web will do although 3" x 3" is better: Get two pieces about 30" long and two about 18" long. Grind or file the faces smooth; radius the corners of two lengths and pin them together. Obtain some lengths and chunks of hardwood (redwood or pine won't get it done) and some tempered masonite. These along with various scraps of aluminum plate, lengths of tube and bar stock, welding bottles, sandbags and clamps can be used to do an amazing variety of things with sheet metal.

BENDING SHEET METAL

Sheet metal can be bent between clamped angle irons in lengths up to about 30" in 18 gauge mild steel and up to about 18" in 14 gauge steel. See Figure (38). Clamp the sheet very firmly indeed between the angles, one end of which is held in a vise. The desired bend line must be exactly positioned at the center of the radius of the angle iron. Use a piece of hardwood at least 2" x 8" as a form with which to bend the sheet. This wooden form must be kept tight against the sheet to avoid wrinkles. Clamp the wood to the sheet. The result of all this will be a fairly generously radiused bend. To tighten the bend, remove the bending board before the bend is completed, place a heavy block (which must be long enough to prevent denting the work) against the sheet and pound on it with a hammer, moving the block along the bend as you go. Never hammer directly on the sheet. Don't try to do it all at once—proceed slowly and gradually.

A large radius can be bent using one angle iron and a length of tube or bar stock of the proper radius Figure (38).

A truly large radius can be hand bent around a welding bottle, sewer pipe or whatever.

Straight flanges can be formed by clamping the work between two angle irons or boards and hammering the flange gradually with a rawhide mallet Figure (39).

Hardwood or tempered masonite blocks or steel bending forms can be used to produce various box, top hat and channel shapes Figure (40) and (41). Don't beat the metal directly over the edge of a vise.

FORMING SHEET METAL

Sheet metal is formed into curves and compound shapes by shrinking or stretching the metal (sometimes both). Figure (42) shows how "flipping blocks" are used to produce drawn shapes. Figure (43) shows how dished tank tops and the like are hammered over a masonite or aluminum form. Curved flanges can be stretched over a hammer block Figure (44) but stretching is more difficult and will usually require cutting vees out of the flange unless form blocks are used Figure (45). The form blocks can be used for either stretching or shrinking. No matter what method is used, it is essential to avoid sharp corners, so whatever hammer form is used must have some radius. This is also true when using the leaf brake or the box and pan brake. In this case a radius sheet of the required thickness is placed between the work and the brake die. Figure (46) lists minimum bend radii for most materials, along with their physical properties and characteristics.

ANNEALING

When metal is shaped it tends to "work harden" and crack. Normally you won't be working enough shape into steel parts to worry about it but, since most non-structural aluminum parts are made from Alloy 3003-H14 which is in the "half hard" condition, for extreme shapes it is best to anneal the sheet (or tube). This can be very simply done with a rosebud tip on the welding torch. With a carburizing flame evenly deposit a thin layer of carbon on the area to be annealed. With a neutral flame, burn the carbon off. Keep the flame well away from the metal and keep it moving. Let the part air cool and it is annealed. The process can be

Figure (28): Types of Welded Joints for Tubing

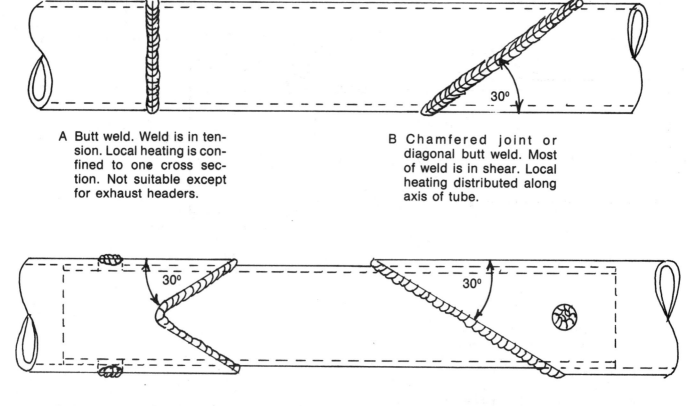

A Butt weld. Weld is in tension. Local heating is confined to one cross section. Not suitable except for exhaust headers.

B Chamfered joint or diagonal butt weld. Most of weld is in shear. Local heating distributed along axis of tube.

C Piloted tubes with fishmouth joint and rosettes.

D Piloted tubes with diagonal butt weld and rosettes.

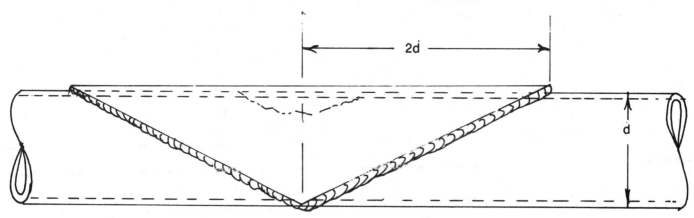

E Welded patch over locally damaged tube. Ideally, damaged area should be no more than 1 tube diameter in length and should extend no more than 90 degrees in circumference,

Figure (29): Finger Plate Reinforcement For Tube Junction With Weld in Tension

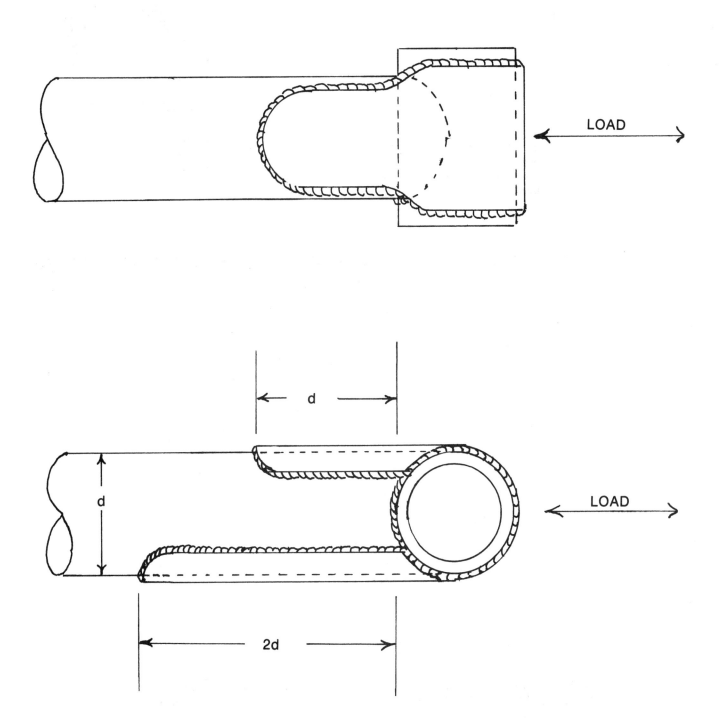

Figure (30): Inner Sleeve Splice at Tube Junction

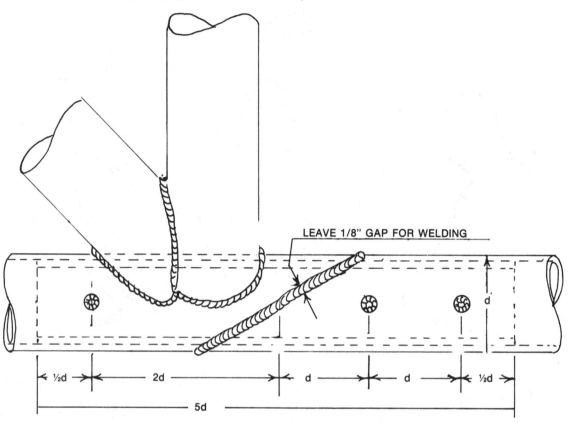

Figure (31): Outer Sleeve Splice at Tube Junction

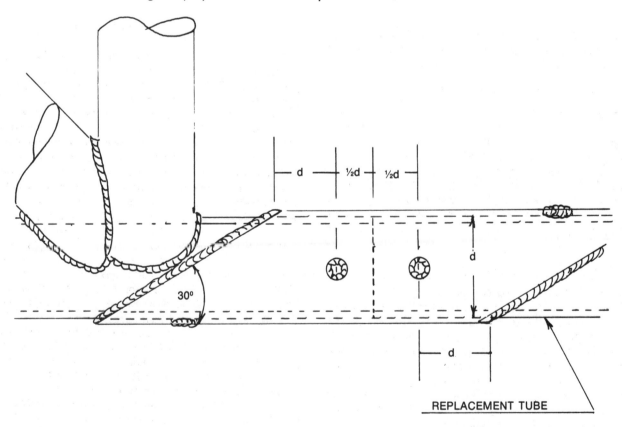

54

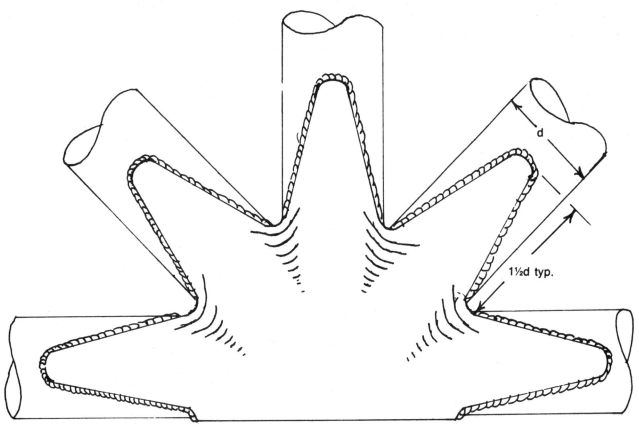

Figure (32): Tube Junction Reinforcement by Finger Plates

repeated as necessary. When forming steel sheet into fairly extreme shapes, as in finger patches and the like, you will do better hot forming it at a dull cherry red.

COMPOUND SHAPES

Despite your most frantic efforts it is not always possible to avoid compound shapes. Short run compound shapes are commercially formed on air hammers, wheeling machines and spinners by very skilled people. We do it by hand, with mallets, planishing hammers, slappers, sandbags, dollies, forms and infinite patience. Start in the center of the area to be formed, and work gradually in a spiral pattern toward the outside. Form in several intermediate stages and do a lot of re-annealing. Gradual work will prevent the bag of walnuts syndrome.

LAYOUT

In making sheet metal parts it is very important to take the time to accurately lay the part out and to work out the sequence of operations before you start. This is the only way that you can be sure that (1) you CAN make the part and (2) that the part will fit when you do get it done. Layout is really pretty simple requiring only a spray can of Dychem, a scribe, a felt pen, a pair of dividers, a prick punch, a machinist's rule and a combination square. A basic knowledge of plane geometry helps, and an understanding of the "bend allowance" procedure is essential.

BEND ALLOWANCE

When metal is bent, the material on the inside of the bend compresses while that on the outside stretches. The neutral axis of the material lies slightly inside the 1/2 thickness line. The compression is greater than the expansion and the metal therefore actually shrinks or loses length when it is bent. Allowance for this shrinkage must be made when the part is layed out or the dimensions will not come out. The formula for this "bend allowance" is B.A.=(.017 x Radius of bend plus .00872 x Thickness of Sheet) x Angle of Bend in Degrees. This is pretty cumbersome. Figure (47) tabulates bend allowances for various radii and sheet thicknesses for one degree of bend. The value selected from the table must be multiplied by the number of degrees in the bend in order to determine the actual bend allowance. We can ignore bend allowance for many non-critical parts. We can always round it off to the nearest 1/64" and usually to the nearest 1/32". But we had best not ignore it for items such as chassis skins. Figure (48) shows bend allowance computation and flat pattern layout for a very simple part.

Flat pattern layouts should be made for all critical parts. The time spent in making the layout will be more than made up for by the time saved in making the part—even if the part made without a layout does fit. If several identical parts are to be made it is worth while making the flat pattern layout from thin tempered aluminum or galvanized steel (cheaper) so that it can serve as a tracing pattern, hole location

Figure (33): Tube Joint Reinforcement by Gussets

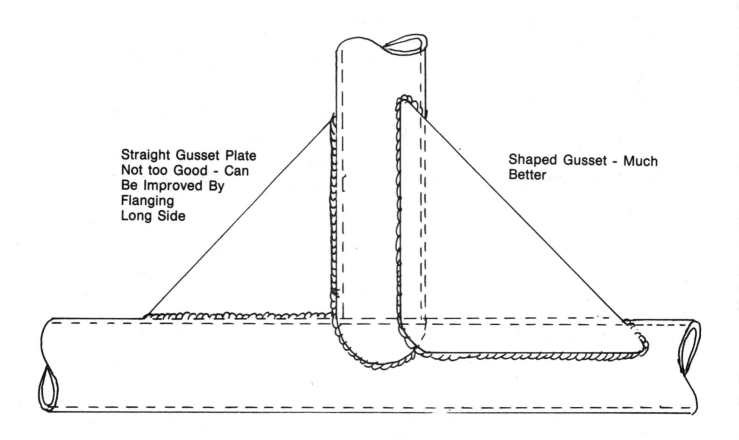

Straight Gusset Plate
Not too Good - Can
Be Improved By
Flanging
Long Side

Shaped Gusset - Much
Better

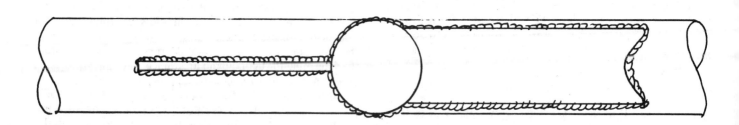

56

Figure (34): Tube Ends - Boss Type

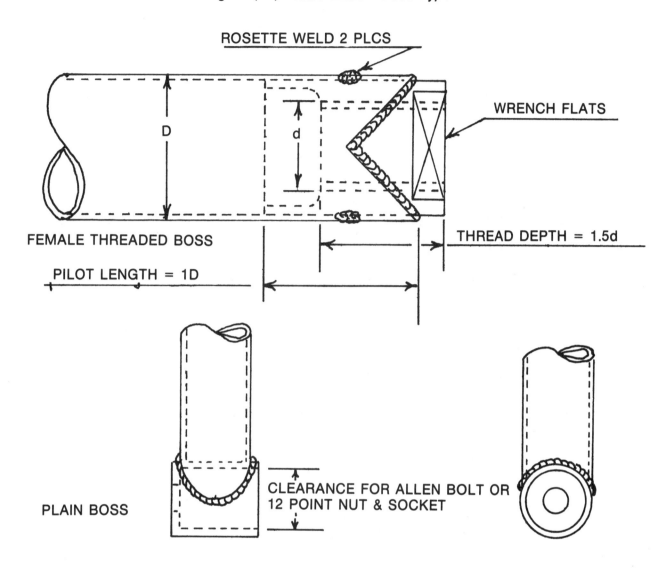

ROSETTE WELD 2 PLCS

WRENCH FLATS

D

d

FEMALE THREADED BOSS

THREAD DEPTH = 1.5d

PILOT LENGTH = 1D

PLAIN BOSS

CLEARANCE FOR ALLEN BOLT OR 12 POINT NUT & SOCKET

pattern and bend line pattern for subsequent parts. You should also mark the direction of each bend and the bending sequence on both the pattern and the work. This will avoid scrapping parts that can't be finished because the last bend can't be made or parts which were bent in the wrong direction. It is remarkable how easy it is to bend a part in the wrong direction. I am expert at it! Bend lines must be marked on the inside of each bend. Obviously this means that some lines will have to be transferred to the opposite side of the work. Bend lines are layed out and marked with a felt tipped pen—never with a scribe. A scribed line is a glorious stress raiser and any part bent at a scribe line will eventually break at that line. Scribed lines indicate cuts only.

REPAIRS

Sooner or later every race car gets more or less severely bent, presenting someone with a problem. We all realize that final repairs take time and may not put the car on the grid tomorrow morning. To reach the grid do whatever is necessary, so long as it is sound. Cover the dents with decals but never forget that the futures of a lot of people are involved in your decision as to whether or not a quick and dirty repair is safe to race.

ANALYZING DAMAGE

The first essential step in repairing a bent one, be it tube or monocoque, is to determine the exact extent of the damage. It is amazing how often this is overlooked. In the event of anything that resembles a major prang, this means stripping the car all the way down and REALLY inspecting it. One of the major advantages of the space frame and even more so of the stressed skin chassis is the way in which impact (i.e. crash) loads are progressively distributed throughout the structure. In addition to the obvious benefits to the hapless occupant of the car at the moment of impact, this means that parts of the structure a long way from the accident may be damaged. Inspect it all, looking for: bent tubes, distorted brackets, cracked welds, sprung or broken rivets, deformed skin or bulkheads and bent bolts. Bolt strength being what it is a bent bolt usually means distorted

57

Figure (35): Tube Ends - Flat and Yoke Types

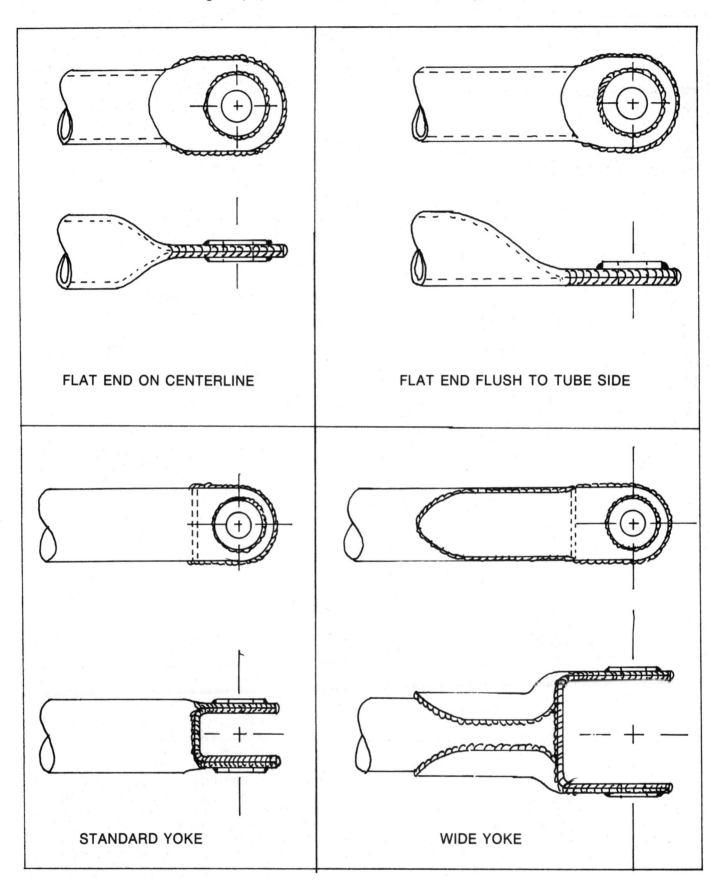

FLAT END ON CENTERLINE

FLAT END FLUSH TO TUBE SIDE

STANDARD YOKE

WIDE YOKE

Figure (36): Ends for Streamline Tube

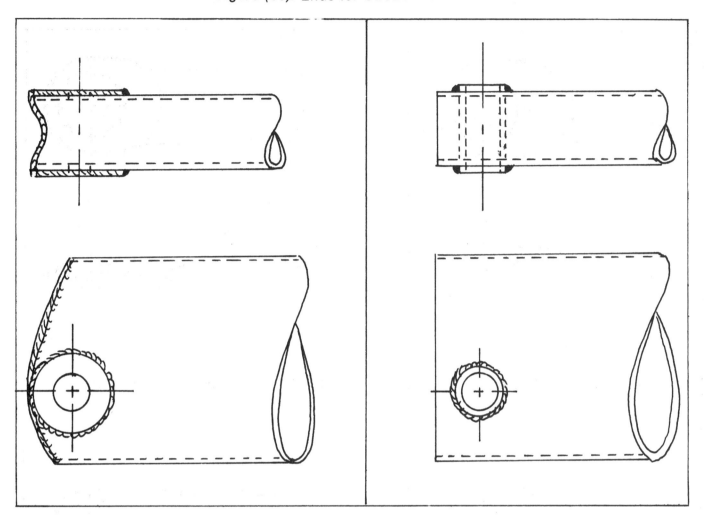

Figure (37): Tubular Clamp ("Dutchman Clamp")

Figure (38): Clamped Angle Irons Used to Bend and Radius Sheet Metal

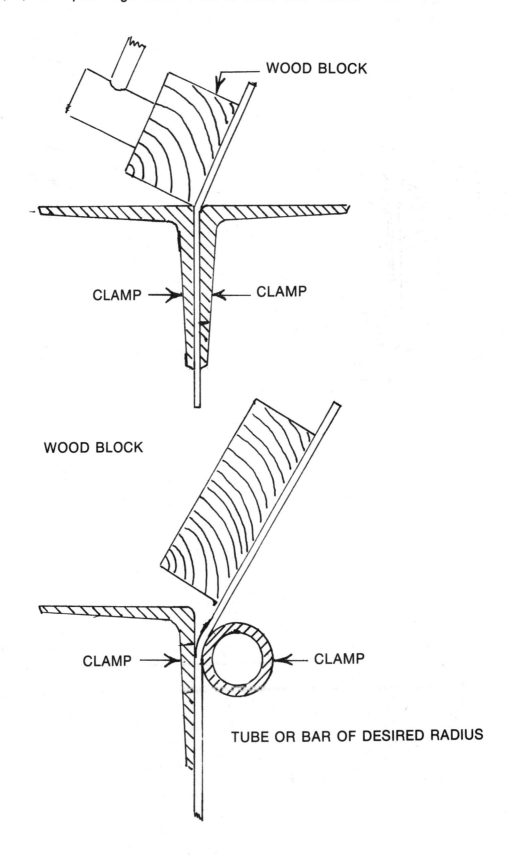

WOOD BLOCK

CLAMP → ← CLAMP

WOOD BLOCK

CLAMP → ← CLAMP

TUBE OR BAR OF DESIRED RADIUS

Figure (39): Use of Clamped Wooden Block for Bending Sheet Metal

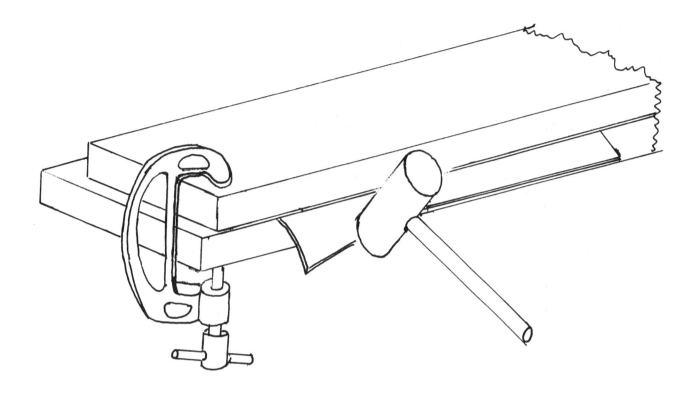

Figure (40): Bending a Box Shape by Means of Blocks and Clamps

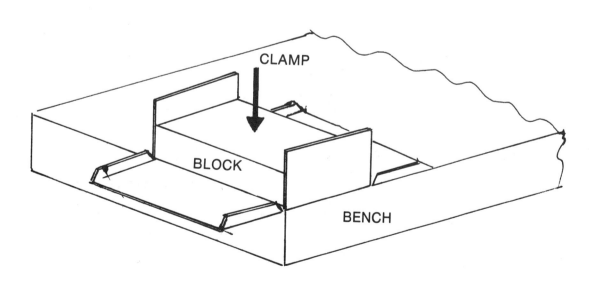

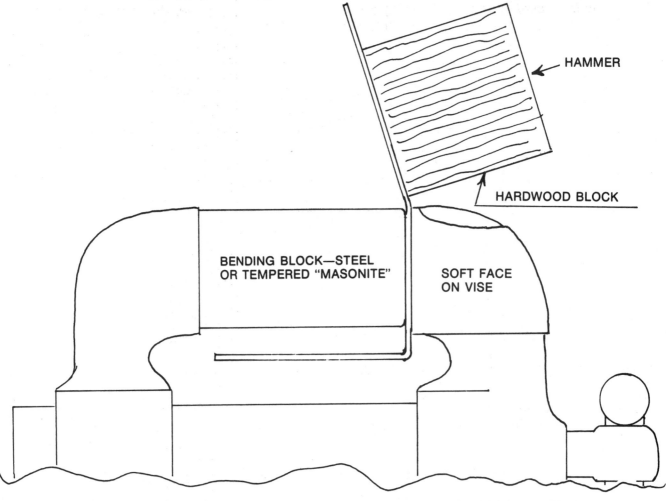

Figure (41): Bending a "U" Shape in a Vise With Bending Block

HAMMER

HARDWOOD BLOCK

BENDING BLOCK—STEEL OR TEMPERED "MASONITE"

SOFT FACE ON VISE

structure where the bolt was. The inertia of the engine and transaxle assembly makes it imperative that their mounts and the structure to which the mounts attach be closely inspected after any crash.

The next step is to take measurements—lots of them, including diagonal ones—of the suspension pick up points to determine if the chassis has been bent or twisted and how much. It is a big help at this time if you took all of these measurements at some time before the season started because now you will have a good reference.

Whatever the damage, it is almost always repairable. Sometimes it is not economically worth it, but whatever someone built, someone else can fix. If it's really bad, check the price of a replacement chassis—it just may be a pleasant surprise.

TUBE FRAME REPAIR

With a tube frame, repair is a pretty straightforward process of cutting until you reach good structure, and replacing the bad bits. If the damage approaches being major, a holding fixture will probably have to be built in order to end up with a straight chassis. The fixture need not be elaborate. Anything that will hold the front and rear suspension pickup points in their designed relationships and locate the various brackets will do.

MONOCOQUE REPAIR

With the stressed skin chassis, the fix is liable to be less obvious—not more complex, or difficult—just less obvious. Good men who will attack a tube frame with joy and anticipation tend to shy away from repair of stressed skin structures. This attitude is, fortunately, unfounded. Damage falls into two major categories—bulkheads and skins. If a bulkhead is distorted or broken, it will have to be removed in order to be repaired. This means nothing more than the removal and subsequent replacement of a lot of rivets. Bulkheads are usually fabricated from steel tubes and are repaired by normal methods. If they happen to be sheet metal fabrications, the job will be more complex and time consuming, but not particularly more difficult.

Since stressed skins are normally formed from tempered alloys, they are not easily straightened. Luckily the vast majority of designers are practical men who avoid compound curves like the plague. This means that small areas of skin damage can be repaired by cutting away the damaged portion and replacing it. Form the patch from 2024-T3 aluminum the same thickness as the original skin (6061-T6 is an acceptable substitute). Install it with a full doubler ring on the inside of the chassis and a double row of flush rivets. Figure (49) llustrates. It is often convenient (and always structurally sound and advisable) to extend the patch to a

Figure (42): Use of Hammer Block or Flipping Blocks to Form Drawn Shapes. This is the Usual Method of Forming Wing Ribs. On a Larger Scale, Bulkheads, Etc. Are Formed in the Same Way.

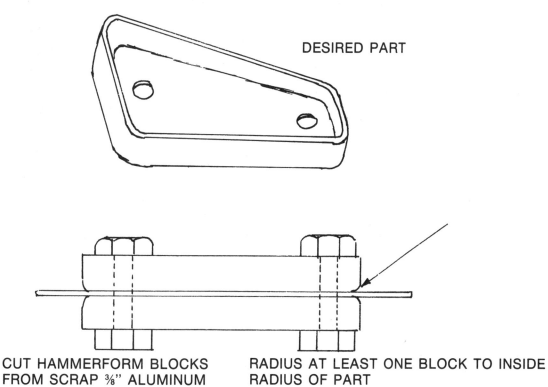

DESIRED PART

CUT HAMMERFORM BLOCKS
FROM SCRAP ⅜" ALUMINUM

RADIUS AT LEAST ONE BLOCK TO INSIDE
RADIUS OF PART

CUT MATERIAL OVERSIZE: HAMMER TO SHAPE:
TRIM & FILE SMOOTH

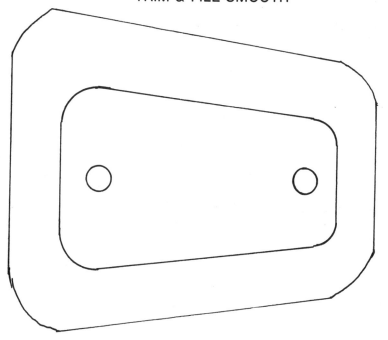

Figure (43): Use of Tempered Masonite or Wooden Hammer Form to Make Dished Tank Top or Similar Parts.

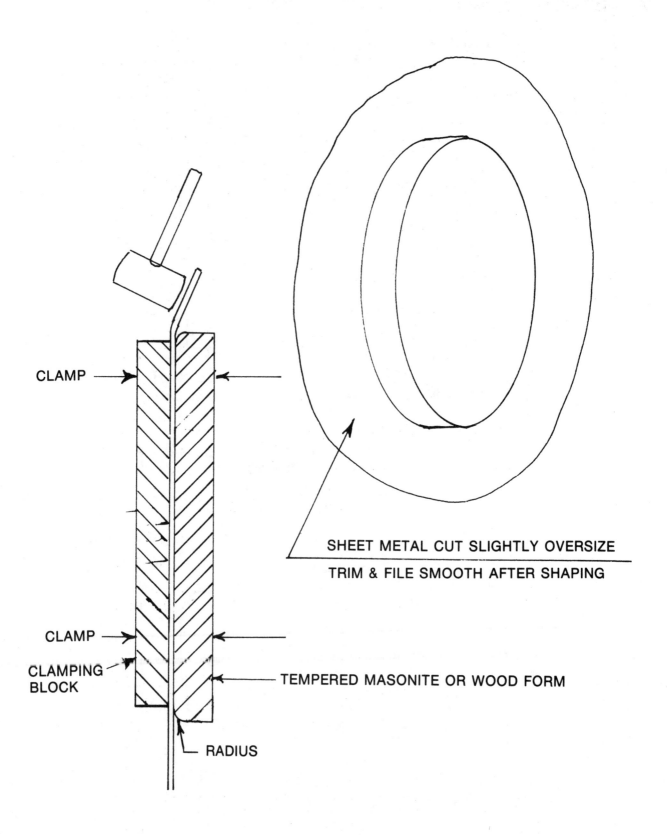

CLAMP

CLAMP

CLAMPING BLOCK

RADIUS

SHEET METAL CUT SLIGHTLY OVERSIZE

TRIM & FILE SMOOTH AFTER SHAPING

TEMPERED MASONITE OR WOOD FORM

Figure (44): Stretching and Shrinking Curved Flanges

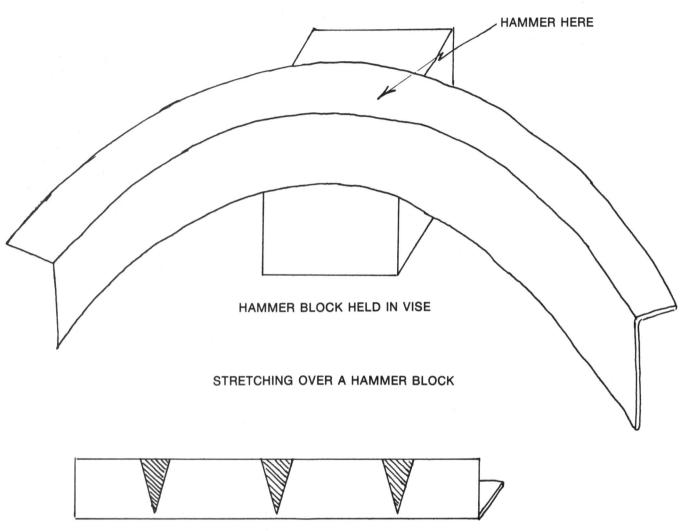

HAMMER HERE

HAMMER BLOCK HELD IN VISE

STRETCHING OVER A HAMMER BLOCK

SHRINKING BY VEE NOTCHES

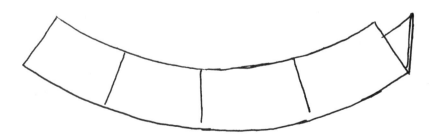

NOTCHES CLOSE WHEN CURVE IS FORMED—CAN BE WELDED IF DESIRED

65

Figure (45): Form Blocks for Stretching or Shrinking a Curved Flange

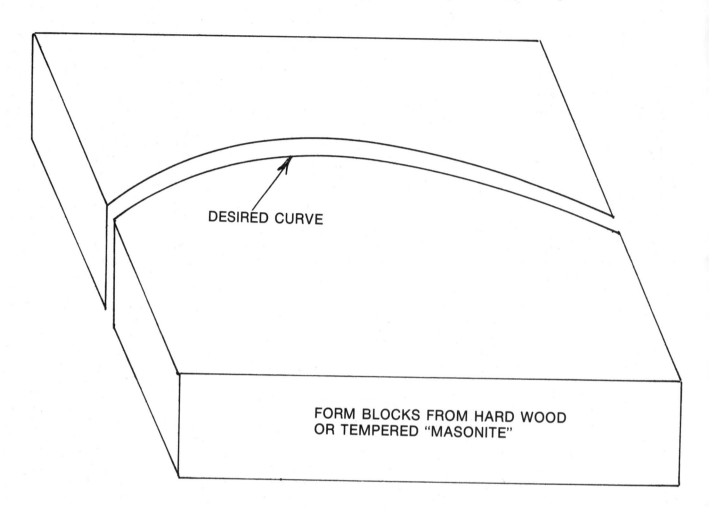

DESIRED CURVE

FORM BLOCKS FROM HARD WOOD
OR TEMPERED "MASONITE"

nearby bulkhead or original rivet joint. Normal body putty treatment (Devcon aluminum putty is better) will completely hide the patch if the area is painted.

If skin damage is extensive, it will be necessary to form and install complete replacement panels. To do this you will need access to a brake and a shear. Your local air conditioning sheet metal shop has them—and a lot more besides. You should cultivate the acquaintance and friendship of the proprietor. Be very careful with your flat pattern layouts for skins and fold up a couple of narrow cross-section tryout pieces before doing the real thing.

You may well find broken or loose rivets with no apparent skin damage. Earlier remarks on the design of riveted joints apply. A dirt or oil ring around the head of a rivet is a dead giveaway. Replace such rivets with the next size larger as their holes are bound to be distorted.

BRACKETS

Of the commonly fabricated items, those most prone to failure are the numerous brackets and braces used to attach various auxiliary items (tanks, coils, wings, exhaust systems, etc.) to the vehicle. Almost invariably the failure is due to poor mechanical design or to poor choice of material or joining methods. Often the reason for the poor design is that the bracket was an afterthought and never was designed at all—it just got built. A race lost because the coil or the oil tank fell off is just as irrevocably lost as one lost for any other reason. Brackets deserve your full attention—and a great deal of thought. The items attached by brackets are liable to vibrate a lot, so only ductile materials should be used. You should give a lot of thought to the alternative methods available before deciding to do much welding in the bracket department. Also bear in mind that the oil tank which you are idly tossing in your hand while you are trying to figure out how and where to mount it is going to weigh 24 pounds more with three gallons of oil in it—and a further 12 under 1.5 g loading. The downforce generated by a wing, and the penalty for losing it make wing mountings a subject for very serious study. Don't forget what happens to the direction of loading on a wing mount when the car spins. Make all of the attachments for failure prone items such as coils and amplifiers really quick change and use isolation mountings of some description for those items which don't like vibration. Here, as in so many areas, a little care and forethought can save a lot of heartache and unnecessary work.

Figure (46): Physical Properties of Common Alloys

ALLOY & TEMPER	TENSILE STRENGTH P.S.I. ULTIMATE	YIELD	ULTIMATE SHEAR STRENGTH P.S.I.	% ELONGATION IN 2"	FORMABILITY	MIN. BEND RADIUS (X THICKNESS)	WELDABILITY	MACHINABILITY	WEIGHT (LB/IN)
ALUMINUM									
3303-H14	22,000	21,000	14,000	16%	GOOD	1+T	EXCELLENT	FAIR	.099
2024-T3	70,000	50,000	41,000	18%	POOR	3+T	NOT RECOMMENDED	EXCELLENT	.100
5052-H34	38,000	31,000	21,000	10%	GOOD	1+T	FAIR	FAIR	.097
6061-T4	35,000	21,000	24,000	22%	FAIR	3T	EXCELLENT	FAIR	.098
6061-T6	45,000	40,000	30,000	12%	FAIR	4T	EXCELLENT	GOOD	.098
7075-T6	83,000	73,000	48,000	11%	NOT RECOMMENDED	10T	NOT RECOMMENDED	EXCELLENT	.101
MAGNESIUM									
AZ31B-H24	42,000	30,000	29,000	15%	POOR	8T	NOT RECOMMENDED	EXCELLENT	.0642
STEEL									
1018 COLD DRAWN	75,000	55,000		20%	EXCELLENT	2T	EXCELLENT	FAIR	.283
4130 NORMALIZED	92,000	75,000		17%	GOOD	2T	EXCELLENT	GOOD	.285
4130 ROCKWELL C30	138,000	116,000		12%	NOT RECOMMENDED	NOT RECOMMENDED	NOT RECOMMENDED	EXCELLENT	.285

Figure (47): Sheet-Metal Bend Allowance Chart for 1-Deg Angle

R \ T	.020 .022	.023 .025	.028 .029	.031 .032	.038 .040	.050 .051	.063 .064	.081	.091 .094	.125 .129
1/32	00072	00073	00076	00079	00086	00094	00104	00117	00125	00154
1/16	00126	00128	00131	00135	00140	00149	00159	00172	00180	00209
3/32	00180	00183	00185	00188	00195	00203	00213	00226	00234	00263
1/8	00235	00237	00240	00243	00249	00258	00268	00281	00289	00317
5/32	00290	00292	00294	00297	00304	00312	00322	00335	00343	00372
3/16	00344	00346	00349	00352	00358	00367	00377	00390	00398	00426
7/32	00398	00401	00403	00406	00412	00421	00431	00444	00452	00481
1/4	00454	00455	00458	00461	00467	00476	00486	00500	00507	00535
9/32	00507	00510	00512	00515	00521	00530	00540	00553	00561	00590
5/16	00562	00564	00567	00570	00576	00584	00595	00608	00616	00644
11/32	00616	00619	00620	00624	00630	00639	00649	00662	00670	00699
3/8	00671	00673	00675	00679	00685	00693	00704	00717	00725	00753
13/32	00725	00728	00730	00733	00739	00748	00758	00771	00779	00808
7/16	00780	00782	00784	00767	00794	00802	00812	00826	00834	00862
15/32	00834	00836	00839	00842	00848	00857	00867	00853	00888	00917
1/2	00889	00891	00893	00896	00903	00911	00921	00935	00943	00971
17/32	00943	00945	00948	00951	00957	00966	00976	00989	00997	01025
9/16	00998	01000	01002	01005	01012	01020	01030	01044	01051	01080
19/32	01051	01054	01055	01058	01065	01073	01083	01098	01105	01133
5/8	01107	01109	01111	01114	01121	01129	01139	01152	01160	01189
21/32	01161	01163	01166	01170	01175	01183	01193	01207	01214	01245
11/16	01216	01218	01220	01223	01230	01238	01248	01261	01269	01298
23/32	01269	01272	01273	01276	01283	01291	01301	01316	01322	01351
3/4	01324	01327	01329	01332	01338	01347	01357	01370	01378	01407
25/32	01378	01381	01383	01386	01392	01401	01411	01425	01432	01461
13/16	01433	01436	01438	01441	01447	01456	01466	01479	01487	01516
27/32	01487	01490	01491	01494	01501	01509	01519	01534	01540	01569
7/8	01542	01545	01548	01550	01556	01565	01575	01588	01596	01625
29/32	01596	01600	01601	01604	01610	01619	01629	01643	01650	01679
15/16	01651	01654	01655	01657	01665	01674	01684	01697	01705	01734
31/32	01705	01708	01709	01712	01718	01727	01737	01752	01758	01787
1	01760	01763	01765	01768	01774	01783	01793	01806	01814	01834

Minimum allowance below line —————— for hard aluminum.

Minimum allowance below line ------------ for soft aluminum and steel.

Multiply value from table by number of degrees in bend to determine actual bend allowance.

Figure (48): Computation and Layout of Bend Allowance

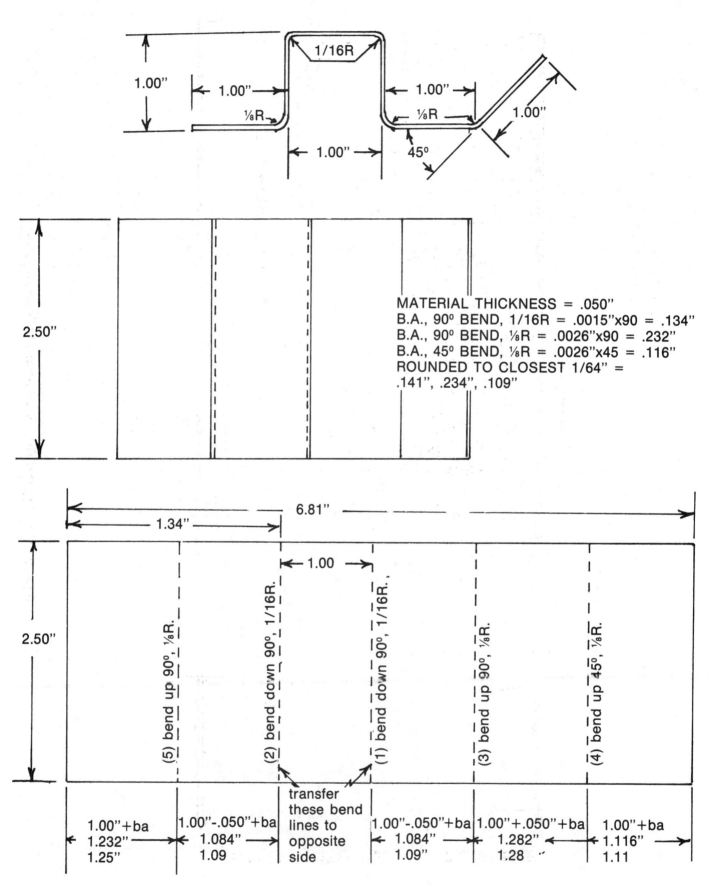

MATERIAL THICKNESS = .050"
B.A., 90° BEND, 1/16R = .0015"x90 = .134"
B.A., 90° BEND, ⅛R = .0026"x90 = .232"
B.A., 45° BEND, ⅛R = .0026"x45 = .116"
ROUNDED TO CLOSEST 1/64" =
.141", .234", .109"

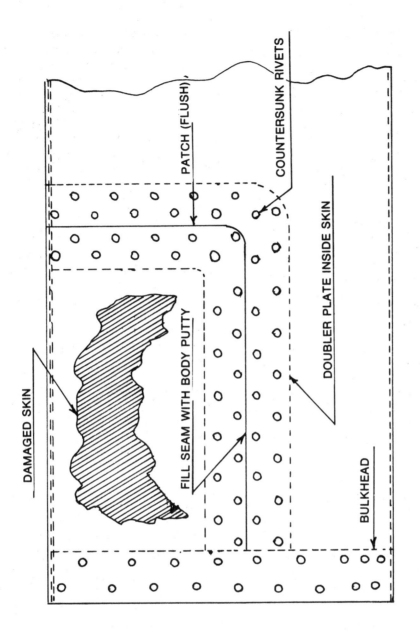

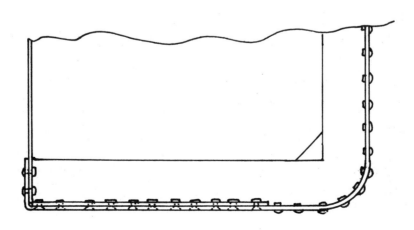

Figure (49): Typical Repair of Stressed Skin Damage

69

THREAD CUTTING

Another aspect of metal work is the cutting of threads. There is very little reason for us to cut male threads as we can buy whatever we want in that line at reasonable cost. This is just as well as the thread die is at best a miserable device which produces a poor thread. Threads can, of course, be turned on a lathe, but this requires a lathe and a fair bit of skill and time. Even then, lathe turned threads are not as strong as rolled threads. Nonetheless, you will have to obtain, eventually, a set of dies because sooner or later you are going to need them. They also serve to repair threads which have been damaged by carelessness or pure bloody mindedness.

The use of the thread die looks simple. It isn't, and experienced and skilled people regularly ruin parts by getting the threads on crooked. First off, make sure that the die is tightly held in the die holder and is installed right side up. The bottom, or starting, side of a die has a larger opening and a less sharply defined thread. It is often marked, "start this end". The top of the die is seated in the die holder. Deburr the stock to be threaded and, if possible, taper the end. Lubricate both the stock and the die ("Rapid Tap", or "Tap Magic" for steel and "Alumitap" for aluminum work very well, but any sulphur based oil for steel and kerosene for aluminum will do). To start the thread, hold the die handle near the middle (a one handed hold at the center seems to work best for me) and, exerting enough downward pressure to make the die cut, start turning it. If you can keep the die straight for the first two or three turns, you've got it made. You must reverse the die every half turn or so to break and clear the chip. Once the thread has started, further down pressure is not necessary or wanted. Let the die thread itself onto the work and do its own thing—it will cut cleaner that way. Keep everything well lubricated and go ahead on. If it is a critical application (which it had better not be, or you have no business threading it with a die), relieve the last thread or two with a radiused groove on the lathe. The last thread cut by a die is one of the all-time great natural stress raisers.

If we don't do much male threading, we make up for it by cutting a lot of internal threads. Normally this is accomplished by the use (or misuse) of the hand tap. If it is accomplished by the correct use of the hand tap, the thread will be a lot better, and the taps—which are expensive—will last a lot longer.

The first rule in tapping a threaded hole is to use a tap drill chart and to drill the hole the correct size and in the required direction. Of equal importance is the tap itself. Cheap taps are junk. They cut lousy threads and they break. Spend the money and buy good taps. There are three configurations of hand taps. The starting tap has a long taper on the point which centers itself and the thread in the hole so that the thread will be straight. Since several teeth are doing the cutting it is easier to use and lasts longer. The second, and most common, tap is the plug tap which has a much less pronounced starting taper. In principle it is used to finish threading through holes and as the second operation on blind holes. In practice it is normally used as a starting tap. Since the plug tap does have a starting taper, it cannot cut threads to the bottom of a blind hole. The bottoming tap,

without a taper, can and does. It cannot be used to successfully start a thread. Good practice calls for using at least two taps on each hole; virtually no one does. A perfectly straight thread can be started with a plug tap if sufficient care is taken with alignment and enough steady downward pressure is exerted to start the tap cutting. As with the threading die, after the thread is started, further downward pressure is not desirable and the tap rotation must be reversed every half turn to break and clear the chip. Straight threads are a damn sight easier to achieve in a drill press or lathe than they are by hand. In both cases the machine is used for alignment and the turning is done by hand—at least by the inexperienced and relatively unskilled.

Use a good tap holder—not a crescent wrench (or any wrench, for that matter) or an El Cheapo special. A Tee handled wrench is handy for the smaller taps. Turn the tap slowly and with even pressure. Use a lubricant—same as for cutting threads with a die. Tapered pipe threads are cut with a tapered pipe die. A tapered hole is required for which pipe reamers are made. This tends to be a pain. Tapered pipe threads are an abomination anyway. Use a straight thread and an "O" ring.

THE LATHE

Beginning Mechanical Engineering students are informed that the screw cutting lathe is the only machine tool capable of reproducing itself. I am personally convinced that a really good machinist with an engine lathe can make anything that can be produced by machining. Attachments can be bought or made which allow both grinding and milling operations to be performed. The good lathe operator's potential is virtually unlimited. The average racer can also produce good parts on the lathe—not as quickly as a machinist can—but he can produce them. What I am trying to say is that if you are going racing seriously, you must obtain a lathe or access to a lathe, and you must learn how to use it. We will not conduct a course in machine work—if for no other reason than that I am not qualified to do so. MACHINERY'S HANDBOOK or KENT'S MECHANICAL ENGINEER'S HANDBOOK—one of which you should have—plus the operator's manual for the lathe in question will tell you, plainly and in great detail, everything you need to know—except for the important bits that can only be learned by experience.

Most of the troubles encountered in lathe turning come from either improperly ground tools for the job in question, improper spindle speeds, trying to take too big a cut, or not using a lubricant/coolant. Figures (50), (51), (52), (53) and (54) illustrate the basics here.

CHATTER

Chatter—of the tool or of the work—is a No No. It ruins the surface finish and breaks tools. Breaking tools is not only expensive; it can get you hurt. Chatter is caused by a lot of things: springiness of the work (mount long, slender parts between centers), springiness of the tool (use a heftier tool, or at least a shorter one), too high a spindle speed, improper depth of cut, too broad a cutting edge in contact with the work, not enough lubricant and a host of others. Preventing it is largely a matter of experience. It must be prevented.

Figure (50): Cutting Tool Nomenclature and Tool Angles

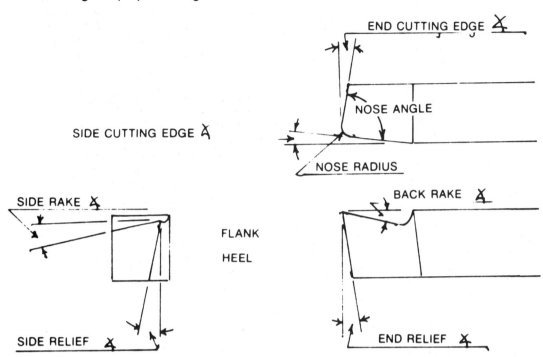

RAKE AND RELIEF ANGLES FOR HIGH SPEED STEEL CUTTING TOOLS

MATERIAL	OPERATION	BACK RAKE DEGREES	SIDE RAKE DEGREES	SIDE RELIEF DEGREES	END RELIEF DEGREES
Steel Soft	Roughing	6-10	14-22	5-9	5-9
	Finishing	14-22	0	0	5-9
	Parting	14-22	0	¹₂-2	5-9
	Forming	14-22	0	0	3-5
Steel Hard	Roughing	4-8	10-14	5-9	5-9
	Finishing	8-14	0	0	5-9
	Parting	8-14	0	¹₂-2	5-9
	Forming	4-8	0	0	3-5
Steel Very Hard	Roughing	3-7	5-10	5-9	5-9
	Finishing	5-10	0	0	5-9
	Parting	5-10	0	¹₂-2	5-9
	Forming	0-5	0	0	3-5
Aluminum	Roughing	8	16-22	5-9	5-9
	Finishing	8	16-22	0	5-9
	Parting	6-12	0	¹₂-2	5-9
	Forming	12-20	0	0	3-5
Magnesium	Roughing	5-8	3-5	6-10	6-10
	Finishing	10-15	0	0	6-10
	Parting	10-15	0	6-10	6-10
	Forming	5-10	0	0	6-10
Bronze	Roughing	6-8	4-10	5-9	5-9
	Finishing	14-22	0	0	5-9
	Parting	6-12	0	¹₂-2	5-9
	Forming	12-20	0	0	3-5

Cast Iron uses similar angles to hard steel. For other metals consult manufacturer's data sheets.

71

Figure (51): Cutting Tool Profiles

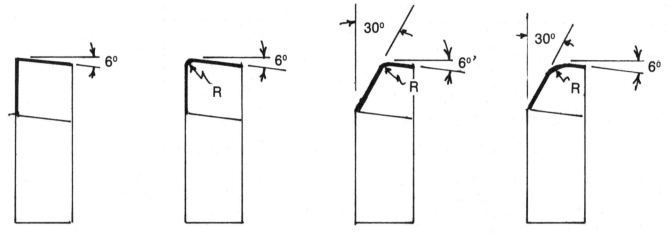

TYPICAL RIGHT-CUT ROUGHING TOOLS—CUTTING EDGE INDICATED BY HEAVY OUTLINES

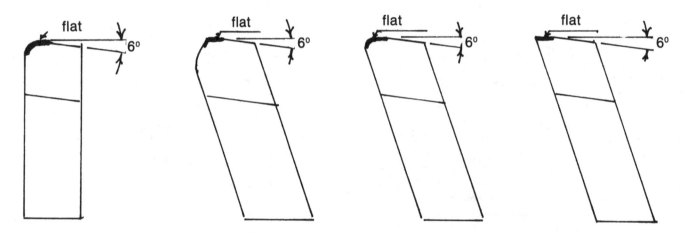

TYPICAL RIGHT-CUT FINISHING TOOLS—CUTTING EDGE INDICATED BY HEAVY OUTLINES.

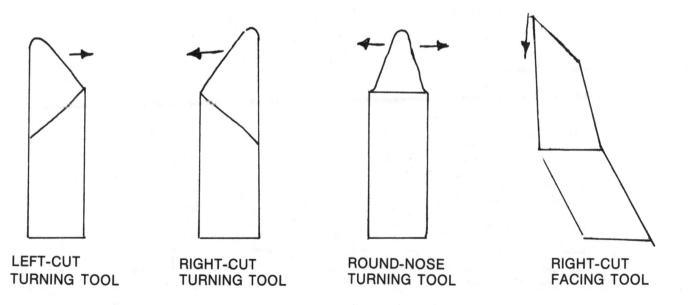

LEFT-CUT
TURNING TOOL

RIGHT-CUT
TURNING TOOL

ROUND-NOSE
TURNING TOOL

RIGHT-CUT
FACING TOOL

Figure (51A): Lathe Turning, Facing, Chamfering and Boring

	Turning to a square shoulder. Straight turning tool—right hand	45° 90°	90° nose angle tool chamfering to 45°
	Facing to a square shoulder Straight turning tool—left hand	60° 120°	120° nose angle tool chamfering to 60°
	Turning to a square shoulder Straight turning tool—left hand	80°	80° nose angle tool finish turning
	Rough turning— square shoulder not required. Rough turning tool— right hand		Cutoff tool
	Rough facing— square shoulder not required. Rough turning tool— left hand		Convex radius form tool
1 2	[1]Facing with broad nosed tool [2]Chamfering with broad nosed tool		Concave radius form tool
	Plunge cutting with broad nosed tool		Boring with boring bar

Figure (52): Lathe Tool Cutting Angles and Spindle Speeds

CUTTING ANGLES FOR STEEL

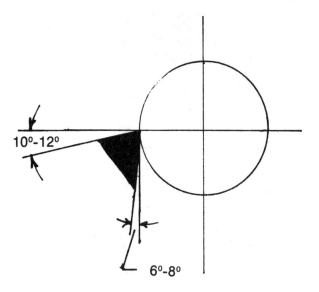

10°-12°

6°-8°

CUTTING ANGLES FOR ALUMINUM

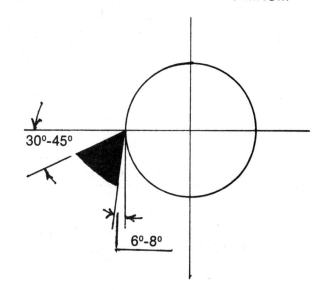

30°-45°

6°-8°

LATHE SPINDLE SPEEDS IN RPM FOR AVERAGE DEPTH OF CUT WITH HIGH SPEED STEEL CUTTING TOOLS

WORK DIAMETER IN INCHES	HARD STEEL OR CAST IRON 75FPM	ALUMINUM AND MAGNESIUM 300 FPM
1	275 RPM	1150 RPM
2	150 RPM	575 RPM
3	100 RPM	380 RPM
4	75 RPM	285 RPM
5	60 RPM	225 RPM
6	50 RPM	190 RPM
7	40 RPM	165 RPM
8	35 RPM	145 RPM
9	32 RPM	125 RPM
10	29 RPM	115 RPM

Figure (53): Use of the Parting Tool

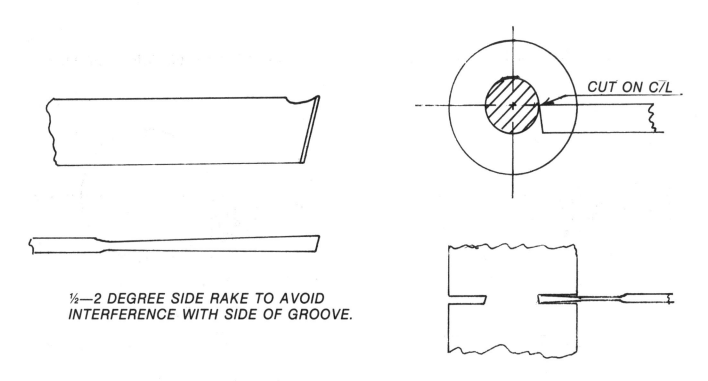

½—2 DEGREE SIDE RAKE TO AVOID
INTERFERENCE WITH SIDE OF GROOVE.

Figure (54): Chip Formation

FRONT RAKE USED WITH DUCTILE MATERIALS SUCH AS NORMAL STEELS
AND ALUMINUM TO PROMOTE CUTTING BYSHEAR. CHIP CURLS AWAY
FROM TOOL IN LONG SPIRAL.

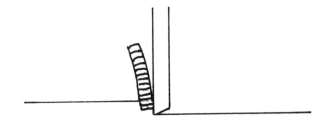

ZERO RAKE USED WITH BRITTLE MATERIALS SUCH AS CAST IRON AND
BRASS. CHIP CRUMBLES AGAINST FACE OF TOOL.

HEAT

A vast amount of friction is generated at the point of the cut, particularly with brittle materials (with ductile materials, as shown in Figure (55), the parting is largely by shear and takes place ahead of the tool, thus saving the tool). This friction generates extreme heat which must be dissipated to obtain good cutting, good surface finish and reasonable tool life. The only way to dissipate the heat is with a combination lubricant/coolant—in quantity. Squirting a drop of oil every so often won't do much good as the heat from the chip will merely boil or drive the oil away from the cut leaving the tool dry. Most lathes have a coolant pump and recirculating system and this is the best answer. Use a water soluble oil at about 40:1. If your lathe doesn't have one, you can improvise one easily enough. It is essential to use a splash guard at high spindle speeds. When turning aluminum the heat causes a deposit of aluminum oxide to form on the tool, dulling it. Lubrication will prevent this.

The cutoff tool is almost always abused. Always use the tailstock to hold the work steady and aligned. Grinding the side rake shown in Figure (52) on to the tool will prevent the tool from binding in the groove and allow most parting operations to be completed in one cut. Use lots of lubricant and feed the tool into the work with authority.

Some of the very basic dos and don'ts of lathe turning are:

DO:
(1) Use the right spindle speed.
(2) Use the right cutting tool—properly set.
(3) Use a lubricant/coolant.
(4) Make very sure that the chuck and tool post are securely tightened.
(5) Wear safety glasses or a face shield.
(6) Remove the chuck wrench before turning the lathe on—every time.
(7) Clean the lathe and its bed after every use. Resharpen tools as necessary.

DON'T:
(1) Take too big a cut.
(2) Let the tool chatter or burn.
(3) Clear the swarf with your bare hand while the lathe is turning.
(4) Wear a tie or anything else that dangles or can get caught.
(5) Stand directly in line with the work.
(6) Work alone in the shop.
(7) Break down someone else's setup on the lathe without asking first.
(8) Leave a setup on the lathe without a note to that effect.

I think it is reasonable to assume that any lathe is better than none. If you can't afford an engine lathe, maybe you can afford a used bench lathe. It is also reasonable to assume that if you have a universal milling machine, you probably know how to operate it. Few racing operations have more than a bench lathe and a drill press. With a little ingenuity and a lot of time a great variety of operations can be successfully carried out with these two pieces of equipment. However, regardless of the size and expertise of the operation and the extent of the equipment, sooner or later machine work is going to be farmed out.

FARM OUT WORK

You can save yourself a lot of money and nasty scenes by carefully selecting the firm to whom you subcontract your work. Low bid is almost always a loser. You must supply good working drawings and material specifications for each part. One of the surest ways to come unstuck is to hand a sample part to a machine shop and tell them to duplicate it. Choose tolerances with care. Close tolerances are expensive and it is a bit silly to spend time and money having the O.D. of a part turned to $\pm$ .001" when $\pm$ .030" would have done just as well. The machinist is going to make the part to your drawing. If the part doesn't match the drawing—he eats it. If it does match the drawing, but doesn't fit—you eat it. Machined parts don't taste good and they make expensive paper weights.

CHAPTER FIVE

THE BRAKING SYSTEM, THE CLUTCH, THROTTLE LINKAGES AND THE COCKPIT

THE BRAKE SYSTEM

In the not very distant past, brakes were generally regarded as one of the most trouble-prone and trouble-causing systems to be found on the race car. Equal braking on all four wheels was difficult to achieve and almost impossible to maintain over the distance of the race. Hard use of the brakes led to fade, rapid wear, or both. Drums were prone to distortion and cracking and fluids boiled frequently. Wet brakes were a disaster. The popular finned aluminum drum with its cast iron friction surface was expensive and demanded frequent replacement. Shoes and linings had to be radius ground and very carefully adjusted. The best of the drivers developed the science of nursing the brakes into a fine art.

THE DISC BRAKE

To our great good fortune the advent of the disc brake and the subsequent rapid and continuous development of discs, calipers, friction materials and hydraulic fluids has changed all that. The basic advantages of discs over drums are: better heat dissipation, insensitivity to water, self-adjustment and ease of replacement of the linings and, if necessary, the discs. These advantages are so overwhelming that no serious race car constructor has used drum brakes for years.

However, even at the present advanced state of brake development, care and attention to detail in selection, assembly and maintenance are necessary if you want your braking system to be really effective. If it is not really effective, you will not win races.

BRAKE FLUID

We'll begin with brake fluid. Here, as in so many cases, the racer's enemy is heat. For our purposes fluids are incompressible. Under normal conditions this works out very well—the incompressible fluid transmits the force exerted on the brake pedal by the driver's foot (multiplied by the mechanical advantage of the pedal and the hydraulic ratio of the system) to the brakes in a progressive manner. You end up with a firm and controllable pedal and the amount of braking force developed is directly proportional to the amount of force applied to the pedal. If the fluid should boil at any point in the system, or if even a small leak should develop, gaseous bubbles will be present in the fluid. The

fluid will no longer be incompressible: the brake pedal will feel "spongy" and may require pumping at each application. The driver will no longer be able to sense, with precision, the amount of braking force developed and will either lock a wheel or (more likely) will no longer be able to modulate the brakes to his own maximum ability.

Obviously only the best available fluids (i.e. those with the highest boiling points) should be used. Any fluid exceeding SAE specification 7OR1 and 7OR3 and meeting Federal Standard 116 will do. These fluids are available from Delco (Delco 550 Supreme), Ford (C6AZ 19542-A), and Wagner Lockheed (FC-59250). All normal brake fluids are hygroscopic— that is, they tend to absorb moisture from the atmosphere. Even the most minute amount of water in the fluid will lower the boiling point of the fluid by an alarming amount. Since most racing car hydraulic reservoirs are vented directly to the atmosphere, the fluid should be replaced at least every 30 days. It is equally important to store the fluid in small containers. A quart of fluid in a gallon container will adsorb enough water vapor to make it useless in a couple of hours. For this reason you should buy your fluid in 12 ounce cans. For the same reason, it doesn't pay to re-use the fluid lost in bleeding (although this fluid is OK for the clutch—where heat isn't much of a problem). Don't be tempted to use the ultra-high boiling point fluids used in the aircraft industry—our master cylinder and caliper seals are not compatible with these fluids and their viscosity characteristics may not be suitable for automotive use. The future solution to the fluid problem lies in the use of silicon based fluids. At the moment, the only such fluid that I know of which is being used semi-successfully in racing is made by Dow Corning. Other brands are available, but troubles have been experienced with viscosity and foaming.

PLUMBING

Plumbing the brake and clutch systems is straightforward and expensive. We covered this aspect in some detail in Chapter One. I would like to re-emphasize that there is no substitute for genuine Aeroquip 66000 series teflon and stainless hose with genuine Aeroquip "super Gem" hose and fittings for the flexible lines. It is also very convenient to substitute this hose for the rigid lines in the system, but it is probably not worth the expense. It is critical that there be no leaks whatever in the system, so you must be extra sure to inspect all fittings, both male and female, for dirt and scratches on the sealing surfaces as you assemble them. It is equally critical that the system be clean. A small particle of dirt can block ports in either the master cylinder or the calipers and the results are disastrous. Make very sure that all hydraulic lines are kept well away from the exhaust system (instant boil) and that nothing gets crimped, kinked or crushed when changing engines. It is also well to ensure that there is no way that a hydraulic line can be damaged or torn off during an off course excursion, or crushed by a jack.

INSTALLATION OF DISCS AND CALIPERS

The installation of the discs and calipers receives very little of the careful attention that it deserves. It is so easy to just bolt the things on and forget about them that that is exactly what most people do. Wrong!

The disc itself is mounted by means of a "top hat" or "bell" to either the hub flange or to the transaxle output shaft flange. The top hat may be an integral part of the disc as on production cars, or it may bolt on to the disc with the torque taken by lugs or straps as on all serious racing cars. In either case we must make sure that the mounting surface of the top hat is absolutely true to the disc surface and that the disc friction surfaces are true to each other. With ventilated discs it is as well to check that the casting is true. It is not unknown for a core shift to result in a disc with its friction surfaces skewed. This not only fouls up the heat sink characteristics of the disc but also causes an incurable dynamic imbalance which will drive the tire busters up the wall as they try to cure it. Run-out of the disc surfaces should not exceed .006" total indicator reading. Remember that any play in the hub bearings will show up as run-out.

DISC FLOAT

The discs of a Formula A, Can Am, Long Distance or heavy production racing car are going to suffer an incredible amount of abuse—mostly in the generation of insane amounts of heat. Almost all of these cars are equipped with discs mounted to separate top hats. The disc should float on the top hat, about .002"/.004" radially and about .006"/.008" axially. This will prevent the inevitable differential heating of the inboard and outboard friction surfaces (the outboard surface on outboard brakes gets hotter, because it is less exposed to airflow) from turning the disc into a giant belleville washer and also will slow down the propagation of radial stress cracks in the disc eminating from the mounting notches. The mounting notches should also be deburred with a stone to get rid of the stress raisers built in during manufacture. All of this is quite laborious but well worth it. In passing I should mention that at least one well known manufacturer uses very deep top hat sections from alloy 356 cast aluminum. These get very hot in use and warp like crazy, resulting in quite a bit of run out. Top hats, at least deep ones, should be machined from something like 7075-T6 aluminum bar stock. It won't hurt a damn thing to at least statically balance the disc and top-hat assembly. The best possible treatment for new discs is to deburr them, mount them true on their top hats, run them for a short test session with old pads and then, after all of the machining oil, etc. has been baked out and they have been stress-relieved

and relaxed by the heat, grind both surfaces true. This can be done in a lathe with a tool post grinder or by blanchard grinding. Every time that run out is detected or the heat checks are really bad or the surfaces measure out of parallel, discs should be reground. Normally they will become badly cracked long before you grind or wear enough off of them to worry about. When radial cracks start to show up, propagation can be retarded by stop drilling the end of the crack with a small drill bit. Milled tangental slots—.060" wide x .030" deep—six per side—will improve brake performance by removing the "fire band".

TRUEING THE CALIPERS

When mounting the calipers, make sure that the pistons are normal to the surface of the disc—in both planes—and that the caliper is centered on the disc. Shim washers will rectify the out of center condition and the alignment condition in the vertical plane. Stamp the required shim thickness on each caliper ear. Misalignment in the horizontal plane must be corrected by machining the offending caliper ears or mount. Pads should fit easily in the caliper but shouldn't have much slop. New pads must not be too thick to slide into place freely with the pistons retracted fully. Mount the calipers with drilled head bolts, torque them and safety wire the bolts. If the caliper bolts to a light alloy casting, use a threaded insert in the casting. Always mount each caliper with the bleed screw at the top. Make sure that your caliper seals are compatible with automotive brake fluids (many replacements, including the ubiquitous "Buna N" compounds, are not) and inspect them frequently. Caliper seals do not like solvents. Calipers should never be soaked in a solvent bath. Any evidence of scoring or cracking of the seal is cause for rejection as is weeping. Extreme care is necessary when installing seals. Clean caliper and seals, and lubricate both the bore and the seal with clean brake fluid. Be very sure that the seal is installed in its groove without twisting. Install the piston absolutely square with the bore to avoid rolling and/or cutting the seal. The caliper bleed screw must be open. Do not use air or hydraulic power to install the piston. If you can't get it in by hand with a flat wooden block to push on, then something is wrong. The design of caliper seals is worth an article in itself. To my knowledge all of the British and Continental racing calipers have properly designed seals. Some of the early Airheart units, however, had trouble with the seals rolling and gulping a minute amount of air. These units required a teflon back up ring with the seal to cure the problem. If you are having seal trouble, your best bet is the Parker Seal Company Field Engineer—if you can get him interested. Yes, they do make square cut seals and, yes, a normal circular section "O" ring works perfectly well—in the right size and compound.

MASTER CYLINDERS

Master cylinders should be mounted with their ports upward and vertical to ensure good bleeding. They must also be attached securely to rigid structure which will not deflect under extreme pedal pressure. Use stock master cylinder pushrods whenever possible. If you must make your own, faithfully copy the profile of the actuating end on the stock unit. A slight machining error here can, and has, caused the brakes to lock on. It is critical to install the dished retaining washer on Girling cylinders with the dish toward the rear of the cylinder. It is important to be sure that the master cylinder bore be aligned with the center of the effective arc of travel of the pivot between pushrod and pedal—otherwise a side load will be placed on the piston producing premature wear and possible scoring of the cylinder. The longer the actuating rod, the less angularity in operation. For progressive actuation it is vital to adjust the pedal position so that during operation, the pedal does not go over center. This changes the mechanical advantage of the pedal itself resulting in a non-linear action which can totally disrupt the driver's efforts. New master cylinders should be disassembled, thoroughly cleaned and lubricated with clean brake fluid before installation. This should also be done to the spares before they are packed away. The man in charge of putting swarf and dirt into the cylinders at the factory sometimes does a hell of a job. Master cylinders should be inspected frequently. Any scoring of the bore is cause for scrapping the unit. Deterioration of the piston seal is rare, but they should be inspected for cracking and checking and discarded as necessary. I use *only* Girling cylinders. Master cylinder seals also do not like solvents.

Hydraulic fluid reservoirs must have sufficient capacity so that it is impossible to run out of fluid with fully worn pads. This means that the volume of the reservoir must exceed the total volume of the caliper cylinders (all of them) at that end of the car, with the pad backing plate rubbing against the disc plus an allowance for lines, etc., and at least an inch of fluid must remain in the reservoir. If you are using remote reservoirs, mount them above the master cylinders (theoretically they should also be above the calipers, but this is difficult to achieve) and connect reservoir and cylinder with minimum 3/16" I.D. line. In this particular application, Aeroquip line and fittings are a waste of money and weight. I favor the use of Nylon or Delrin semihard tubing with aluminum AN compression fittings. In order for the pedal to return, master cylinder reservoirs must be vented. The best system is the flexible bellows within the reservoir cap as provided by Repco, Lockheed, Kelsey Hayes and Airheart. This provision keeps the fluid away from direct contact with the atmosphere and prevents absorbtion of water vapor. Remember, though, that the cap itself must be vented to the atmosphere. This method also prevents spillage of the fluid under heavy g loads. All of the other commercial systems, in addition to venting the system, vent fluid which makes a mess of the paint. The usual solution is to tape a piece of tag or rubber foam over the reservoir caps and hope for the best. A better method is to solder or epoxy a length of bundy tube, formed into a pigtail and leading to an overflow can (35mm film cans are ideal), onto the cap. Another way is a straight piece of bundy about 4" tall with the top plugged and radial vent holes drilled into it quite high on the tube. Filling the reservoir with clean fuel cell foam, cut to shape, will reduce surge, but it has to be very clean—we don't need foam scraps floating around in the system.

HEAT & COOLING

The brake is nothing more or less than a device which slows the moving vehicle by converting kinetic energy into heat energy. The amount of heat generated by racing type retardation from high speeds boggles the mind. This heat has to be dissipated for several reasons—disc life and avoidance of fluid boiling being prime among them. The pads must also be kept below their critical operating temperature (beyond which we find pad fade). We want to dissipate this heat into the atmosphere—not into the calipers, hub carriers, wheels, tires, etc. Radiation won't get it done! In any application faster and heavier than a Formula Ford, this means ducting forced air to the brakes. A beautiful duct directing multi cubic feet of air per second to the brakes won't do much good if the air can't get out. This is why the solid disc spun aluminum wheels don't work on powerful race cars with outboard brakes. It is also why Ford spent a fortune on the turbine bladed wheels for the Mk IV Le Mans car (yes, they did work, but the increase in efficiency was of a low order). The first law of ducting is that fluids only move from a region of high pressure to a region of lower pressure—stuff flows down hill. Two quite different types of ducts are required in racing—depending on whether you have solid discs or vented discs.

SOLID DISC COOLING

The solid disc requires that cooling air be forced to both inboard and outboard friction surgaces. Otherwise you end up with the outboard friction surface and pad operating a couple of hundred degres hotter than the inboard surface. This makes a thermostat of the disc, putting a radial curve into it and also means that one pad or the other is not operating at maximum efficiency. The way to avoid this is to end the duct in a can which directs air onto both disc surfaces Figure (55). The leading edge of this can should be steel and should be as close as possible to the disc surface (like .010") in order to scrape as much as possible of the hot boundary layer from the surfaces. The duct should be as close to the leading edge of the caliper as the installation permits.

VENTED DISC COOLING

With the vented disc—as found on Formula A and bigger cars—the problem is somewhat different. Here the idea is to force the cooling air into the "eye" of the disc so that it will pass out through the radial slots, assisted by the centrifugal action of the rotating disc, and cool both surfaces from the inside. The problem is often complicated by the fact that the eye of the disc may be more or less masked by hub carrier, steering arm or whatever. Nonetheless, we want to force as much air as possible into the eye with minimum leakage. The best solution to this problem that I have seen is on the front brakes of the Lotus 70 Figure (56). Air is ducted into the eye and leakage is prevented by a "seal plate" secured to the hub carrier. Like so many of the good Mr. Chapman's details it is simple, effective, light and cheap.

There is a theory prevalent among open wheel racers that ducting to the brakes is not necessary on Formula Cars. This may have been true once—although not in my experience. In this day of super wide wheels with the brakes hidden inside the wheels, or the body work, or sitting next to the tranaxle the theory doesn't hold water. It is true, however, that much more simple ducts are required on open

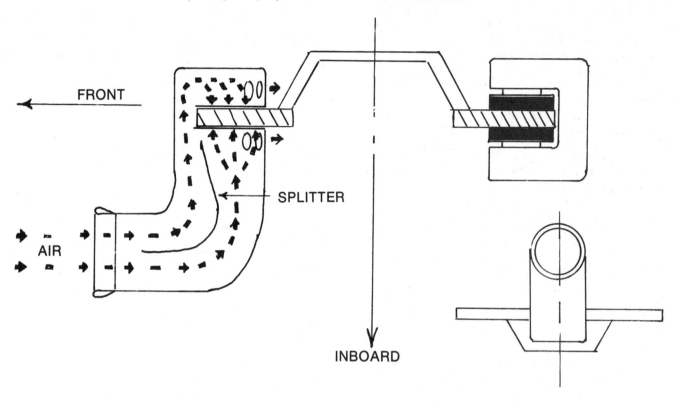

Figure (55): Duct for Solid Brake Disc

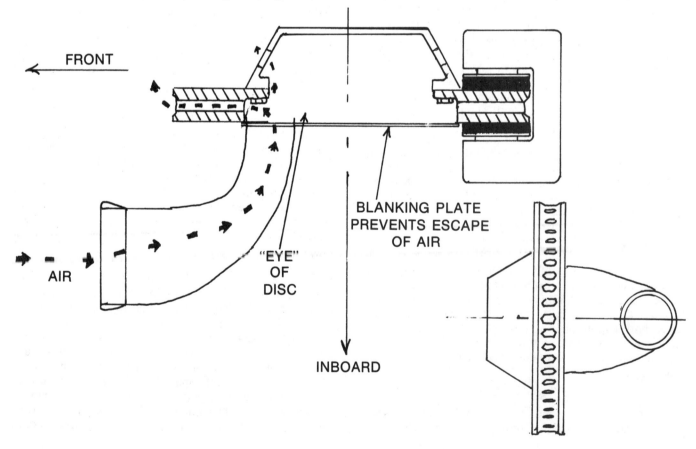

Figure (56): Duct for Ventilated Brake Disc

wheeled cars than on closed wheel cars. At least the system isn't totally hidden from the rushing air. Open wheelers (REAL race cars?) require only a horn attached to the hub carrier and extending into the airstream. This can be an aluminum fabrication or a fibreglass moulding (I once saw a pair made from beer cans which worked fine and set a new all time record for cost, class and light weight). In any case make sure that they clear everything as the wheel does its travel thing. On a car with fenders, some sort of flexible ducting is going to be necessary. It must be at least 3" in diameter and must begin in a high pressure area. Take a good look at the works McLaren Can-Am cars—both ends. The flexible ducting won't do much good if it is cut, abraded or otherwise full of holes, so inspect it often. Repairs can be effectively made with racer's tape. The ducting has a nasty tendency to flop around and interfere with things so it must be pretty well secured. It smells bad if it burns—which it will if it is allowed to rub on a wheel rim.

The efficiency of your brake (or other) cooling system can be conveniently checked at low cost by the use of temperature sensitive paints or crayons available from your welding supply house. Remember that the ubiquitous Ferodo DS-11 pad material stops working at 1050°F. and that Raybestos 19M doesn't start to work until 800°F. (it is still effective at 1600°F. but is expensive, hard to find and hell on discs). What is usually not appreciated is that the coefficient of friction between any pad material and the disc varies with operating temperature. This is not a straight line relationship, but a curve. For ideally effective and progressive braking it is necessary that the front and rear brakes operate at nearly the same temperature and that they reach their temperatures at nearly the same rate. This will keep the front to rear braking ratio constant during deceleration from very high to very low speeds and allow maximum utilization of the braking system by the very sensitive driver. Damned few drivers are that sensitive, but I have worked with a few and it has been a pleasure. Achieving this balance—which is not to be confused with front to rear proportioning of braking effort, or pad wear— is a question of more air to the fronts and/or less to the rears.

SLOTS

Lately you may have seen discs with tangential slots milled in the friction surfaces or with holes drilled in a tangential pattern normal to the friction surface. This is an effort to wipe the "fireband" or boundary layer off the disc before it reaches the point of contact with the pad and to provide the very hot particles of friction material worn off with some place to go other than into the operating area. The holes don't work as effectively but do lighten the disc notably. They also make the disc difficult to balance. The slots increase system efficiency and decrease operating temperature along with pad wear. Much the same result, to a lesser extent, is achieved by the slots in the pad itself. All pads come with a radial slot about 1/8" wide cut in the pad. In my experience, the addition of a longitudinal slot at 90° to this one helps a lot. It can be done in a mill. Pads are very expensive. The belief that they can only be used until they are about 1/2 worn is prevalent. It is also mistaken. In long distance racing pad wear is projected to about 3/32" of friction

surface remaining. Often, projections being what they are, I have removed pads with less than 1/32" remaining. They still work fine. The trick is to avoid taper wear. Taper wear is caused by caliper flex, skewed caliper mounting (in either plane) or differential cooling between the friction surfaces on opposite faces of the disc. There really isn't a hell of a lot you can do about caliper flex except use Lockheed calipers which may not be practical. Some of the flexible flyer calipers can be helped considerably by the addition of stiffening bridges, but it is difficult. Most of the manufacturers have caught on now, and the present generation of calipers is much stiffer than was previously the case. The rest of the problem is a case of attention to detail. Anyway, don't discard worn pads until they are really worn—they may not do a race, but they're OK for testing and practice.

BLEEDING

In order for the braking system to function efficiently, it is necessary that the hydraulic system be free not only of moisture, but also of air and air bubbles. Fluid may be incompressible, but air is not. This means proper and frequent bleeding of the system. Everyone has his own pet system for bleeding brakes—mine is to bleed one front and one rear caliper simultaneously which ensures full travel of each master cylinder piston and precludes the possibility of trapping a bubble in the master cylinder itself. It also allows you to check (by closing the bleed screw at each end independently) that the bias bar will permit each end to function independently in case of failure. Keep the reservoirs full by slowly pouring in fresh fluid (slowly to avoid creating bubbles) and slowly pump the pedal (no flutter foot, please) until no bubbles are observed in the bleeder lines and the fluid coming out of the calipers is clean. If the caliper has twin bleed screws (and it should have), bleed the inboard (closer to the feed line) side first. When this part of the operation is complete, hold maximum pressure on the pedal while the bleed screws are released and retightened. When no more bubbles appear, bleeding is complete but you should pump maximum pedal pressure while someone visually checks the whole system for leaks. Continued formation of air bubbles, evidenced by a spongy pedal, may be caused by leaks somewhere in the system (including the often ignored joints between the reservoirs and the suction ports of the master cylinders), faulty or worn master cylinder or caliper seals (both evidenced by weeping) or by local boiling of the fluid either in the calipers or somewhere in the lines. Internal leaks in caliper castings are not unknown.

BEDDING

Linings, for both disc and drum brakes, require bedding in before they will deliver good or consistent performance. This is due to the so-called green fade characteristic which manifests itself (like all fade characteristics) by a pronounced lack of braking effect even though the pedal remains high and firm. It can get you into the trees in a hurry. Many a driver has been caught completely unawares by green fade which, unlike normal fade due to excessive heat, gives no warning at all. This phenomenon is caused by the more volatile parts of the bonding agents which hold the pad material together boiling out when extreme heat is first generated and forming a liquid layer between the pad and the disc. This layer of liquid has very poor frictional properties. This boiling out process continues throughout the life of the pad, but most of it happens in the first few heating cycles. A new pad, viewed on edge, is a uniform very dark grey or black color. A properly bedded pad will show a grey-brown flinty appearing color from the friction surface down about 1/8" to 3/16". This layer is the "bedded" portion of the pad and stays at a constant depth as the pad wears.

The best method I have found to bed pads is through many medium brake applications to increase pad temperature gradually, followed after a couple of mild "green fade" periods have been gone through—by one tremendous "burning on" from high speed (picking a place on the track where fade will not put the car into the wall and checking the mirrors carefully so that an unexpected severe braking effort is not going to result in getting hit from behind). The car should then be parked for 10 minutes or so to let the pads cool. Until the driver catches on to how to bed pads, and how to sense when they are ready, the process may have to be repeated a few times. Visual examination will tell you whether or not a pad is bedded. When the car arrives at the pit with hot brakes, get the driver's foot off the brake pedal and rock the car slowly back and forth until the brakes cool down. This prevents pad material from forming "pick up" on the discs which leads to rough braking and shortens disc life. Disc surfaces should never be exposed to anything containing oil and should be cleaned of any pick up with a flat scraper, not with emery cloth. For very obvious reasons, a race should never be started with unbedded pads. Not only is the risk of green fade putting the car into the weeds very high, but the chances of pads bedded during a race ever performing well is remote. Use test sessions or early practice sessions to bed pads. He who waits until the Sunday morning warm-up to bed his pads is often going to be caught out. Don't bother trying to bed them when it's wet. I carry a full set of bedded pads in my briefcase against the inevitable day.

It is best not to run new discs and new pads together because either scoring of the disc or heavy pick up on its surface will result. Examination of worn pads for taper wear is an excellent indication of caliper rigidity and trueness of mounting. When re-using old pads, install them in their original positions.

BRAKE BIAS

To finish the discussion of braking systems, we will briefly consider the front to rear braking bias. To achieve optimum braking each wheel should have braking force applied to it in proportion to its dynamic ability to transmit that force to the track. Until such time as automatic four wheel independently operating anti-lock brake systems come into use on racing cars, our best method of achieving approximation of this ideal is by adjusting the front to rear brake bias. If too great a proportion of the total braking effort being developed is applied to either pair of wheels, then the opposite pair is not doing its share. If more pedal effort is applied, the biased pair will lock. If this happens to be the front pair the car will merely plow straight ahead until such

time as the pedal effort is reduced and steering control is regained. This situation may be embarrassing, but it is preferable to locking the rears—which instantly slews the car sideways. This front to rear bias is more complex than it might appear. Due to forward weight transfer under braking, one needs a fair old bit of bias toward the front in order to achieve the optimum condition where the front wheels lock just before the rears. This optimum setting varies with tire cross-section, compound and construction, track condition, suspension ride rate, driver technique and fuel state. It is gotten into the ball park by selecting master cylinder sizes and caliper piston sizes and it is finally adjusted by the brake bias bar. Almost all racing cars are delivered with master cylinder and caliper bores correctly sized and proportioned. If you can't develop enough total braking force, increase the mechanical advantage of the pedal or change to smaller master cylinders. If too much force is developed with too little pedal effort, reverse the procedure. The bias bar is schematically shown in Figure (57). It is adjusted by moving the pivot toward the cylinder which you wish to bias. In making adjustments take care to maintain sufficient clearance between the bearing housing tube and the bias bar clevises so that a mechanical bind cannot occurr. On the other hand, excessive clearance will allow the bearing to move back and forth on its own, thus changing the adjustment. Make very certain that the bearing is securely retained on the bar and that the clevises are locked to the bar. It is also essential to lock the push rods to the clevises and to adjust the push rod length so that both master cylinder pistons start to exert pressure at the same time. To adjust the pedal position to the driver, the best method is the foot pad which screws into the pedal shaft Figure (58). If this is combined with a couple of alternate pivot locations, then the static pedal position can be almost infinitely adjusted while the pedal and push rod geometry is kept at its optimum, and the over center condition is avoided. Brake pedals and their mountings have been known to both bend and break. Make certain that yours won't.

To roughly set the bias, steadily increase the pedal pressure with the car on jack stands until the front wheels are just locked. At this point, the same man who determined that the front was locked should still be able to turn the rear wheels, although with notable effort (make sure that the car is out of gear). The differences in tire diameter and section width will come pretty close to the weight transfer effect and you will be close.

Brake bias must finally be set on the race track. Using a set of tires of the same compound, construction and size that you will race on, but which you don't value too highly, have the driver brake hard (very hard) on a smooth, level and clean surface where you—or someone else who is capable of telling which end locks up first—can observe him at close range. It helps to have one observer on each side of the car. Adjust the bias bar until the fronts lock first—but just barely. The more experienced and sensitive the driver becomes, the less he is going to flat spot the tires while he is doing all this—until you eventually arrive at the point where it is safe to do it with good tires. It is as well to start beginning drivers with a slight excess of front bias and work toward optimum as his skill, judgement and sensitivity increase. It is also as well to remember that fuel load has a lot to do with

Figure (57): Brake Bias Bar—Plan View Schematic

TO ADJUST, TURN BIAS BAR IN DIRECTION THAT WILL MOVE BEARING CLOSER TOWARD MASTER CYLINDER OF PAIR OF BRAKES WHICH NEED MORE EFFORT.

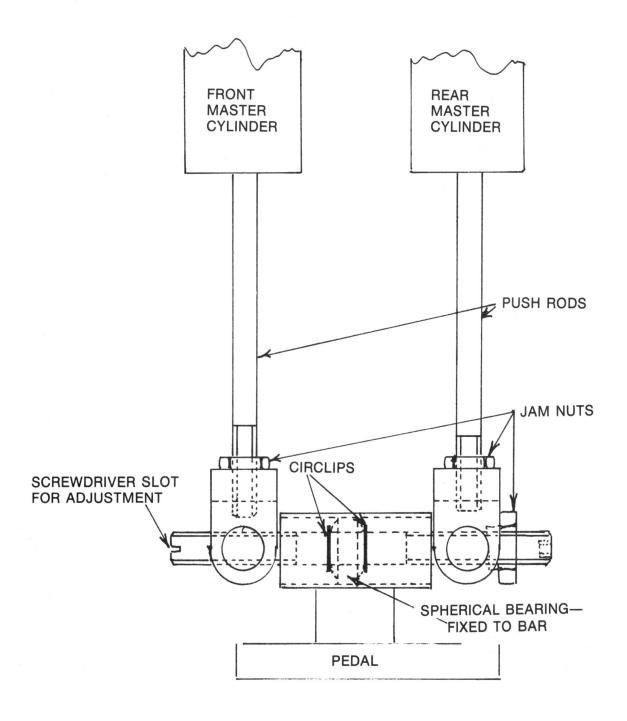

Figure (58): Brake Pedal Adjustment

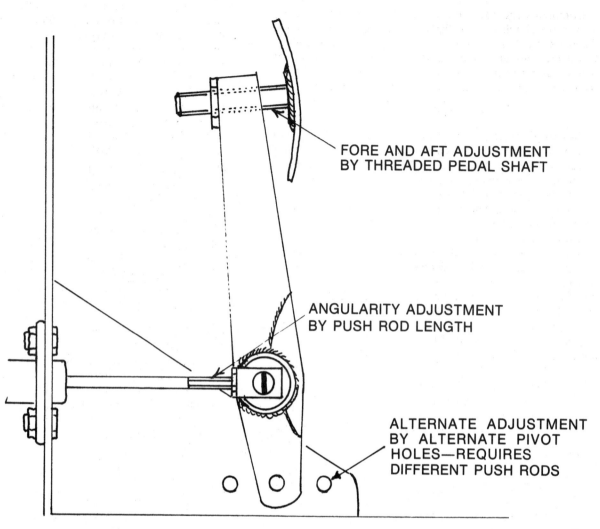

FORE AND AFT ADJUSTMENT
BY THREADED PEDAL SHAFT

ANGULARITY ADJUSTMENT
BY PUSH ROD LENGTH

ALTERNATE ADJUSTMENT
BY ALTERNATE PIVOT
HOLES—REQUIRES
DIFFERENT PUSH RODS

optimum proportioning and that a car set up light on fuel may well have a rearward bias when it is full. Find out about this sort of thing, and make damned sure that your driver remembers.

One last caution—when you install a fresh set of pads to be bedded, tape a sign to the steering wheel that says "NEW PADS" and don't let anyone take it off until you push the car away from the pit. Thus no-one can forget to tell the driver. Every so often someone manages to install a pad with the steel backing plate against the disc. The results are never good. It is the chief mechanic's responsibility to make sure that this has not happened by visually checking— every time.

Once the bias has been adjusted to the point where everyone is happy it is a good idea to take a pressure gauge reading and record it. In that way, if you ever lose it, for whatever reason, you can get back very close to where you want to be without testing and adjusting. It could come in handy some day . . .

ERRATIC BRAKING

Erratic braking can have many causes. Most of them, if they have to do with the braking system itself, are evidenced by inconsistent pedal height and/or firmness. Assuming that there are no leaks in the system, disc run out is not excessive, hub bearings are properly adjusted, pads are not excessively tapered, the reservoirs are freely vented, and all pedal joints and connections are sound, erratic pedal height is caused by soft pressure lines, spindle flex, caliper flex or improperly designed caliper seals. Erratic performance on the track—instability, darting or weaving under the brakes—can be caused by improperly adjusted bias, the suspension running hard on the bump stops under braking, front bump steer, uneven shock adjustment and/or uneven wheel weights.

The wheel weight bit can be either spring perch height or an improperly adjusted sway bar.

THE CLUTCH SYSTEM

Comments regarding the brake hydraulic system apply also to the clutch system. Remember that clutch actuation displaces much more fluid than does brake application. Consequently clutch lines should be larger in diameter or you are going to have a slow operating clutch. 3/16" I.D. seems to be about right.

CLUTCH STOP

To prevent overtraveling the clutch fingers or diaphragm (and wasting foot travel and time— assuming that your driver uses the clutch) a positive mechanical stop should be installed somewhere in the clutch system. I prefer to put it at the pedal and thus avoid the generation of extreme hydraulic pressure which could bend or break something. Most people put it directly on the clutch actuating rod where it seems to work fine. I'm conservative.

It is also important to provide a really stout clutch return spring at the clutch end. I use an extension spring on the actuating rod in addition to the stock Hewland mousetrap spring. Free-play adjustment should be provided at an easily accessible portion of the clutch actuating rod between the slave cylinder and the throw-out fork. This adjustment must be positively locked. Make sure that the actuating rod cannot jump out of the throw-out fork. For this reason I prefer to use a rod end bearing to attach the rod to the fork rather than the normal ball and socket arrangement Figure (59). If at all possible install the slave cylinder so that the cylinder bore is in line with the actuating rod. This prevents putting a side load on the slave cylinder piston and greatly increases the life of the cylinder assembly.

When selecting the clutch for your car remember that the lighter the clutch and flywheel unit and the smaller its diameter, the faster your shifts will be. Also, of course, the smaller the diameter, the lower you can install your engine—sump depth, tire diameter, axle enter and drive shaft angularity permitting. This means that for maximum performance you must use a Borg and Beck multi-plate clutch. They are expensive, but they last virtually forever.

The manufacturer of your clutch will provide information regarding installation torque, flywheel configuration, release distance, type and configuration of release mechanism required, free play, wear measurement, etc. Obtain this information and use it. When installing the Borg and Beck multi-plate clutch it is essential to avoid overtightening the mounting bolts. Correct torque is 15 to 18 lb/ft. Over torqueing will distort the magnesium housing and prevent free release of the clutch. The driven discs are clearly marked "flywheel side". They mean it. "Riding the clutch" must be avoided at all costs so some sort of left foot rest whould be provided. Clutch pedal travel can be reduced—at the expense of pedal effort by using a larger master cylinder or a smaller slave cylinder. The system is bled in the same fashion as the brakes, and, like the brakes, the slave cylinder should be mounted with the bleed fitting upward. With inboard rear brakes, make sure that the hydraulic line does not get overheated. We'll discuss the actual mounting of the clutch in the chapter dealing with engines and the final drive. If the clutch plates are burned, it is because the driver was riding or slipping the clutch, or it was installed witn insufficient free play.

Money can be saved by buying both clutch and brake spares either at the time you purchase the car in England (The constructor should pass most of his discount along to you—after all you are doing him a favor by buying the damned thing)—but don't expect him to do so after the car is delivered or from the U.S. representatives of the corporations concerned. It is usually not a very good idea to buy from your race car importer as his mark up is usually (and rightfully) higher. Sources are listed in Table (10).

THROTTLE CABLES AND LINKAGES

Throttle linkages and cables are a genuine pain! Good ones are worth the trouble and can result in quite dramatic improvements in lap time.

The best throttle cable is American Chain and Cable Co.'s push-pull unit now marketed for racing use through Meyer Engineering in Speedway, Indiana. Three day service in any length for about $30.00— you can't beat it. This little dandy is a twisted wire cable enclosed in a teflon lined spiral wound steel wire housing which has threaded abutments at each end. The cable ends are ball and socket affairs which provide about 16° of misalignment capability. The ends themselves are #10-32 threaded rods. Stock stroke is 3". The unit is remarkably heat resistant, friction free and smooth in operation. It is damned near indestructible.

A similar, although inferior, unit is manufactured by the Morse Instrument Co., Hudson, Ohio. It is not so smooth in operation, cannot be bent in anywhere near as tight a radius and tends to bind when exposed to heat. It is, however, found in boat shops all over the country. Price is slightly less.

Motorcycle "Bowden Cables" are readily available, very cheap and can get you hurt. I will not allow one on a race car. You can make a decent cable from stainless aircraft control cable enclosed in bundy tubing. You can also use music wire in bundy tube, but only for straight runs. When making your own, soft solder the ends to avoid heat embrittlement and pay particular attention to the ends of the housing which is how you will attach the thing to the chassis. Commercial ends as used on bowden cables are usually chrome plated soft brass and they are deadly.

THROTTLE STOPS AND ADJUSTMENT

Stretching the cable is a No No! The only way to prevent it is to use an adjustable full-throttle stop at the pedal and one at the engine. They must be synchronized, or rather, the one at the engine is set at full-open throttle and the one at the pedal is matched to it. Since the optimum throttle pedal travel will vary from driver to driver, and also with the engine's power curve characteristics, it is best to provide a series of cable attachment holes at varying distances from both the pedal pivot and the throttle arm pivot. Remember that moving the attachment to the pedal or throttle arm up or down will probably require moving the attachment of the housing to the chassis a like amount to prevent running out of angularity. As the pedal and the throttle arm normally move through an arc, the cable ends should be rod end bearings locked to the cable shaft with jam nuts. This also provides a limited adjustment to the off-throttle position of the pedal. More is easily achieved by the provision of a left and right handed coupler in the cable system. This is usually more convenient at the throttle end. When possible it is a good idea to place the rear attachment of the housing to the chassis at the firewall bulkhead. It is more convenient and prevents the cable from being damaged when changing engines. You must be very sure that no part of the cable, throttle or linkage can in any way bind, interfere with or get caught on anything—including the driver's leg. Throttle cables are not meant to be stepped on when getting in and out of the car, nor are they meant to be sat on. They do not like bends. While it is almost impossible to achieve a straight run, the bend radii can be kept very gentle. Throttle cables do not like heat and they must be kept well away from exhaust systems. For adjustment purposes the cable housing is usually secured to the chassis with a bulkhead type fitting Figure (60). If it is desirable to let the housing end swing freely, it can also be put through an el-cheapo rod end or sherical bearing.

Figure (59): Stock and Modified Clutch Release Forks

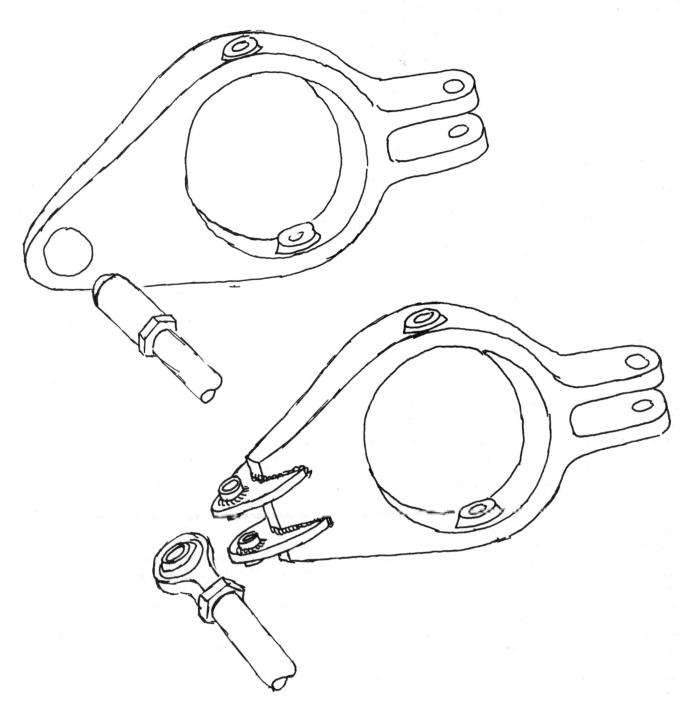

Figure (60): Attachment of Throttle Cable to Chassis

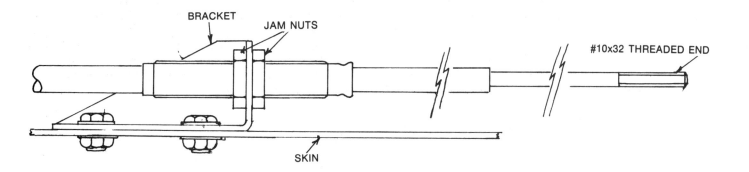

RETURN SPRINGS

Don't buy your throttle return springs at the local hardware store. Use good quality springs, preferably of stainless, and use at least two—at two different places in the linkage. Three is better. Form the ends of the springs carefully with generous radii, and make sure that they do not interfere with anything or each other through the full range of throttle movement. The best set up I have seen (and the only one I have used since I first saw it) is the compression spring set up first used on the works McLaren Can-Am cars Figure(61).Even with this system, which will function if the compression spring breaks, use a safety spring at another location.

THROTTLE SHAFTS AND BUSHINGS

Throttle butterfly shafts should run in either bearings or bushings and should not extend the full length of the manifold. Torqueing the manifold and the heat of running invariably distorts the shaft bores enough to cause some binding. Split them in the middle and use some sort of coupling. Pull the throttle from the center of the shafts rather than from one end to prevent shaft wind-up. Butterflies should be carefully centered in their bore and the screws loctited AND staked or safety wired.

THROTTLE SYNCHRONIZATION

Everyone realizes the importance of synchronizing throttles at idle, and almost everyone realizes that they should be also synchronized at full throttle. It is equally important, but not widely appreciated, that they remain synchronized throughout the range of operation. This not only affects mid-range power but, more important, throttle response. Many of the commercially available manifolds and linkages ignore this little fact. Check yours and, if the butterflies do not stay synchronized as they open, spend a couple of days making a geometrically correct linkage. It is a simple exercise in plane geometry but may require turning two of the carbs around so that they all face the same direction. From full open to idle the average butterfly moves

through an arc of around 83 degress. This is because the idle position (which should be individually adjustable for each pair of butterflies) is normally around 7 degrees. The operating arm must not be allowed to move over-center or you run the risk of either having the throttles jam open or not being able to consistently close them to the idle position. Additionally, with big hairy engines it may be necessary to arrange a varying ratio of pedal travel to butterfly opening so that the first 15 or so degrees of throttle opening requires 50% of pedal travel. Some engines develop God-Awful percentages of total power with relatively small throttle openings and in extreme cases a straight line relationship between pedal and butterfly can result in a really ticklish part throttle control problem. The solution lies in the use of bellcranks, which may be required anyway simply to change the direction of motion of the linkage. They are easy to make, using a Fafnir BCP-10 bearing as the pivot, and they are both fun and educational to play with. The cross-link between the left and right banks of a V-8 must be left and right hand threaded for adjusting the synchronization and, like the throttle pull, it should be mounted in the center of the shaft assembly rather than at one end. I have never seen a hydraulic throttle control that I would be willing to put on a car. I wish someone would make one.

THE COCKPIT

Now it's the driver's turn. It is just not reasonable to expect any driver to operate at his maximum capability if he is uncomfortable or has to brace himself in the car. Non-racers refuse to believe that it is possible for the human being to be at all comfortable in our little lie-down racers. In actuality, they are a lot more comfortable and offer better support and perception than the old sit-up styles. It is every bit as important to adjust the cockpit to the driver as it is to adjust the suspension to the track—and it's a damn sight easier.

Start with the seat. What we don't need is a lot of padding between driver and seat. Flat sheet metal or fibreglass, providing it is shaped and proportioned right, is pretty damned comfortable to sit on—or in. What we do need is

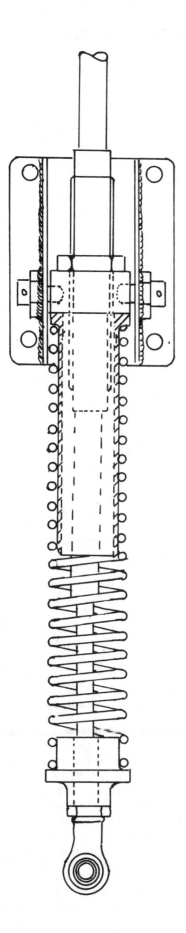
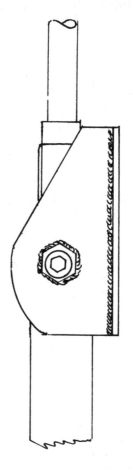

Figure (61): Compression Spring Throttle Cable Abutment with Swivel Mount

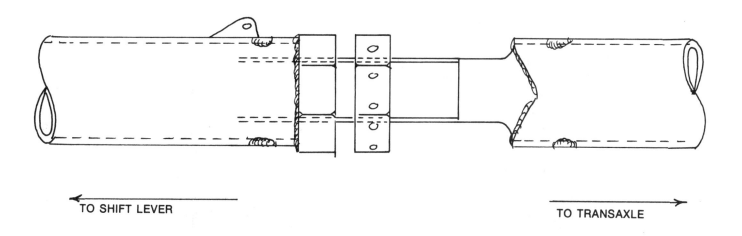

Figure (62): Gearshift Linkage Adjuster Permitting Radial and Fore & Aft Adjustment

◄──────────── TO SHIFT LEVER

TO TRANSAXLE ────────────►

maximum lateral support of the driver's hips and torso while leaving his arms free. This means that he should be a press fit in the cockpit. Most of the current crop of cockpits, with or without separate seats, are pretty well designed, but it is necessary to do some individual tailoring. Closed cell polystyrene foam and tape will do a reasonable job but shaped aluminum or fibreglass is better. It is usually necessary to provide extra support under the thighs in order to prevent fatigue and sliding forward under braking and also around the rib-cage under the arms to prevent being thrown around or having to brace under lateral loads.

The steering column should be adjustable both longitudinally and vertically to provide comfortable arm positioning, and the gearshift should be positioned in line with the steering wheel in the natural position so that the driver's hand falls naturally onto the knob. It should be close to the wheel, but there must be plenty of hand clearance when the shift lever is in whatever gear is closest to the wheel. Don't worry about clearance in reverse except to make sure that reverse can be selected. The same is true of first in five speed Formula A and Can Am cars—you'll never use it on the race track. A threaded coupling, with a positive lock somewhere in the gear linkage will provide both fore and aft and radial adjustment Figure (62). Gear linkages must be very strong indeed and must not bind at all. The use of "Apex" brand heavy duty universal joints is a must. Make sure that the driver cannot bind or move the shift linkage by leaning against it or the seat. The driver's hand must have at least 1/2" of clearance from anything and everything, including the skin and the windshield while shifting and steering.

The brake and accelerator pedals' relative positions must allow your individual driver to blip the throttle during downshifts while retaining constant and controlled brake pedal pressure. They must be close enough to allow heel and toe or foot rolling action (whichever the driver prefers) but they must be far enough apart so that there is no way he is going to make a mistake or get his right foot caught. Variations will be necessary due to driver preference and foot and ankle construction, but the throttle pedal should normally be about 1/8" below the brake pedal with normal braking pressure exerted, and they should have about 1" of lateral separation. Most drivers prefer pedals which pivot at the bottom, because pendant pedal geometry and the human ankle function when in the lie down position are not fully compatible. Low pivot pedals also make mounting master cylinders, rack and pinion assemblies and the like easier. The pivot bolts can be a bear to get at though . . .

Instruments, particularly the tachometer and the oil pressure gauge, must be positioned so that they can be seen regardless of hand position. They should also be mounted high so that he doesn't have to change his eye positioning to read them (glance at them would be a better term). Don't over-instrument the car. He doesn't ever need to know more than rpm, oil pressure, fuel pressure and water temperature. Turn the gauges so that the normal needle position is at 12 o'clock. The oil temperature gauge can be mounted on the tank and you can read it when he stops. Make sure that he can reach all of the switches while strapped in but cannot accidentally turn them off. They should be clearly labeled in large and prominent letters. The ignition switch should be a good long ways away from the others (steering wheel is best) as should the master switch and the fire system control. Speaking of fire system controls, for the sake of economy (freon systems cost a fortune to refill) they should have a safety pin incorporated in the control to prevent accidental discharge. They should also have a big red streamer on the safety pin, and the pin should be removed before the car leaves the pit. The driver will not have time to pull the pin if he needs the system—even if he does remember it. He should be instructed to activate the system when it looks like he is going to hit something hard and not to worry about the cost of refilling it if it turns out that it wasn't needed. If he manages to avoid the crash that he was sure was coming, the stuff won't hurt or even disturb him. If he doesn't activate it, and he doesn't happen to be conscious when he needs it, it's too bad. The chances of most crash crews getting an unconscious driver out of a fire are pretty remote.

COOLING

Even in the mid-engined car the cockpit can be a pretty hot place. Heat is debilitating. Hot people, particularly very hot people, do not perform as well as cool people. Therefore it is incumbent upon us to supply cooling air to the driver—not for humanitarian reasons, but in order to improve performance. The most effective place is usually at his feet; it will then find its own way out the top of the cockpit, cooling as it goes. NASA ducts, located in a good, high pressure area of laminar flow not only look trick—they work. In coupes it is vital to remember that it won't do any good to provide inlet ducts if you don't also provide a route of exit. Top radiator air exit ducts must not be allowed to direct hot air into the cockpit or onto the driver's face. Some playing around with splitters and shields may be necessary here. The windshield height may also have to be adjusted to prevent buffeting of the driver's head. An outward curled lip or a longitudinal rib on the cockpit sides goes a long way toward preventing buffeting. Done right it will also stiffen a typically flimsy area. Take a look at the Tyrell 006 Formula One Car or the Repco Matich A 50 Formula 5000 Car.

MIRRORS

Mirrors must be mounted rigidly enough to prevent vibration and high enough to provide a view. The mirror mounted on the side of the windscreen may look neat and may provide an excellent view of the wing and/or rear tire but look at where Jackie Stewart used to put his—and think about how often he had logical reason to look for someone coming up on him. There must be a clue there . . . The same is true of Mario Andretti's mirrors.

THE ROLLOVER BAR

The constructor has supplied a nice little plate on the roll over bar which claims that it meets all sorts of neat specifications. In many cases he is a damned liar. In no way will I defend SCCA's roll over bar requirements which are idiotic. I will admit, however, that if anyone ever built one to conform to those specs, it would be a good one. Let your conscience be your guide. One sure thing is that conduit and poprivets to .051" skin aren't going to do much good. If you are clever about it you can use the back braces to help the engine mounting system more than a little. You have to have them anyway, so they may as well do some good.

Don't take chances with safety harness. SCCA has finally seen the light and requires a six point system. You can hold it on with pop rivets, but it has to be six point. Most stressed skin chassis come with totally inadequate lap belt mounts. The snap type attachments featured by most sedan type belts are too bulky for race car cockpits. The plate type works OK, or you can loop the belt around a tube. Do not attach the shoulder harness to the engine. Engines have been known to come undone in severe crashes. If your lap belt is secured to the chassis and your shoulder harness is secured to the engine—and the engine goes away . . . This is also why the Grand Prix constructor's Association is against rearward roll over bar braces in the typical chassis in which the tub ends at the firewall and the engine is attached only to the firewall, it bears thinking about, although with one notable exception, all of the Formula A and Can Am cars have good tubular structure holding the engine in. The best American safety harnesses (as well as gloves and boots) are made by Whetstone Research—if you can find them.

In virtually no case should it take more than two hours to fit the driver to the car. Minor modifications will be necessary after he has driven it. It is rare that you get to do anything in that amount of time that will have an equal effect on performance or on the driver's mental outlook which is part and parcel of the same thing.

CHAPTER SIX

SUSPENSION BEARINGS AND BEARING INSTALLATIONS

The suspension system of the racing car contains a considerable number of precise and expensive bearings of various types. Ideally all of these bearings should work in harmony to ensure that the wheels rotate smoothly with minimal friction, that the suspension links swing freely through their appointed arcs with minimal compliance and that dynamic wheel motion closely approximates the paths intended by the designer. The selection, inspection and proper installation of these items is one of the places where both performance and money can be saved—or wasted.

HUB BEARINGS

Hub—or axle—bearings are obviously critical items. They fall into three broad categories: tapered roller bearings, deep groove ball bearings and needle roller bearings. Regardless of type, the purpose of the hub bearing system remains the same:

> (1) To permit free rotation of the road wheels with minimal frictional resistance and no deviation from the plane of rotation.
> (2) To transmit the loads, both radial and thrust, developed by the static and dynamic weights of the vehicle and its vertical, lateral and longitudinal accelerations through the suspension system and into the chassis.

The efficient achievement of these ends can be accomplished only when the bearing system has been well designed, the bearings themselves have been properly selected, lubricated and installed and the assembly is correctly maintained.

While the actual design of the hub, hub carrier and bearing system is beyond the scope of this book, the basic considerations are worth mentioning.

The assembly must be capable of accepting both the radial loads imposed by the dynamic weight of the vehicle and the thrust loads imposed by the side forces generated while cornering. Any play within the assembly under dynamic conditions will not only generate undesirable wheel motion and/or deflection but will eventually lead to component failure.

The larger the bearings and the closer the axial center of the bearing assembly to the wheel centerline, the greater will be the radial capacity of the system. The larger the bearings and the greater the axial spacing between them, the greater will be the thrust capacity. In both cases it is necessary to obtain and maintain the proper preload on the bearings themselves.

While it is difficult to conceive of a racing installation which could be deficient in radial capacity (ignoring the existence of high bankings), thrust capacity is another thing entirely. The problem became acute in the mid-sixties when tires first began to approach their present indecent widths and lateral capacities.

The immediate solution was to save the existing systems, whether tapered roller or deep groove ball bearings, by fitting a carefully machined steel spacer between the inner races or cones of the bearings in order to maintain preload adjustment. This temporary solution was followed by a general move toward large diameter tubular steel hubs, invariably of the "live axle" variety, with attendant larger diameter bearings and greater axial spacing.

TYPES OF HUB BEARINGS

Figure (63) illustrates the principle and construction of the tapered roller bearing and Figure (65) shows a typical installation. Since this bearing combines excellent radial capacity with almost equal thrust capacity at moderate cost, it is a very good solution to the problem. The only disadvantages to the tapered roller bearing installation are the difficulty in sealing the bearings (the best method is probably the English "Nylos seal" which resembles a very thin steel saucer, is difficult to obtain and does not provide a positive seal, but takes up very little room) and the difficulty of obtaining optimum preload between the inboard and outboard cones. Due to manufacturing tolerances on the bearings themselves, it is sometimes necessary to refit the preload spacer when replacing bearings. Each preload spacer must be kept as a partner with its individual hub carrier (not with the axle). It is also critical to use cones and cups of the same manufacture as slight geometrical differences exist.

Except for Lola, most of the racing car manufacturers have now drifted away from the tapered roller bearing and use either a pair of opposed deep groove ball bearings Figure (66) or a combination of a deep groove ball bearing inboard to take the thrust load with a needle roller bearing outboard to take the radial load Figure 67).

As shown in Figure (64), ball bearings come in three basic configurations, maximum capacity, angular contact and Conrad or deep groove. The Conrad or deep groove bearing is eminently suitable for racing car hub or axle bearing applications. It has excellent bi-directional thrust capacity combined with typical ball bearing radial capability. Further, it is available in a wide range of standard sizes in a prelubricated permanently sealed configuration. Manufacturing tolerances are such that, once the preload spacer has been properly fitted to the individual hub carrier, bearings can be changed without upsetting the preload. Determining

Figure (63): Tapered Roller Bearing Nomenclature and Geometry

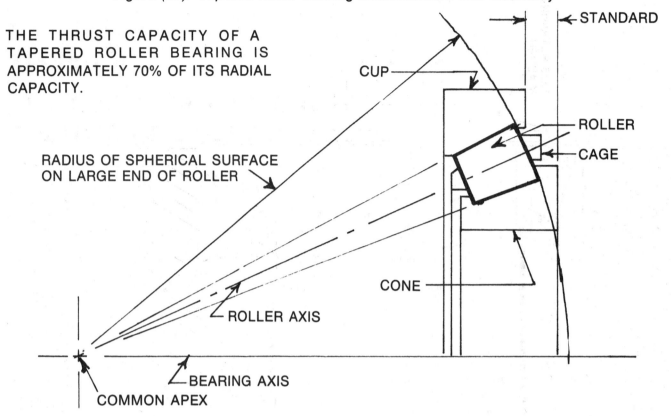

THE THRUST CAPACITY OF A TAPERED ROLLER BEARING IS APPROXIMATELY 70% OF ITS RADIAL CAPACITY.

STANDARD

CUP

ROLLER

CAGE

RADIUS OF SPHERICAL SURFACE ON LARGE END OF ROLLER

CONE

ROLLER AXIS

BEARING AXIS

COMMON APEX

Figure (64): : Ball Bearing Configurations and Characteristics

TYPE		APPROX. RANGE OF BORE SIZES (INCHES)		RELATIVE CAPACITY		LIMITING SPEED FACTOR	MISALIGN. TOLERANCE
		MIN.	MAX.	RADIAL	THRUST		
CONRAD or DEEP GROOVE		.012	41.72	1.00	0.7 2 DIRECTIONAL	1.0	+0 15'
MAXIMUM CAPACITY or FILLING NOTCH		0.39	5.12	1.2/1.4	0.2 2 DIRECTIONAL	1.0	+0 3'
ANGULAR CONTACT		0.39	12.60	1.00/1.15	1.5/2.3 1 DIRECTION		±0 2'

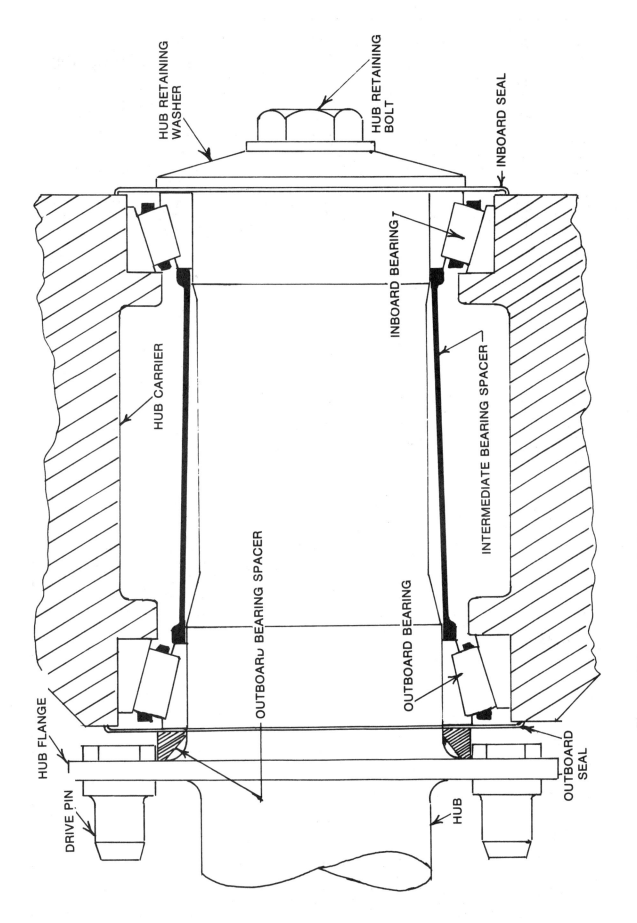

Figure (65): Hub Assembly Using Tapered Roller Bearings. Intermediate Bearing Spacer is Ground to Fit Assembly. Replacing Bearings May Require Refitting Spacer. Do Not Use Cones of One Make With Cups of Another. Do Not Over-lubricate.

93

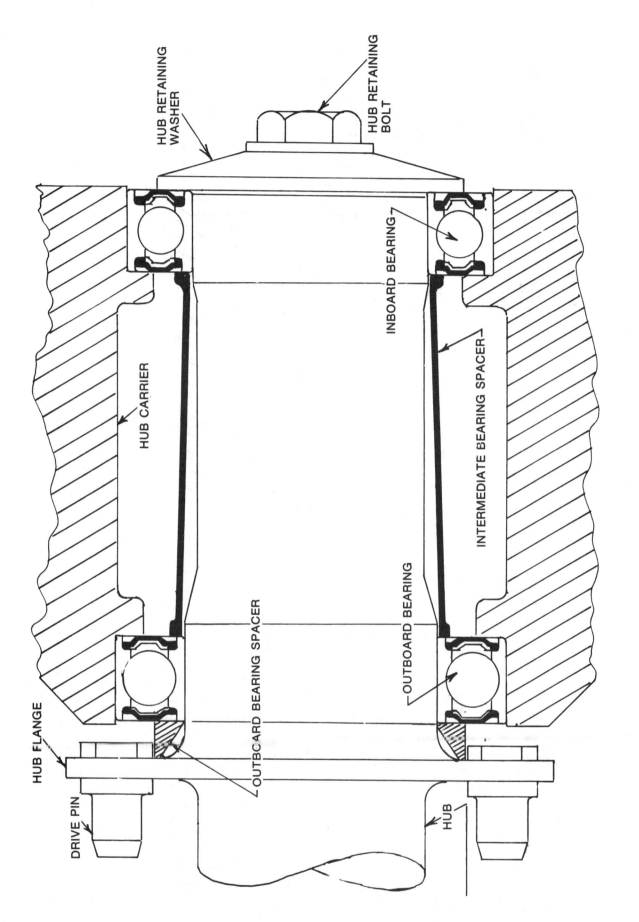

HUB RETAINING WASHER

HUB RETAINING BOLT

INBOARD BEARING

HUB CARRIER

INTERMEDIATE BEARING SPACER

OUTBOARD BEARING

OUTBOARD BEARING SPACER

HUB FLANGE

DRIVE PIN

HUB

Figure (66): Hub Assembly Using Double Sealed Deep Groove Ball Bearings. Intermediate Bearing Spacer is Ground To Fit Hub Carrier. Bearings Can Be Changed Without Disturbing Assembly Tolerance.

94

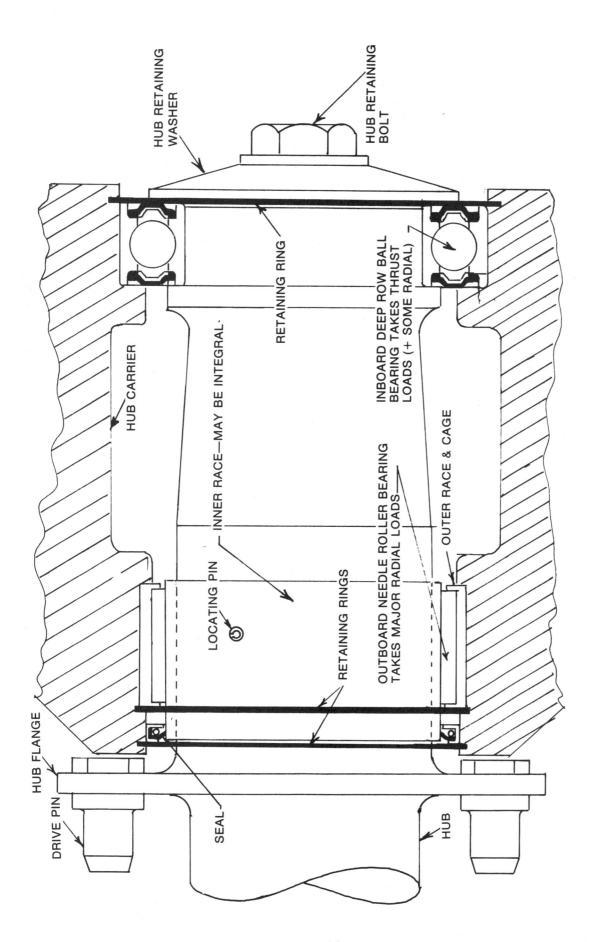

HUB RETAINING WASHER

HUB RETAINING BOLT

RETAINING RING

INBOARD DEEP ROW BALL BEARING TAKES THRUST LOADS (+ SOME RADIAL)

HUB CARRIER

INNER RACE—MAY BE INTEGRAL.

LOCATING PIN

OUTER RACE & CAGE

RETAINING RINGS

OUTBOARD NEEDLE ROLLER BEARING TAKES MAJOR RADIAL LOADS

HUB FLANGE

DRIVE PIN

SEAL

HUB

Figure (67): Hub Assembly Using Needle Roller Bearing for Major Radial Loads With Deep Row Ball Bearing for Thrust Loads. No Spacer Required.

optimum spacer length is a simple matter of measuring the exact distance between the bearing bore shoulders in the hub carrier and machining the spacer to that dimension. The only disadvantages are those of size and cost. For equal capacity the Conrad bearing will be greater in diameter than a tapered roller bearing and will cost about twice as much.

When buying replacement bearings it is absolutely necessary to be sure that you obtain Conrad type bearings manufactured to ABEC-1 tolerances. The maximum capacity ball bearing has virtually no thrust capability and the angular contact bearing has a thrust capability in one direction only. Substitution of either of these bearings will lead to an accident. A fourth type does exist, the split inner race ball bearing. It has the greatest bi-directional thrust capability of all of the ball bearings, but has limited radial capacity. They are not available sealed, are hard to find and won't fit anyway. The only common application for this type of bearing is as the pinion thrust bearing in the Hewland DG 300 transaxle. Unfortunately the bearing selected for this application is too small for the job and is a source of trouble. It is also essential to buy quality bearings. The best that I know of are manufactured by MRC and by New Departure. The bible is MRC's catalog 60.

My own preference in hub bearing systems is the combination needle roller/deep groove ball bearing configuration originated by McLaren and now used by All American Racers, McRae Cars, Matich, Talon and others. I feel that this system offers the best combination of size, simplicity and load capacity yet devised. It offers the further advantage of not requiring a preload spacer as the needle roller is allowed to float on the hub journal to accomodate differences in thermal expansion. It is also a damn sight easier to install and take apart. Most McLaren innovations are. The bible for needle rollers is INA's catalog #E301.

LUBRICATION

Irrespective of the type of bearings used, certain ground rules apply. In order to function, all bearings must be lubricated. In order to prevent loss of lubricant and ingress of dirt, all bearings must be sealed. While virtually all of the ball bearings used in hubs are sealed for life, the needle rollers and tapered roller bearings are not and the user (or installer) is required to lubricate them before installation as well as to install separate seals. The best grease I know of is Shell's Aeroshell 16 which is available in five pound cans from your Shell Aviation Products Distributor and is the only grease you are going to need except for assembly lube and Molygrease for constant velocity type drive shafts, should you be so fortunate as to have them.

The cardinal sins of bearing lubrication are both sins of excess—too much grease and too much dirt. The storage, packing and assembly of both grease and bearings must be carried out in a clean environment with clean hands. A plastic garbage bag on a bench a long way away from grinders, hacksaws, etc. makes an acceptable clean environment. Lacking a bearing packer, a golf ball sized glob of grease is placed in the palm of one clean hand and the bearing is scooped across the palm forcing the grease into the spaces between the rollers. Lightly coat the bearing races, hub and the inside of the hub carrier with the same grease

and install the bearings. The old "If a little bit is good, then a lot must be better." attitude just does not hold true. Excess grease will merely be pumped around inside the cavity generating heat and will finally be forced out past the seals creating a mess.

Recommended fits onto shafts and into housings of different materials are given in the bearing manufacturers' catalogs. Note that the fit differs depending on which part of the bearing is going to rotate. As shown in Figure (67) some ball bearings are retained in their housings by a retainer ring. In these applications it is essential to check that the bearing is a tight axial fit between the shoulder of the bearing bore and the retaining ring. If it is not, the bearing will move in its housing which will both damage the housing and allow compliance in the system as well as inconsistent brake pedal height. The condition is corrected by cutting shim rings to suit from stainless shim stock and placing them between the bearing's outer race and the retaining ring.

SHRINKING BEARINGS IN AND OUT

Due to the fact that magnesium and aluminum hub carriers (and gearbox casings) have a much higher coefficient of thermal expansion than do steel bearing races, all bearings are heat shrunk into light alloy housings. The best way to heat the housing in order to remove or install bearings is in an oven at 250°F. to 275°F. Since virtually no one has access to an oven, the normal method is to slowly and evenly heat the operating area with a rosebud tip on an oxyacetylene torch. A 250°F. temperature crayon from your local welding supply house will tell you when the proper temperature has been reached. Also, at about 250°F. a mark made with a bar of hand soap will go away and spit will sizzle and pop. This is hot enough to cause severe burns so asbestos gloves are a big help. If both temperature and fit are correct the bearings will literally fall in or out (especially in, as in that case the bearing is still cold). Tapping the housing, hard, on a piece of wood with the bearing facing down will usually remove a recalcitrant bearing. Conversely, tapping on the outer race of a bearing with a suitable piece of tubing will install a bearing if necessary. Don't use much force and make sure that the bearing is square in the housing before you start beating. Most hub carriers have small reliefs machined in the bearing housings to aid removal. If your car does not have this provision, do it. A rat tailed file will get it done.

Hub carriers tend to be expensive. A unit with a damaged bearing bore can often be saved by machining the bore oversize, shrinking in a new seat of the same material, then machining the sleeve to fit the bearing. Use a tighter fit on the sleeve than on the bearing. Loc-Tite bearing mount will solve a loose bearing fit in an emergency but don't think of it as a permanent repair.

DISASSEMBLY

Disassembly of the hub, hub carrier and bearing system is mainly a matter of common sense. In order to remove the hub from the hub carrier it is first necessary to remove the retaining bolt and then to either tap or press the hub from the inboard end. This will also (in most applications) remove the inboard bearing from the hub. Ideally a press

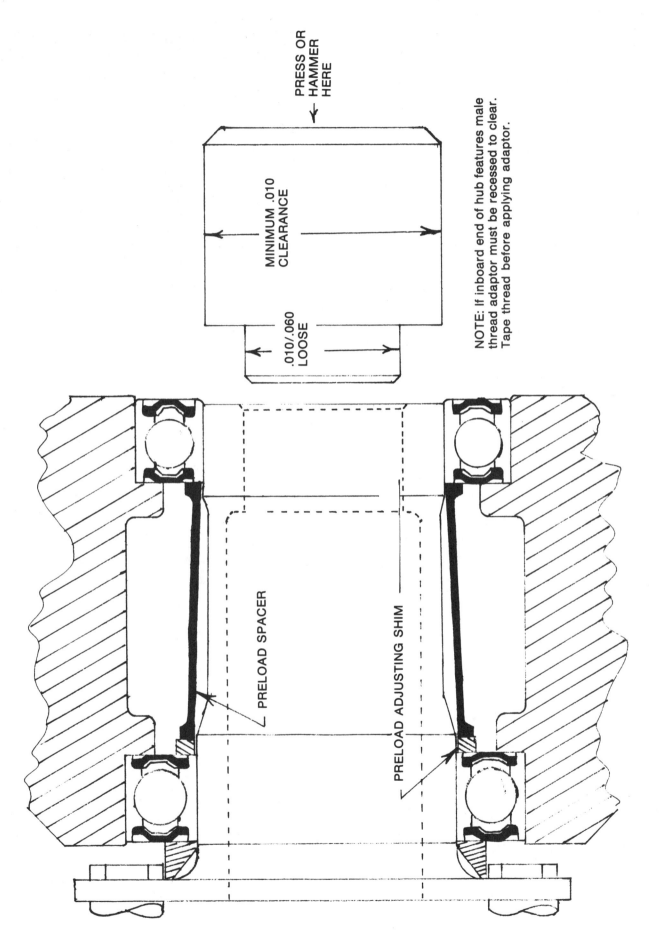

PRESS OR HAMMER HERE

MINIMUM .010 CLEARANCE

.010/.060 LOOSE

NOTE: If inboard end of hub features male thread adaptor must be recessed to clear. Tape thread before applying adaptor.

PRELOAD SPACER

PRELOAD ADJUSTING SHIM

Figure (68): Hub Removal Adaptor & Shim Preload Adjustment

97

should be used. In the absence of a press a large brass or copper hammer will do the job. In the not uncommon case of a slightly too tight fit between the bearing I.D. and the hub journal, the hammer treatment will usually shock the bearing loose where the press will fail. In either case, do not beat or press directly on the end of the hub as serious damage is guaranteed. Make an adaptor of mild steel or, preferably, aluminum bar that will spigot into the hub I.D. or fit over the male thread. The O.D. of the adaptor must be smaller than the bearing bore. With the adaptor held firmly and square against the hub face, have at it. Figure (68) illustrates.

The outboard bearing will probably be a line to line fit with the hub journal. A "clamshell bearing puller" is the best way to achieve separation. In some cases it may be necessary to machine the puller to obtain the clearance necessary for insertion. Again a press is better but a large soft hammer will do and an adaptor must be used. If it is possible to position the puller so that it contacts only the inner race of the bearing, bearing removal can almost always be accomplished without damage. Sometimes this is just not practical and a tight bearing will be ruined during removal. Often removal of the wheel drive pins from the hub flange will allow better access and puller positioning.

Needle roller bearings are a relatively loose fit on their journals and will remain in the hub carrier as the hub is withdrawn.

ASSEMBLY

To install the outboard bearing on the hub, first make sure that both the hub and the bearing are free of dirt and scratches, are lubricated and that the outboard bearing spacer is installed. Using a tubular spacer which is a loose fit on the hub journal and which contacts only the inner race of the bearing, press or tap the bearing into place until it is firmly seated against the spacer. Never tap or press on the outer race or on a cage when installing a bearing onto a journal. It may be necessary to slightly warm the inner race. It is essential to make sure that the bearing starts onto the journal square. Figure (70) illustrates.

PRELOAD SPACING

Where a preload spacer is used, the most practical method I have found to determine proper spacing (if it cannot be measured) is to construct some sort of fixture which will allow the hub or the hub carrier to be firmly held in place. Usually a large vise with soft jaws clamping either the hub flange (if it is square or rectangular) or the caliper mounting ears will do. Assemble and torque the unit and measure the axial play with a dial indicator. Naturally the magnesium hub carrier will expand more at operating temperature than the spacer so it is best to set the preload slightly on the tight side. This is not true with fabricated steel hub carriers. Most bearing applications call for zero preload. This is almost impossible to measure. I have found that .001" to .002" loose or tight makes no functional difference. Never succumb to the temptation to adjust preload with thin shim washers. They will pound out in service and leave you with a loose assembly filled with steel dust. The same is true of the crush spacers used in proprietary rear end assemblies. It is, however, permissible to use a series of relatively hefty machined shims, say between .090" and .100" in increments of .001" to adjust preload. This is both less expensive and less time consuming than machining spacer sleeves and allows adjustment at the track. Figure (68) illustrates.

When installing a McLaren type hub into the hub carrier, make damned sure that it starts square and don't force it. If it won't go with the pressure of your body, something is wrong. Slight heating of the upright will encourage the union. With new bearings, this type of unit may feel stiff when first assembled. Warm the entire assembly to 150°F. or so. If it feels OK at this temperature it will wear in and be happy in a few laps. If it doesn't (especially with a new hub carrier) the bearing boss for the needle roller is very slightly undersize and I hope that you know a good machinist. When replacing hubs, make sure that the needle roller is an easy fit on the journal before assembly. If not, send the hub back.

INSPECTION

Bearing inspection is simple. Thoroughly clean bearing and race with solvent. Scotchbright will remove grundge. Any sign of pitting, brinelling or skuffing on any working surface is cause for rejection. A matt surface on the working area of a tapered roller bearing cone is normal. Rough spots felt while rotating clean and oiled bearings by hand mean trouble. Sealed bearings should be inspected for loss of lubricant, axial play, damaged seals and roughness in rotation. Some sealed bearings can be disassembled for inspection —most cannot.

PURCHASING BEARINGS

Many racers buy their hub bearings and seals from the manufacturer or dealer for their car. This is almost invariably a mistake. Bearing and seal sizes are international and your local bearing house, given a manufacturer and a part number can obtain virtually any bearing or its exact equivalent. The same applies to seals. The exceptions are some of the Hewland transaxle bearings and the previously mentioned Nylos type seals. Additionally if you talk nicely, cry a little and order in any sort of quantity at all, you can probably get a good discount. Obtain the catalogs and handbooks. They are full of all sorts of helpful and fascinating bits of information. Don't take the rotational speed limitations listed too seriously—they are plenty conservative. If you have a real bearing problem, I have found that the bearing company field engineers (not salesmen) are almost invariably expert and helpful. Your bearing house can help you to contact one.

ROD END AND SPHERICAL BEARINGS

Suspension linkage bearings of the rod-end and spherical variety present a problem in that there are a lot of them; they do wear out; good ones are expensive and bad ones are an abomination. Even slightly loose bearings in a critical spot will destroy the handling of your car. The only tip is to figure out which applications are critical and use first quality bearings in those applications while saving money on the

Figure (69): Use of Clamshell Puller to Remove Bearing from Hub

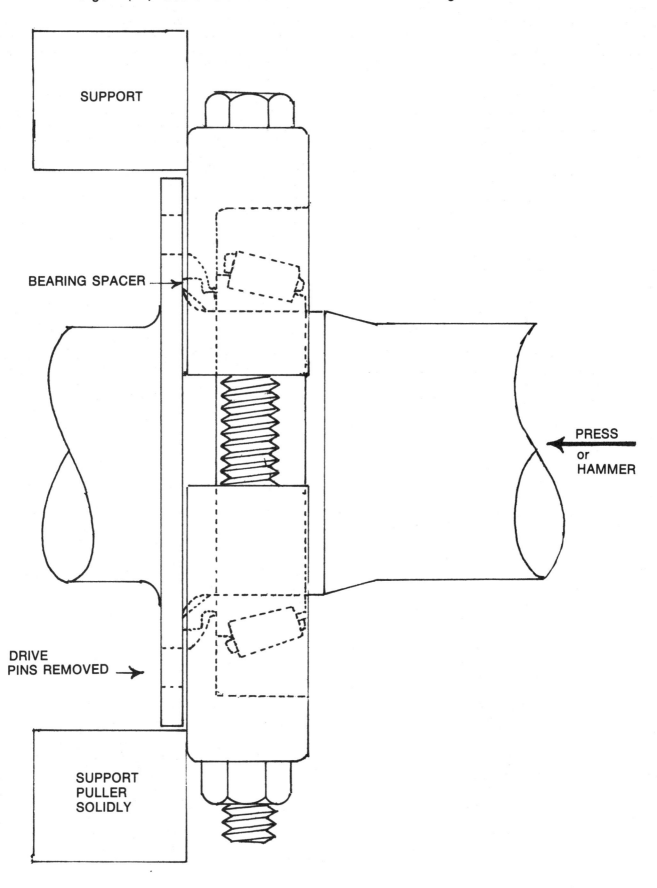

SUPPORT

BEARING SPACER →

PRESS
or
HAMMER

DRIVE
PINS REMOVED →

SUPPORT
PULLER
SOLIDLY

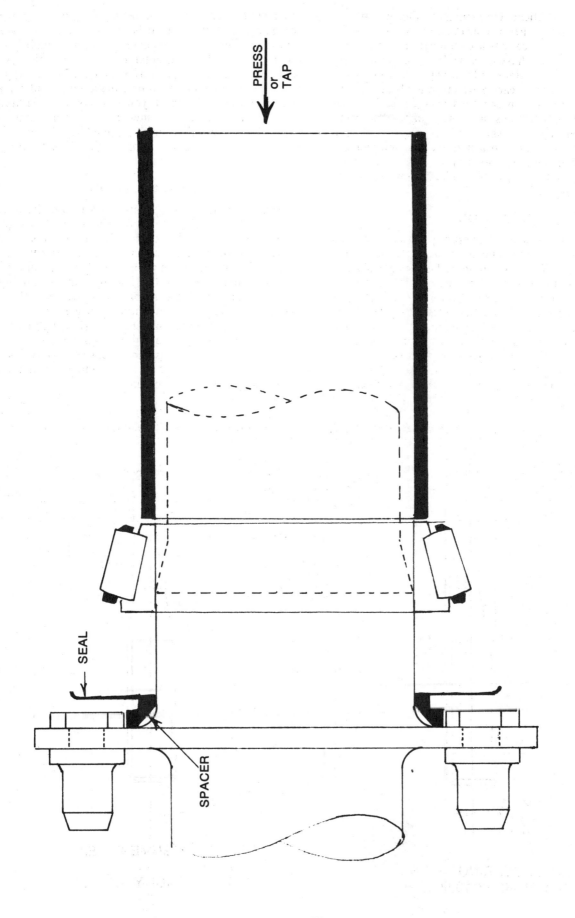

PRESS or TAP

SEAL

SPACER

Figure (70): Use of Heavy Wall Tube to Install Bearing on Hub

100

ones that are non-critical. Unfortunately the non-critical ones are few in number, never wear out and don't cost much to start with. Critical locations are all locations which connect the wheels to the chassis, i.e. wishbones, radius rods, parallel links, transverse links and steering track rods. Most critical of these are any bearing which controls rear toe-in —rear lower wishbones, lower radius rods, or rear parallel links. Non-critical locations are sway bar links, wing mount stays and adjustors, shock adsorber eyes and shift linkage. In fact, nice sloppy bearings are a definite advantage in the shift linkage. Do not confuse nice sloppy shift linkage bearings with sloppy shift linkage universal joints which must be avoided.

SELECTION

For the non-critical items, the best buy is Heim's bronze on steel line. For critical applications my preference is for NMB's series of teflon lined bearings. The price is slightly less than Fabroid, the quality is lots better and the longevity is just about twice. The best bearings available are Southwest Products' Dyflon line but unless you get lucky at a surplus outlet, both price and availability are ridiculous. Shafer-Rexlon, Fafnir (faflon line) and Heim also make good bearings. Sperco is to be avoided. I have found the ubiquitous Fabroid to have spotty quality control and the life expectancy is not good. The English Ampep bearing looks nasty but is, in fact, very good and, in England, reasonable. All of the good bearings have a thin layer of flouride or flouride impregnated fibreglass bonded to the outer race. Further, the outer race is in one piece and is somehow or other extruded over the ball. The basic rule is not to use a metal on metal or a metal on moulded plastic bearing in a critical place. If you have a friend in Military or Commercial aviation maintenance, cultivate him. Occasionally you may find some very good buys in surplus outlets, particularly at Earl's Supply and at Joe Factor's.

INSTALLATION

Proper installation will greatly increase the life of these bearings. Never lubricate a flouride lined bearing. No lubrication is required and the oil will merely serve as a carrier to introduce grit into the working surfaces. To prevent beating out the bearing, check each individual installation to make sure that the bearing cannot run out of angularity during normal suspension movement. If it can, either rotate the bearing mounting 90 degrees (as on a rear upright clevis pin), use a high angularity bearing Figure (71) or use conical spacers to avoid bottoming Figure (71) and (72). It does no good to use an expensive bearing if it is a loose fit in its housing or if the mounting bolt is loose in either the bearing or the mount.

Figure (71): Standard and High-Misalignment Rod End Bearings

STANDARD BEARING—⅜" BORE
RADIAL CAPACITY 10,000 LB.

HIGH-MISALIGNMENT BEARING
⅜" BORE
RADIAL CAPACITY 5500 LB.

Figure (72): Conical Clearance Spacers for Rod End Mounted in Clevis

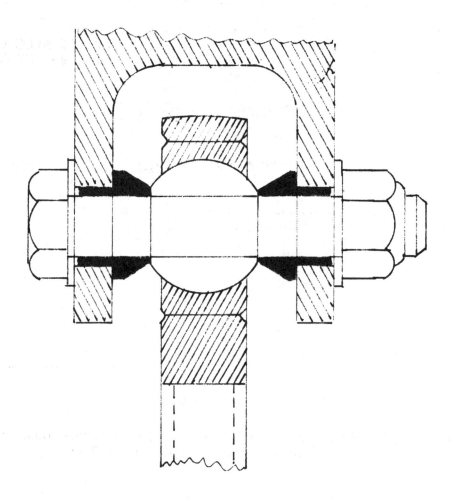

When installing rod end bearings use AN 316 series aircraft check nuts to lock the bearing in place. The presence of an NAS keyway in the shank of a rod end does not affect its utility. Do not loc-tite the threads of either the check nut or the rod end. Safety wire is not necessary. A red nail polish line across the check nut and the adjoining link will give a visual indication that the check nut is still tight. Many mechanics wrap the check nut and the end of the link with black plastic electrical tape after tightening the check nut to indicate that it has been done. I have never had a check nut loosen so I no longer do any of the above. I do, however, religiously tighten each check nut immediately every time that I loosen it while adjusting things so that there is no possibility of my forgetting to do so later.

SPHERICAL BEARING INSTALLATION

When installing spherical bearings use the catalog recommended fits, aided when necessary by bearing mount and shim stock. During installation use a tubular adaptor and press or pound only on the outer race. A bench vise should be all of the press needed. The axial fit of spherical bearings in their housings very often requires adjustment with shim stock.

SLEEVES

When it is necessary to sleeve the I.D. of a rod end or spherical bearing, make the sleeve a precise fit, both I.D. and O.D. With flanged sleeves, leave at least 1/16" gap between the sleeve ends so that they can be punched out later. Figure (73) illustrates.

Figure (74) shows the basic nomenclature of rod ends. Spherical bearings are merely rod ends without the body. Both are available in both standard and high misalignment configuration Figure (71) and the rod ends are available with both left and right hand threads. Standard rod ends have the shank size equal to the bore and heavy duty rod ends feature a shank 1/16" larger than bore diameter. It is not unusual to find surplus rod ends of very good quality with the shank 1/8" larger than the bore. With rod ends it is essential to inspect each one individually to ensure that the body has the rolled stake ring which positively locks the liner into the body. From time to time this operation gets left out and the inevitable result is separation of the liner from the body and disaster. SCCA requires any rod end or spherical bearing not in double shear to have a safety washer on the open end with a diameter great enough to prevent total separation. This is a good idea although what they

Figure (73): Rod End Bushing/Spacer

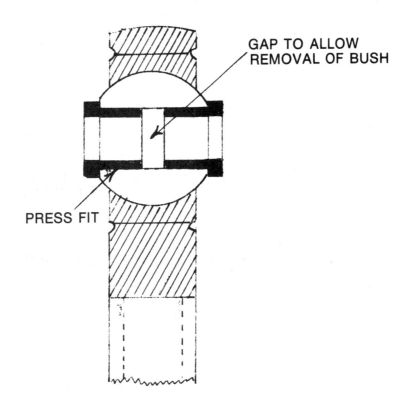

GAP TO ALLOW
REMOVAL OF BUSH

PRESS FIT

*Figure (74): Rod End Bearing Nomenclature Showing Positive Retention of Race
in Housing by Means of "Grumman Ring".*

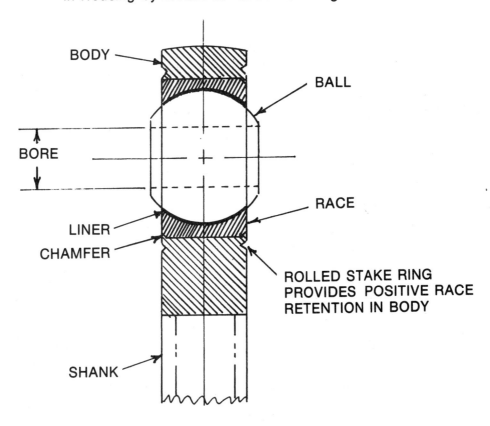

BODY

BALL

BORE

RACE

LINER

CHAMFER

ROLLED STAKE RING
PROVIDES POSITIVE RACE
RETENTION IN BODY

SHANK

should do is to outlaw single shear mounting. Unfortunately SCCA doesn't much care what the washer is made from or how thick it is. If you must use such a thing, make one that will do the job should it ever become necessary. Most of these devices need tapering on the side next to the bearing so that you don't lose bearing angularity.

BALL JOINTS

Subconsciously I have left the upper and lower front suspension ball joint until last. This is because I dislike the ubiquitous English "Thompson Joints" so much that I don't even want to talk about them. I am for sure not going to make a drawing of them so no Figure illustrates. Similar to most U.S. production car ball joints they differ in that they are adjustable for wear which is a good thing. The O.D. of the joint housing is axially serrated to provide positive location in the wishbone bore (and to require extreme pressure to install or remove the joint). It is axially retained by a spiral-lock clip. Adjustment is by means of a threaded upper cap which pushes the nylon bearing onto the ball stud. The cap is then wired in place. The trouble is that, in stock configuration, the only means of turning the upper cap is by means of two tabs which, if the car is not new, are guaranteed to have been knocked off by some idiot who tried to adjust it with a punch. If the car is new, the cap was probably installed dry and the threads are locked. The quick way to make a tool is to file a slot in a conveniently sized socket so that you can turn the thing. The holes in the tabs are radial so that you have to either drill a lot of holes in the circumference of the housing so that the safety wire will line up as you adjust, or take the cap out and drill new holes at 90 degrees to the existing ones or silver solder a drilled bolt head to the center of the cap. No tap or die exists to repair damaged threads. Having done all of the above, you can now adjust the damned things every hundred miles or so for the rest of your life. These joints are dirt cheap in England, very expensive here and a first class pain. Most English race cars feature them and you are pretty much stuck with them as an inordinate amount of machining is necessary to substitute a spherical bearing as should have been done to start with. Lubricate them with a little moly grease and adjust them to just snug—often. When your camber readings won't repeat or you think you can feel wheel bearing play, or when you can't keep your front wheels in balance—adjust them again.

With the suspension bearings in order, it is time to consider the suspension components themselves. As the consequences of suspension component failure are inevitably disastrous, frequent and meticulous inspection is mandatory.

HUBS

The hubs (or axles, or spindles) are almost invariably high quality steel forgings, heat treated after machining with the bearing journals ground after heat treating. All radii should be extra generous, there should be no large or sudden changes in wall thickness, there should be no machining marks, inside or out, and the unit should be shot peened (except for the bearing journals and threads) by a company which really knows what it is doing. Shot peening is a complex and fascinating subject. Done properly it can greatly in-

crease the fatigue life of almost any ferrous part. Done improperly it is almost useless. Shot peening, contrary to popular opinion, is not even related to glass bead blasting which is basically a cleaning process. As a matter of course I have all of my hubs (and ring and pinion sets) redone by a local aerospace firm. When I can afford it I also have new hubs, hub carriers, wheels, input and output shafts X-ray inspected. In order to avoid the insidious effects of corrosion stress, it is vitally important that the hubs (or any other part) not be allowed to rust. Frequent spraying of the bores and all visible parts with any of the proprietary aerosol anti-rust products will do the job. It is even more important to avoid nicks and scratches which will serve as stress raisers and will lead to the generation of cracks. Handle with care and without chisels and such. Bare hubs must be both well oiled and well wrapped for storage, especially if they are to be carried on board the truck. It is a well known fact that all race trucks, and particularly the side boxes affixed thereto leak like sieves.

HUB CARRIERS

Cast magnesium (or any other kind) hub carriers must be inspected when received—by X-ray if you can afford it and by Zyglo if you can't. If cracks or excessive porosity are evident, send them back. All of the magnesium alloys are very notch sensitive—careful deburring and radiusing of new units will pay off in increased life. Small cracks which show up in service can very often be filed out—if caught while they are still small. Both the English Electron C and the American AZ 91 and AZ 92 alloys are weldable—by an expert who knows how to preheat. Welding on a hub carrier, will, of course, destroy the heat treatment in the area of the weld so that this is definitely an area where expert advice should be sought.

CORROSION

In addition to being notch sensitive, magnesium is very corrosion prone. Corrosion can destroy the strength of a magnesium casting from the inside without your being aware of it. Frequent and liberal spraying with one of the aerosol rust preventitives will not only prevent the start of corrosion, but will also keep the casting looking good. It is essential not to let water stand on magnesium overnight. When spraying, make sure that you reach the interior surfaces through the core holes and make equally certain that you do not oil the brake discs and pads.

Hub carriers invariably contain lots of shrunk or pressed in steel bushings. In order to prevent galvanic corrosion, as well as seizing, both the bushing and its bore should be coated with some sort of anti-seize prior to installation. These bushings are normally shrunk in at about 250°F. As with hub bearings, they must be started square with their bores and some sort of adaptor should be used for installation. If the bushing is not designed so that it is positively retained in the casting it should be locked in place with a coarse threaded grub screw. This retention bit is worth some detailed examination as some designers are quite lax in this respect.

Most rear hub carriers feature through pins or clevises top and bottom to mount the radius rods. Under torque loads, these pins, particularly the lower ones, tend to rotate and thus to bind the rod end bearings at the ends of the radius rods. They should be positively located with lock screws as in Figure (75).

Most of the threaded bores in hub carrier castings come with Heilcoils installed. Look at yours and, if there are any threads without helicoils, install them (or Rosans, or Keeserts or whatever).

SUSPENSION LINKS

Wishbones and suspension links are usually fabrications of welded tubular and sheet mild steel. Comments in chapter two regarding finger plates, gussets, wraps and the avoidance of butt welds apply. All bosses welded to tubes with the bore of the boss normal to the centerline of the tube must be wrapped. Particularly in the smaller English Formula cars, few come that way from the manufacturer. All ears mounting suspension links, shock adsorbers, etc. should be boxed or gussetted. The same applies to attachment points on the chassis. No attachment should be in single shear. The addition of another ear or tube will usually convert a single shear mounting to double shear neatly and economically. Most link and/or attachment failures not caused by hitting something are due to poor detail design rather than to lack of material strength. Look your vehicle over carefully and strengthen questionable areas before they fail—it's a damn sight cheaper.

THE RACK AND PINION

One of the most vexing elements to deal with is the steering rack and pinion assembly. The problem here is to adjust the preload and back lash of the gears, the fit of the rack end bushes and the mounting of the housing to the chassis so that play is reduced to a minimum while free motion is maintained throughout the travel of the rack.

The only answer that I have found is patience, fortitude and a lot of hardened shims. Start by magnafluxing both rack and pinion and by making very sure that the rack is straight (if it isn't, straighten it carefully, in a press, with vee blocks) and that all of the gear teeth are free of nicks and burrs. Lubricate the rack with a good grade of grease and make sure that the rack housing mounts are normal to both the housing and the chassis (otherwise the rack housing will be distorted when the mounts are tightened and the unit will bind).

Most racks feature some sort of a follower which rides on the rack surface opposite the teeth and above the pinion. The purpose of this device, whatever its configuration, is partially to keep the lash constant but mainly to positively prevent the rack from jumping a pinion tooth which will lead to instant disaster. It must not be left out! Most of these devices are either oilite or teflon sliders or rollers. They may or may not be spring loaded and they are adjusted by means of a thread on their housing or by shims. Some units are supplied with a ball bearing as a roller. I don't trust the ball bearing types as the outer races tend to be very hard and have been known to shatter in service causing the rack to lock. I replace them with an oilite roller. Properly adjusted, the rack and pinion will have no tight spots, virtually no play and will be free in operation. Bruce McLaren's test

for steering freeness was as good as any I have found. He felt that if everything was right you should be able to jack up the front of the car (wheels on), wind the steering all the way to one stop, flip the steering wheel hard toward the other lock, release the wheel and have the unit bounce off the opposite stop and return about half way.

Some cars come through with enough steering travel so that at full lock, the wheel rim contacts part of the lower wishbone. Although full lock will never be applied on the race track, it is often used while pushing or driving the cars in the pits, shop or paddock. Rubbing the wheel on the suspension cannot help anything, removes the tape from wheel weights, scrapes the plating and makes a really nasty noise. A little thought and five minutes on the lathe will come up with a rack stop to prevent this.

Try to adjust front bump steer at the rod ends so that you don't have to move the rack itself. This will be covered in detail in Chapter 10.

Most steering shafts are provided with a universal joint at the pinion end. This joint must be free of play but no so tight that it binds. They tend to be fairly nasty proprietary units. Time and money permitting I usually replace them with a good surplus aircraft unit which requires some machining and the welding of the female spine from the stock unit onto the surplus unit. This is a pain and probably not worth doing, but I do it anyway. The steering shaft is attached to the pinion by an involute spline and secured by either a pinch bolt or a lock screw which seats in an annular groove in the pinion shaft. The only way to make sure that the lock screw is in the groove is to look down the hole with a light. The lock screw must be safety wired. The consequence of carelessness in this detail is separation of the shaft from the pinion which is not pleasant at all. An added safety precaution which costs nothing and takes five minutes is the installation of a #10-32 bolt and nut in a hole drilled through the steering shaft just in front of the rear bearing or bushing. In the unlikely event of failure of whatever retains the shaft to the pinion, this will prevent the shaft being pulled off the pinion. It is, however, necessary to locate the hole in the shaft so that the bolt head or nut cannot touch the bearing housing.

NON DESTRUCTIVE TESTING

Since we've been talking about inspection of components for most of this chapter, this is as good a time as any to get into the non-destructive testing of metal bit—i.e. ways in which we can validly inspect the parts of the vehicle for faults without destroying the pieces.

X-RAY

X-ray examination is the best single method of inspection. If taken from the right angles and interpreted by an expert, X-ray will show up casting, forging or welding faults, grain structure deficiencies, internal or external stress cracks, porosities, cold shots and any other nasty things you can think of. Unfortunately X-ray examination tends to be very expensive and requires expert interpretation. Pretty much the same applies to ultra sonic inspection.

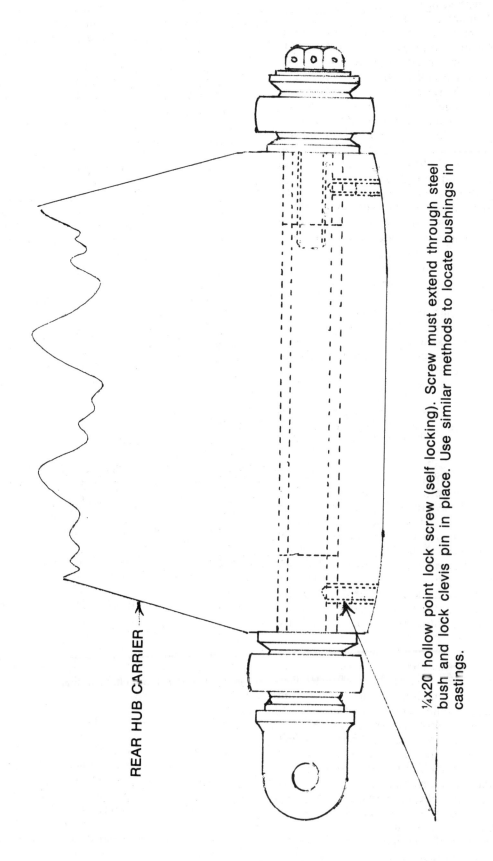

REAR HUB CARRIER

¼x20 hollow point lock screw (self locking). Screw must extend through steel bush and lock clevis pin in place. Use similar methods to locate bushings in castings.

Figure (75): *Use of Hollow Point Lock Screw to Prevent Rotation of Rear Hub Carrier Clevis*

MAGNAFLUX

The most popular method in inspecting ferrous parts is magnetic particle examination or magnaflux. In this method a clean ferrous part is magnetized and a fluorescent fluid containing microscopic particles of iron is poured over the part. The fluorescent iron particles are drawn into any surface cracks, the part is cleaned and then examined under black light. The black light shows up cracks as red lines. Considerable practice is required to intelligently interpret magnaflux readings. The equipment is readily available throughout the country and the cost is nominal. A good portable 110 volt unit is available from Magnaflux Corporation. Magnaflux will not work through oil, paint or dirt. If the current is turned up high enough, it will work through most types of plating. Properly interpreted, magnetic particle inspection is an excellent method and will show up external stress cracks before catastrophic failure occurs. Make sure that all parts are demagnetized after inspection. Any USAC or FAA certified inspection station can be trusted implicitly.

ZYGLOW

For non-ferrous metals the equivalent of magnaflux is Zyglow which substitutes a fluorescent dye for the iron particles. Most corporations which offer magnaflux also do Zyglow and again the cost is nominal. Zyglow equipment is also available with the portable magnaflux unit.

Your cost for having any non destructive testing done can be considerably reduced by stripping all paint, oil, grease, dirt and corrosion from the parts and delivering them to the inspection station in a really clean condition. I do not consider it necessary to remove rod ends from links for inspection.

DYE PENETRANT KITS

Relatively inexpensive aerosol kits of dye penetrant inspection materials good for both ferrous and non-ferrous materials are available at most welding supply houses and should be a part of every racer's road kit. Follow the instructions religiously or you will be wasting your time and building up a false sense of security. Parts to be inspected must be *really* clean.

A really thorough visual inspection of clean unpainted parts under strong light and with a good ten power magnifying glass costs nothing and will reveal a large number of the defects found by the more scientific methods. It will also show up stretched bolts.

The ideal inspection schedule (budget permitting) is X-ray inspection of all forged and cast parts when received, followed by visual and magnaflux or zyglow inspections every 500 to 1000 miles of running depending on the nature of the part. Very careful aerosol kit inspection can be substituted for Magnaflux and Zyglo. Critical parts are: hubs and hub carriers, hub carrier cleviess, rack and pinion, drive shafts, universal joints and their yokes, transmission input and output shafts, ring and pinion units, intermediate gears, engine valves, connecting rods, pistons, piston pins and crankshafts. If your schedule does not permit regular inspection of critical items, you should race less often.

Now comes the question of what to do after your careful inspection has discovered a crack. Don't panic—the red tag from the Magnaflux station does not necessarily mean that all is lost! First of all, all FAA certified stations will reject a part for *any* flaw. Porosity in a non-critical portion of an upright will produce the familiar red tag but is nothing to worry about. Small cracks can often be ground or filed out and carefully radiused. A cold lap on a portion of a weld can often be safely ignored or, at worst, re-welded. The problem, as always, lies in the decision making process. Until you have enough experience to have valid confidence in your own judgement, find someone to make the decision for you. Your Magnaflux/Zyglow station will always let you inspect a rejected part yourself so that you can see whether or not it can be saved. If the part is not salvageable, don't put it on the shelf. If you throw it away, you *know* that it will never end up on the car.

Suspension links fail in four modes: (1) A crack is detected before the piece breaks. (2) A tube bends or a sheet metal fabrication welded to a tube bends. (3) A weld, or the area immediately adjacent to a weld fails. (4) The crack is not detected in time and the tube or whatever breaks.

Repairs can usually be effected without scrapping the whole part. Follow the general guidelines given in chapters two and three. Give lots of consideration to the usually ignored question of why the part failed. In non crash associated failures it is unlikely that bolting on an identical new part is going to be much of a permanent fix.

Bending of a tube, as in radius rod, is usually a compression failure and can almost always be rectified by going up 1/8" in tube diameter while retaining the same wall thickness.

Bending of a sheet metal attachment can be either a compression or tension failure or a lack of angularity allowance at the end of whatever is attached. Compressive or tension strength can be increased by making the attachment three dimensional or by increasing the thickness of the material. Angularity allowance is increased by whatever means is possible—higher angularity bearings, cone spacers, increased axial spacing, etc.

Weld failures are caused by improper weld design (welds in tension, usually) or improper welding (insufficient penetration, undercutting or failure to turn the corner at the end of a weld with fusion welding and improperly cleaned material, too much heat, too little heat or insufficient bead area with low temperature nickel bronze welding).

Whatever the failure mode, don't throw the whole part away. At worst, the threaded bosses at the ends can be saved. With wishbones, very often the point of the triangle, which is the most difficult bit to make, can often be saved and new tubes added on. It is amazing how much can be saved at the race track.

When rewelding, make very sure that all plating has been removed—especially chrome, which shouldn't be used anyway. Muriatic acid will remove cadmium plate. Nitric acid or files and emery cloth will remove chrome and nickel. Thinner, acetone, wire brushes and emery will remove paint. Always re-enforce any patch area by whatever combination of the methods described in Chapter Three seems applicable. With anything other than a straight tube use some sort of a holding fixture, however crude it may be, or the chances are very good that you won't be able to make the repaired part fit.

CHAPTER SEVEN

THE WHEELS AND THE TIRES

My original intention was to cover wheels and tires in a couple of paragraphs in one of the other chapters. This season's outbreak of broken wheels and flat tires has caused me to change my mind. Besides, writing a short chapter can't be that much trouble.

First the tires. The last time I can remember having a blow out on a race car was in 1955. I was running a gas station recap on an Austin Healy in a one hour endurance race (yes, one hour was considered an endurance race in the S.C.C.A. of that era). I deserved everything that happened to me. Every other "blow out" that I have been near since was caused either by running on a slowly deflating tire until it built up enough heat to fail (not too smart on the driver's part) or by wheel failure.

Slow leaks are caused by porous wheels, leaking wheel safety studs, loose or damaged valve cores, lack of valve core caps, improper mounting of the tire on the rim and by cuts and stone bruises which occur on the track, in the paddock and coming on and off the trailer. They are also caused by those damned fools who do not collect and properly dispose of their pop rivet nails and little scraps of sheet metal. What occurs on the race track comes under the heading of an act of God. What we do to our tires off the race track comes under the heading of human carelessness, laziness, ignorance or stupidity.

The present generation of wide, soft, thin and floppy tires are very susceptible to stone damage. Since many of our paddocks are full of very sharp stones (as are the verges of many of our race tracks), it is essential that all stones be removed from the tread of the tires before the car goes on the track. The easy way to do this is to drive the car into the pits on rain or tow tires and, at the end of the practice session, to take the race tires off and return to the paddock on rain or tow tires. When inspecting the tires for stones you will usually find bits of broken glass, snipped ends of safety wire and the like in some quantity. For this reason it is as well to use something other than your hand to clean the tire. Blood does not improve the coefficient of adhesion! An old hacksaw blade works fine.

It helps a lot if you can discipline your people to put all of their scraps into a trash can instead of onto the ground. Good Luck! Even if you succeed in convincing your crew that it is a good thing to do, very few other crews do it so the paddock area and the pit lane tend to be a sort of a torture trail. The only way to avoid picking up this junk is by not driving over it with the race tires. If the pit marshals don't like the idea, that is their problem. If they were really interested in and informed about safety, they would be on your side.

It also pays not to transport the car on race rubber.

Sidewalls are very thin and very delicate and do not like rubbing against ramps and such.

This advice is all very well and good but what do you do when you do eventually get a leak in an otherwise perfectly serviceable and very expensive racing tire. If you are a member of a big team in professional racing and your tires are free, you put on a new tire. If you were a member of a big team in professional racing you wouldn't be reading this book. If you are buying your tires, you locate the hole and, if it is a little one and not on the sidewall, you put a good hot patch on it and keep using the damned thing! The tire companies don't like the idea much, but it works just fine. The other solution, used by itself or with the hot patch is to pour a bottle of Androp Tire Sealant (Androp Inc., La Habra, Calif.) through the valve core hole and hope for the best. This glop is far and away the best of the tire sealants and really works—as long as the hole is small.

THE WHEELS

Steel wheels are, by definition, not porous. Cast magnesium wheels may or may not be, depending on the quality of the casting. If you roughen the inner surface of your wheel with emery cloth and then paint it with any epoxy paint (a very thin coat will suffice) your wheel will be reasonably sealed. Actually most of the present generation of racing mag wheels are a damn sight less porous than the present generation of racing tires. Most of our leaks now come from the safety studs which exist to keep a deflating tire from pulling off the rim. They also help to keep a fully inflated tire from pulling off the rim. The side forces presently being generated are quite terrifying as a close look at any photo of a Formula One or Formula 5000 car being cornered hard will show. Anyway, the studs and the plates which attach them to the rims tend to leak. The studs leak because the only method which will positively seal them is the use of Parker Seal Co.'s Stat-O-Seals which are not well known and are relatively expensive. They do, however, seal the studs and should be used. Most people tend to use plain "O" rings, which do not work because they get all distorted and torn, or some kind of gasket glop which doesn't work either. Use the Stat-O-Seals and inspect them every time a tire is dismounted.

The other reason that the safety studs leak is because whoever installed the stud holding plates did a lousy job. The most common method is to remove the nylon locking ring from a suitably sized nut plate, bore a hole in the rim and rivet the nut plate to the rim. This is fine if the nut plate has enough surface area to provide a positive seal between the nut plate and the rim and if a good epoxy is used to fully bond the nut plate to the rim. Unfortunately most nut plates do not have sufficient surface area and most people do not use good epoxy. Once again I use the 3M structural adhesive. I also make my own plates from mile steel with a full round flange and attach them with 4 rivets where there is room and 3 where there is not. It is a lot of work but the rims do not leak. If your tires are rotating on the rims, secure them to the vertical rim lips with at least 4 sheet metal screws per side.

Tire valve cores tend to loosen due to the very heavy centrifugal force exerted on them at racing speeds. They must be checked frequently. Valve caps are an absolute necessity.

Every time a tire is dismounted, remove your own safety studs. Take them all the way out, inspect the seal, and then replace them with a maximum of two threads engaged. If you do it yourself, and do it this way, there is no chance that a stud will be left extending into the drop when the tire is dismounted. If this should happen, the tire machine is guaranteed to ruin your wheel.

After the new tire is mounted, tighten your own studs (just snug is fine as the Stat-O-Seal acts as a locking device and should not be crushed absolutely flat) and then leak check the entire wheel. A spray bottle of Fantastik, 409 or the like does fine and prevents you from bothering the tire busters by borrowing their soap solution.

After the tire is balanced, tape your own weights. Tape will not stick to anything that is not absolutely clean and grease free so use steel wool and acetone before applying tape. Apply the tape in a cross pattern and make sure that it is stuck. Also make sure that the weights on the inboard face of the rim are going to clear the calipers, wishbones, etc. It helps to tell the man balancing the tires where the weights have to go.

It is to your advantage to cultivate the tire busters. These poor devils work very hard and somehow manage to remain cheerful—most of the time. They do not, however, enjoy redoing work because of your stupidity. They need to have your wheels marked with your car number; they need to have someone present to turn the safety studs when they are ready for them to be turned. They also need to know what size and compound you want mounted on what rim and whether it is to go on the left or right side of the car. If you help them, they will help you. It also doesn't hurt a thing to say thank you at the end of the weekend—or even to buy a drink.

Before delivering a rim for dismounting, remove the weights and clean the rim. This falls under the heading of common courtesy.

If your wheels are of the bolt together type, check the bolt torque weekly.

In Formula 5000 racing, the Melmag wheel is growing in popularity. I am willing to admit that it is a light and relatively economical wheel and that it is the only wheel with anything that resembles a reasonable delivery time. I am also willing to admit that adhesive bonding keeps airplanes together. I do not, however, consider the Melmag, in its present state of development to be a safe wheel. I use them—because I can't get anything else—but I worry a lot. The trouble, as I see it, is that bonding is very strong—in the shear plane only. If we could guarantee that loadings, especially impact loadings, would take place only in the shear plane, the wheels would probably last forever. But we cannot. The side forces generated by the tires place the bond interface in tension as does the impact everytime we drop a wheel off the road. Eventually the bond deteriorates. Usually we get lots of warning because the spray bottle of soap starts to show leaks in the hub area. Sometimes, when we ignore the warning, or when it doesn't show up, catastrophic failure results. This is always unpleasant. The best insurance is to bolt the wheel together through the hub area so that if failure does occur, the halves will not separate. The new Eagle does it the right way by using the drive pins, which live where God meant them to live—in the wheel, not in the hub flang—to mechanically hold the wheel components together.

Anyway, forewarned is forearmed. If you must use Melmags, do a lot of checking.

Repair of damaged wheels is a very dodgy business. Some rims, notably Lola's, come as a multi-piece assembly. This is a good deal as repair can be effected by replacing the damaged bit only, thus saving a large chunk of cash. Crash damage is usually readily apparent to the naked eye and usually not repairable. The broken wheels make good lamp bases, coffee table bases and bar stool bottoms. They are not good for much else. Fatigue cracks show up in the bead rim area and where the spokes join the hub. Magnesium rims can be welded, but only by a genius. Small distortions can also be straightened—by the same genius. Don't try to do either yourself—unless, of course, you happen to be a genius.

CHAPTER EIGHT

THE CARE AND FEEDING OF THE RACING ENGINE

All too obviously the racing engine, Formula Ford or Formula One, is a very highly stressed piece of machinery. As such it is subject to rapid wear, fatigue, gross abuse and sudden expensive failure. This is particularly true of stock blocks— at least the designer of the pure racing engine knew what we were going to do to his brainchild. In this chapter we will attempt to help the reader prolong the useful life of his propulsion unit and, possibly, to point the way to increased performance—through the thoughtful use of his equipment rather than by demon tweaking. The building and tuning of competition engines has been written about by those more expert than I and no attempt will be made to cover these areas.

Enginewise, racers are divided into only two classes—those who buy their engines and those who build them. Those who buy are subdivided into those who send the engine back to its birthplace for rebuild and those who do it themselves. Which group you fall into is a matter of personal preference, ability, equipment available and budget. For our purposes it really doesn't matter as maintenance procedures are identical in all cases.

CHOOSING AND USING THE ENGINE BUILDER

In each class of racing it is pretty obvious which engine builders and component builders are producing winning pieces. It makes no sense at all to save money by purchasing an engine, or the bits to build one, from a builder or supplier whose products have not been proven competitive.

To my knowledge, all of the reputable firms are more than helpful (to their customers) with information, advice and rebuild services. They are, however, usually not very good at time scheduling. It is wise to check with the people who are using the engines that you intend to buy regarding the builder's performance in getting the piece back to you after you have worn it out.

When you buy an engine make sure that you get a dynamometer sheet with it and take the time to graph both corrected horsepower and corrected torque. It is just not possible to intelligently gear a race car without this information. Don't pay a lot of attention to claimed horsepower for two reasons. The validity of some horsepower figures is subject to some doubt and peak horsepower, even if it is accurate, is largely of academic value. "Horsepower sells engines and torque wins motor races.", the man told me twenty years ago and nothing has proved him wrong yet! The area under the power curve in the operating rpm range is a lot more important than peak horsepower and always

will be.

You should also obtain from the engine builder the following information:

(1) Static ignition timing and the rpm at which the ignition is fully advanced.
(2) Fully advanced ignition timing.
(3) Recommended spark plugs—for warm up, for racing and, just maybe, for helping an oiling cylinder. You also need to know what gap they should be set at.
(4) Distributor dwell or point gap.
(5) Cam timing, valve lift and both hot and cold valve lash.
(6) Piston, piston ring, main and rod bearing clearances as well as part numbers for these items.
(7) Engine fastener torque and torqueing sequenced.
(8) Valve spring height and tension (at both nose and heel of cam).
(9) Recommended oil, oil filter, oil system layout and line size.
(10) Anything else that the builder feels you ought to know.

CARE AND FEEDING OF THE ENGINE BUILDER

Having obtained all of this information from your engine builder, it is now time to give some thought about what he needs to know from you. The first thing that he needs to know is that you are going to pay your bill—on time! The number of racers who don't is amazing and is very good reason why many builders require cash in hand before the rebuilt engine goes out the door—which is not always convenient. The second thing that he would like to know is that you are not going to bad mouth him for your lack of success—or for your maltreatment of the engine. If you feel that you have a legitimate gripe with your engine builder discuss it with him frankly and in private. The third thing that he needs is information. When you send an engine back send a note with it telling him how many hours the unit has on it, what its operating temperatures and pressures have been, any vicious over revs and any meaningful comments you may have on its performance—or lack of it. If it is possible to ship the racing ignition and inlet system with the engine (exhaust is too much to ask), you will be rewarded with better performance. Always insist that the engine be dynoed. Until the thing comes off the dyno stand, the builder is responsible for his errors. It is a damn sight better to have one come unglued on the dyno than on the track—and not just for financial reasons. Any assembly errors have about a 99% chance of becoming glaringly obvious on the dyno and being rectified at the builder's expense. Leaks have no better than a 50/50 shot of being noticed on the dyno as every builder has spent years developing a blind eye in this department.

THE FLYWHEEL

Except for the big V-8s, the builder will normally provide a flywheel balanced to the engine. If the flywheel is not counterweighted, ask for it to be zero balanced and do the same to your clutches so that all units will be interchangeable from engine to engine. Virtually all of the V-8s used in road racing use the multi-plate Borg and Beck clutch. This gives you two choices in the flywheel department—buy it at great cost from the car supplier or make the thing. Making a flywheel (or having it made, if you don't have access to a good lathe) is no big thing. Finding a standard starter ring gear of suitable diameter and pitch is. Most of the V-8 engined cars use the brutally expensive Lola compound drive starter motor, which, naturally enough, meshes with the Lola ring gear. I am convinced that this ring gear is a standard English something or other, but have never been able to find out what. Sometimes Carl Haas is able to supply the ring gear all by itself and sometimes he is not. Since perfect mesh between ring gear and starter pinion is not an absolute necessity, I have successfully used ring gears obtained from such diverse sources as Saab, racing Cortina and Fiat. I have also been known to cut and weld ring gears to reduce the diameter. It all works.

Flywheels can be made from Aluminum alloys 6061-T6, 2024-T3, 7075-T6 or from Lo Carbon steel. The aluminum tends to be a bit more expensive, requires some sort of steel friction facing and is no lighter than a steel wheel when the steel is drilled full of thoughtfully located holes. I use either, depending on what is available. Remember that the trick in flywheel design is not only light overall weight but also a low moment of inertia. This means that weight must be kept away from the O.D. of the wheel.

It is essential to make sure that the mounting hole pattern precisely matches the crankshaft and that the mounting flange surface is absolutely parallel with the friction surface. The ring gear must be shrunk on and should then be positively located. I use 1/8" roll pins inserted axially with half the pin in the ring gear and half in the wheel. If you are a little bit clever in the design of the engine facing side of the flywheel you will be able to prevent rotation of the heads of the clutch bolts by means of annular locating shoulder.

THE STARTER

The whole starter problem on V-8s with shallow dry sumps tends to be vexatious—if only from the cost standpoint. My next move in this direction is going to be the compound Chrysler starter motor (light, powerful, cheap and available) mounted in a saddle bracket at the right front of the engine and operating a bendix and pinion in the normal position by means of a jointed drive shaft. I am convinced that this can be done very reasonably and will weigh less than any of the alternatives. It will also reduce the vehicle's longitudinal polar moment of inertia and get the whole mess out of the way of the exhaust system.

While on the subject of starters, most serious race cars use some sort of auxiliary starting battery to save the Varley. Even the SCCA club rules allow auxiliary starts except on the grid and during the race. Any kind of plug can be used— they are available from your welding supply house.

The trick is to locate the onboard plug somewhere so that minimal additional cable is necessary, the onboard battery can be charged through the starting plug, and so that the poor devil pulling out the plug is not going to get his eardrums ruptured by a blipping exhaust. Work out some idiot proof system with the driver so that it is not possible for him to depart with the starting battery plugged in. This is very embarrassing for all concerned and can even be painful. It is also a good idea to keep the starting battery fully charged. If it is down, it will drain the onboard battery to its level the instant that it is plugged in. The auxiliary power pack can be anything from another Varley with a carrying strap to a cart containing battery, fire extinguisher, spark plug tray and small tool box.

ENGINE INSTALLATION

When you receive your engine, first seal all ports, oil, water and fuel passages until it is installed. Next make some kind of stand for it to sit on and be transported on. Leaving an engine sitting on its oil pan is asking for it to be knocked over—or at least to crush the oil pan gasket. On the subject of oil pan gaskets, never use a cork gasket—they will crush, they will disintegrate and they will plug your oil screens with pieces of cork.

With the engine sitting on its stand, check to make sure that the Top Dead Center mark is accurate. If it isn't—and it very well may not be—any attempts on your part to set or check ignition timing, cam timing or valve lash won't be either. The engine builder probably did not use the mark now on the engine when he built it. It is worth the time and money to have the vibration dampener, crankshaft pulley, or flywheel accurately marked with at least TDC for each cylinder and with ignition timing marks for #1. A fully degreed unit allows cam timing to be checked in the car without mounting a degree wheel which is probably next to impossible. Why you would want to check cam timing in the car is beyond me.

The common rubber bonded torsional vibration dampener must be marked with a radius line on both the inner and outer rings so that you will have a visual reference to indicate bond failure before the outer ring flies off. Check it frequently— and especially after any over-revs. This type of failure is by no means uncommon and, if not detected before separation is achieved, the results are both spectacular and painful.

FLYWHEEL INSTALLATION

Before installing the flywheel, the clutch shaft pilot bearing must be installed in the crankshaft. For the Chevies I use Al Bartz's clever device which features an oilite bush in a steel housing containing internal threads so that the whole thing can be removed with a slide hammer. It can also be easily machined so that its length will match up with that of the gearbox input shaft. This dimension should be checked now so that you will not remove the crankshaft thrust bearings by having insufficient clearance. I use 1/8" clearance. The stock pilot bush, if it is still in place, can be removed with an internal puller. If you don't have one, pack the cavity behind the bush solid with grease, insert a tight fitting length of bar stock in the hole and pound on the bar with a heavy hammer. The pilot bush will eventually hydraulic out—as will the grease, making a lovely mess.

Make very sure that both the crankshaft flange and the mounting face of the flywheel are clean and free from burrs before mounting the flywheel. I have found no better bolts for the purpose than the stock Ford/Chevy flywheel bolts (they also make excellent Hewland ring gear bolts). Do not use tab washers to lock the flywheel bolts as they are soft iron and will beat out in service resulting in a loose flywheel. Instead use either red Loctite or safety wire. Torque the bolts 20 lb/ft at a time in a criss cross pattern

CLUTCH INSTALLATION

An old clutch shaft is the best way to align the clutch driven disc or discs—although a splined shaft is not necessary. Chevrolet units fit Borg and Beck clutches. Lacking a clutch shaft, turn a length of bar stock to the configuration of your clutch shaft so that the pilot is a snug fit in the pilot bearing and the major diameter is a close fit to the I.D. of the clutch disc spline. It will work just fine. Do not use the Auto Parts Store wooden cheapy tool or you will have hell stabbing the transmission onto the engine.

Make sure that the driven discs are installed the right way around and in the proper sequence. Borg and Beck multi plate clutch discs are scribed "flywheel side" at the factory and the sequence is: master driven disc, steel plate, driven disc, steel plate, etc. until the end is reached. The last piece is the heavy ridged steel plate which is installed with the annular ridge which serves as the fulcrum for the diaphragm toward the rear. This plate will have a red line painted on it which is meant to line up with the corresponding line on the diaphragm plate and the magnesium ring in order to achieve zero balance. Do not overtighten the mounting bolts (18 lb/ft is specified) and draw them up evenly. Make sure that the pilot shaft will slip in and out of the assembled clutch smoothly. If it won't, you didn't tighten the bolts evenly and you get to do it over. If your particular beast features nuts on the forward face of the flywheel, rotate the flywheel to make sure that the nuts or bolt ends clear the block.

Sintered Borg and Beck driven discs come with a new thickness of .104/.106". They can safely be run down to .090". Despite Borg and Beck's best intents and efforts the driven discs do not wear quite evenly and the useful life of the discs can be extended by swapping them around to even out the wear. After they have worn down to .090" the life can be even further extended by machining .020" from the back face of a spare magnesium clutch ring. The discs can then be used, with the machined ring, down to .083". It is, however, essential to positively identify the machined ring so that it cannot inadvertently be used with new discs. These clutches should last half a season in a Formula 5000 or Can Am car. If not, there is something terribly wrong—either you are not running sufficient free play or the driver is abusing the clutch. Drivers abuse clutches by slipping them, by keeping the clutch in while in gear at rest and by using the clutch pedal as a left foot rest. Many really fast drivers don't use them.

One last suggestion, clutch driven discs can be bought as a set very reasonably in England. This is not true in this country.

BELLHOUSING INSTALLATION

Make sure that the front and rear faces of your bellhousing are parallel. Next, mount the bellhousing to the block and, with a dial indicator, check that the input shaft bearing boss is central with the crankshaft. Due to Mr. Hewland's genius, this is not at all critical with his gearboxes (the clutch shaft is very small and floats in the constant motion shaft) but it is critical in most front engined cars. If the bellhousing is more than about .006" out of concentricity it should be fixed. Offset bellhousing to block locating dowels with a screwdriver slot for relatively easy adjustment will do the trick. If the mounting faces are not parallel to a few thousandths, either send it back or take a trueing cut on a mill.

GEARBOX INSTALLATION

Before installing the gearbox again carefully measure the clutch shaft to make very sure that it cannot bottom against the pilot bearing and remove the crankshaft thrust clearance. It is equally important that the pilot extend at least 1/4" into the bush or bearing. Adjusting either the bush or the shaft will cure most deficiencies, although if the shaft is too short, a new pilot bush may well be in order. At this time make sure that the throw out mechanism adjustment will give both sufficient free play and sufficient travel to fully release the clutch. Some spacing of components may be necessary. It is much easier to correct any such problems now with the engine and gearbox laying on the floor than it will be after they are in the car and the half shafts and suspension are installed.

ENGINE INSTALLATION

It is well worth the time involved to make a good engine installation system. Makeshift methods have been known to allow engines to fall—on the floor—on the chassis—or on someone. A portable cherrypicker falls into the "nice but not necessary" category. Rear engined cars usually require nothing more elaborate than a couple of 4"x4"s to hold the chassis level and off the ground and a floor jack with some sort of fixture which fits the oil pan and spreads the load over the pan rails. The engine can then be wheeled directly into position on the jack and raised or lowered to the correct height. This method has its shortcomings in the dirt and/or mud. In that case it is best to support the engine on the jack and roll the chassis into place.

With front engined cars and the older mid engined cars with full chassis, some type of lifting device will be necessary. Formula Fords and such require a couple of 2"x4"s, some rope and a couple of willing friends or spectators. V-8s require a come along, an engine sling and some sort of skyhook to attach the come along to (come alongs are cheaper and lighter than chainfalls). Ingenious people with time and forethought construct tubular take-down tripods and such. The rest of us count on finding a strong ceiling beam, convenient tree limb or a friend with a cherry picker.

The actual installation of the engine is, or should be, a straightforward mechanical exercise. Care must be taken to avoid breaking distributor caps, alternators and the like against the chassis and to avoid pinching fluid and electrical lines between the engine and the chassis. Throttle cables are particularly vulnerable in this respect—as are hands and fingers. If the engine mounts don't line up, find out why and fix it. Forcing the issue, particularly with solid mounts, is inviting trouble.

Every fastener in the engine and engine auxiliary system that does not incorporate a self locking nut should be safety wired or properly loc-tited. Do not trust lock washers. The vibrations involved are of very high and varying frequency and have been known to cause the most carefully torqued bolts to back off.

THE EXHAUST SYSTEM

If you use exhaust header gaskets, do not safety wire the header bolts until the engine has been warmed up and the bolts tightened with the heads hot. I prefer not to use header gaskets as they are forever blowing out which causes a large exhaust leak to the detriment of exhaust valves and rocker cover gaskets. I have had much better results by trueing the surface of the header flanges against a large disc grinder, coating them with coppercoat or silicon seal and bolting them directly onto the heads. An even better method, popular with the drag racers, is to machine a small groove in either the head or the header flange and then to seal the port with soft copper wire in the groove. If you must use gaskets, avoid the cardboard ones and use the kind that has a wire core. Gasket life can be extended almost indefinitely by the use of silicon seal on both sides of the gasket.

While we are on the subject, do not bolt the exhaust collectors tightly to the primary pipes. This is one of the areas where things must be allowed to rattle around a bit to prevent vibration cracking, Castle nuts and drilled shank bolts with cowling clips instead of cotter pins are the hot ticket. Leave the bolts at least 1/32" loose. If your car uses the popular 4 into 1 system, installation of the collector will be considerably eased by staggering the primary lengths 1/8" or so at the collector end so that the collector can be slipped over one primary tube at a time. Leave the exhaust flange bolts loose until the collector is on. The collector itself should be attached to the chassis by springs over a saddle bracket to avoid vibration failure.

Making an exhaust system is a pain. Every so often each of us gets to do it. The experts do it by sand bending the tubing in one piece. The rest of us buy U bends of various radii from our friendly header maker and start cutting and welding. .049" tubing is plenty thick enough, Stainless and titanium are for those with both moderate wealth and lots of expertise or with lots of wealth. Before you start to cut and weld, figure out where each pipe is going to go and how it is going to get there while remaining the same length as the others without running into something. The only way that I know of to do this is to have the car complete less springs (so that you can swing the suspension), plug the ports with modeling clay and start bending welding rod into your dream shapes until it all comes out. A lot better than welding rod is the tube benders' trick of twisted soft aluminum wire. Buy a bunch of 3/16" 1100 aluminum welding rod. Clamp one end in a vise and chuck the other end into a 3/8" drill motor. Pull the trigger and you have instantly created a twisted length of aluminum wire which can be bent readily into any shape you desire and which, unlike welding rod, will retain that shape.

Make very sure that your collectors clear the drive shafts at both full bump and full droop. Local reliefs may be necessary and won't hurt the power. It is also necessary that the collectors clear the lower wishbones or parallel links at full bump.

When installing an engine in a car designed around another engine, a certain amount of forethought and planning is necessary to avoid vast amounts of grief. Wholesale removal or modification of chassis tubes or stressed skin panels and/or relocation of engine mounts may well result in serious weakening of the chassis. This is one of those areas where the inexperienced had better seek competent advice.

PLUMBING

Engine plumbing was generally covered in Chapter One. However, a few specific words are in order at this time. In all probability you will have two pressure lines running from the engine to the instrument panel—fuel pressure and oil pressure. The oil pressure fitting on the engine should be somewhere in the main oil gallery before the oil goes to the bearings. I often locate it on the "Pressure Out" fitting on the dry sump pump for convenience. Wherever you decide to put it, make it easy to get at. The fuel pressure fitting should be located just before the injection metering unit or carburetors. Since fuel injection pressures seem to be higher than the safe limits of either Stewart Warner or Smith's gauges and since a ruptured fuel pressure gauge diaphragm is a nasty business indeed, I put a driver operable shut off valve on all of my fuel pressure lines. You may laugh, but I've had four or five gauge failures over the past ten years.

THE FUEL SYSTEM

Most racing cars now use some sort of "surge tank" fuel pick up system. Fuel is forced from the rear of the fuel cell or cells under acceleration through one or more one way valves into a two to four quart "make up tank" from which it is picked up by the feed pump. The make up tank usually incorporates a filter and also receives the bypassed fuel (only if it has been cooled—uncooled bypassed fuel goes directly back into a fuel cell) from the fuel injection metering unit. There must be a return from the top of the make up can back to one of the fuel cells in order to vent the tank. The tank is fed by inertial surge thus ensuring, supposing that the fuel cell outlets are properly located at the very bottom of the fuel cells and at the rear inboard or outboard corners (or the very front corners if you want to pick up under braking rather than acceleration), that all of the fuel on board can indeed be picked up. Fuel that cannot be picked up is a particularly inefficient form of ballast. Since the make up tank is protected from emptying back to the fuel cells by one way valves and is vented from its top to a fuel cell, it should always be full thus providing a solid head of fuel to the feed pump and providing insurance against momentary fuel starvation during those periods when the fuel cell outlets may be uncovered during cornering, braking or acceleration with a low fuel state.

The make up tank should be as tall as practicable and should incorporate a good large area filter which can be easily removed with the tank in place. The tank should be provided with large draughts of cooling air in order to prevent the dreaded vapour lock. In fact the fuel pumps, both electrical and mechanical, should be located in places where they are not subjected to high temperatures and they should be supplied with cool air. All of this is normally easier said than done, particularly as we normally mount our Lucas mechanical pumps down low at the front of the engine and belt drive them from the nose of the crank. This is necessary in order to provide a positive head of fuel to the pump. I particularly admire the REPCO system in which the Lucas Metering Unit is driven by a skew gear on the distributor shaft and the mechanical pump is driven by the same gear on the other side of the distributor. This system does, however, require a low pressure auxiliary pump.

Anyway, in the matter of mechanical fuel pump location, we are pretty much stuck with what we have and the problem becomes one of cooling. The best method I have found is a NACA duct (or ducts) strategically located in the bottom of the tub. The outlets of these ducts must be provided with pretty fine mesh screens. Otherwise, sooner or later, you will trap a small stone between a Gilmer Belt and its gear resulting in an instantly broken belt. Properly located these ducts will provide a lot of air which, while not very cold, is a damn sight cooler than the ambient air inside the engine compartment. This is also a good way of circulating air inside the cockpit.

CURING VAPOUR LOCK

None of the above will do anything to prevent vapour lock when your racer arrives at the pits hot, has the engine shut off and proceeds to heat soak everything in sight, including the fuel pumps. One way to help is to locate the electric high pressure pump outside the engine area. This type of vapour lock, which is particularly prevalent on the grid (Murphy's Law strikes again) is evidenced by lack of fuel pressure when you try to start the engine and is cured by dousing the fuel pumps with cold water or a good blast from a CO_2 fire extinguisher. In order to effect this cure it is necessary to have sufficient amounts of the cooling fluid with you plus some convenient passage allowing you to apply the fluid directly to the afflicted area. Neither method will make you overly popular with grid or pit stewards, but either will get the car running. Once the car is moving and fuel is circulating everything will be all right.

Figures (76) and (77) schematically show fuel system layouts for injected and carbureted engines respectively.

THE OIL SYSTEM — THEORY

Oil lubricates and oil cools. Most racing engines (all serious ones) use a dry sump lubrication system. The advantages of a good dry sump system over a good wet sump system are two fold—a much lower engine installation can be achieved and, due to the hope that the oil will not be whipped around by the crankshaft, better oil control is achieved resulting in improved lubrication and cooling.

The dry sump oil system, schematically shown in Figure (78), consists of a remote reservoir or tank, a pressure pump which picks up stored oil from the tank and supplies it under proper pressure to the engine and a scavenge pump or pumps which collect the oil from the engine crankcase and return it to the reservoir. The scavenge pump capacity must be at least twice that of the pressure pump. Three times is better. Somewhere in the system will be one or more heat exchangers to cool the oil and a filter or filters to clean it. Since, at least theoretically, there is little or no oil left standing around in the crankcase looking for trouble, the oil cannot be whipped by the crankshaft. As the oil pan is merely a collection point, not a storage area, its depth need only be sufficient to clear the path of travel of the connecting rods (rod locus) which allows the engine to be installed lower in the car—assuming that axle center height and drive shaft angularity permit. This will lower the vehicle's center of gravity and reduce the vehicle's roll moment, both of which are good things to do. Additionally, since the reservoir also serves as a de-aeration device, the efficiency of engine lubrication will be improved as the pressure pump will be picking up solid de-aerated oil (a combination of oil and air is neither as good a lubricant nor as good a heat transfer medium as oil by itself). Finally, the engine's power output should be increased throughout the range by the fact that the crankshaft assembly is now rotating in air rather than in an oil bath. When the crank starts to pump oil around in the crankcase the drop in power is as startling as is the increase in oil temperature.

THE OIL SYSTEM — PRACTICAL — PUMPS AND DRIVES

It is much easier to talk about a good dry sump system than it is to build one. Fortunately most of the hard and expensive work has been done for us (and done very well) by Joe and Jerry Weaver of Weaver Brothers and by Tommy Davis of Aviaid. Both of these companies manufacture and sell excellent combined pressure and scavenge pumps of modular design (which means that you can have as many scavenge stages as you want—I use either three or four). They also market gear belt drives with about any drive ratio and center distance you can think up. Aviaid will also fabricate pans to your specification or theirs and has a really neat in-line screen filter which should be installed in every scavenge oil line to protect the pump from trash and debris. Pumps should be driven as slowly as you can get away with.

THE RESERVOIR

Reservoir design is pretty simple, now that we have figured out that, in order to avoid uncovering the pick up and to promote deaeration, the thing wants to be as tall and skinny as we can make it. The most popular design used to be a tall cylinder as shown in Figure (79). The scavenge oil line enters tangentally at the top and scavenge oil is swirled onto the vertical tank wall to promote deaeration (the thing is basically a centrifuge). Two baffles are generally incorporated—a downward facing conical plate with the center cut out and a series of flanged holes in its surface is located one to two inches above the running oil level to help deaeration and to keep the oil from riding up the side of the tank under accelerative forces. A similar baffle without the flanged holes is located a couple of inches above the pick up.

114

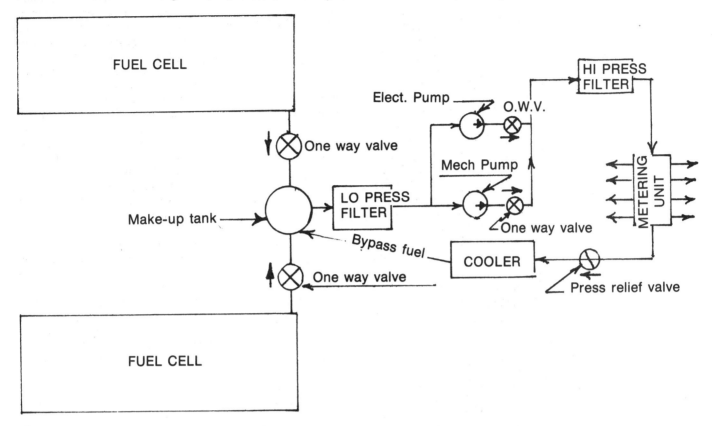

Figure (76): Fuel Feed System Schematic—Fuel Injection

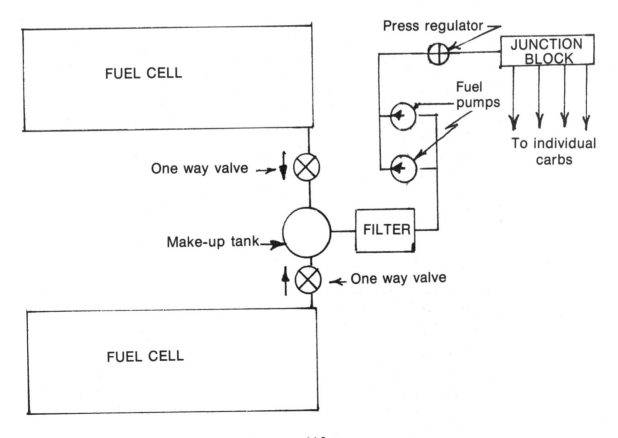

Figure (77): Fuel Feed System Schematic—Carburetors

115

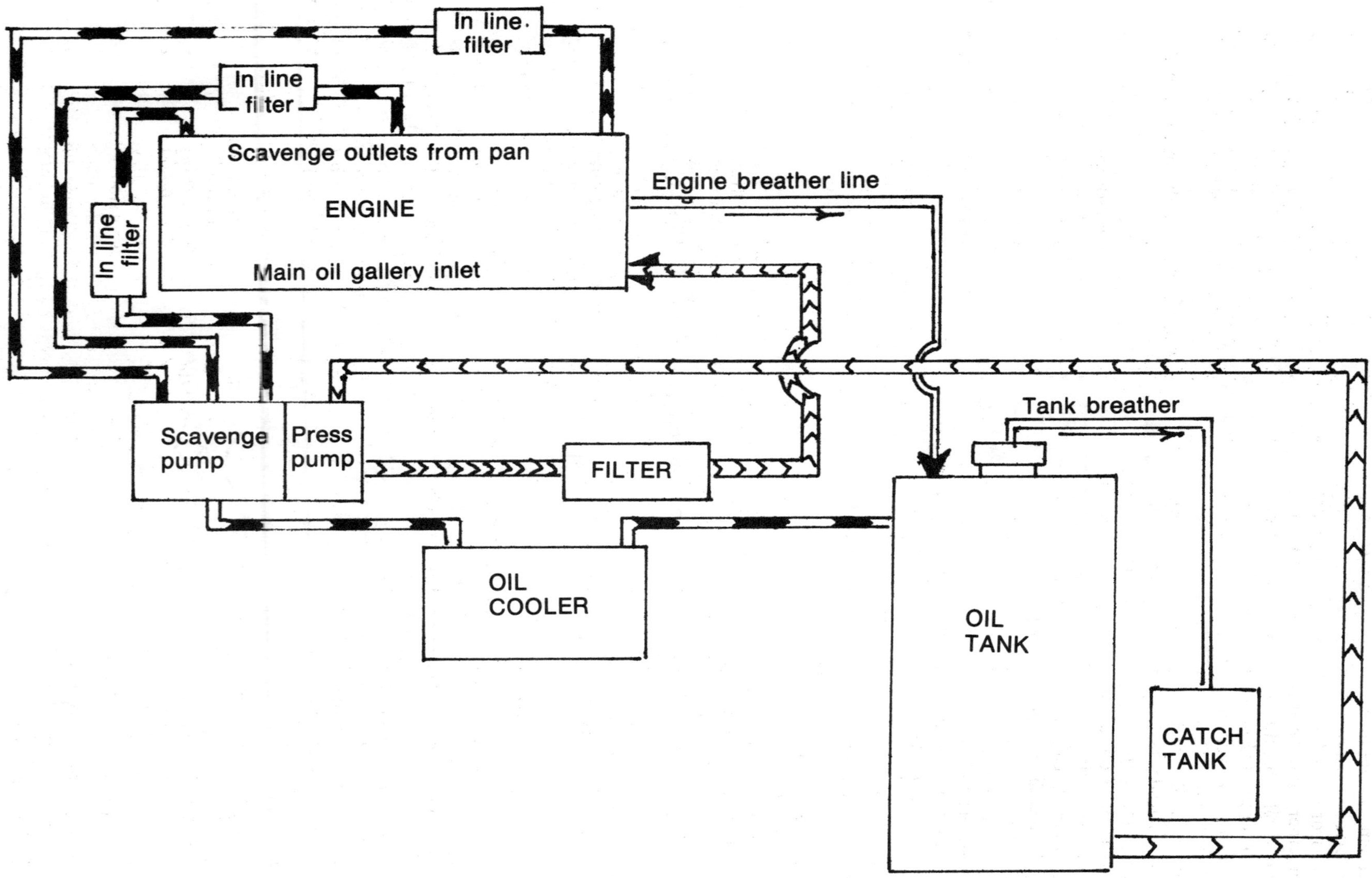

Figure (78): Oil System Schematic

CATCH TANK

OIL TANK

Tank breather

Engine breather line

FILTER

OIL COOLER

In line filter

In line filter

Scavenge outlets from pan

ENGINE

Main oil gallery inlet

In line filter

Press pump

Scavenge pump

The lower baffle exists to prevent the pick up from being uncovered. The oil temperature probe is usually located in the bottom of the reservoir and a removable plate of fairly large area should be incorporated in the bottom to facilitate cleaning. The breather from the engine enters the top of the tank and the tank itself is breathed to the catch can through a baffled device incorporated in the filler cap. It is an excellent idea to attach a 110 volt heating pad to the reservoir in order to preheat the oil. These cylindrical reservoirs are usually mounted on saddle brackets in the bellhousing area. They used to live alongside the transaxle. At about the time that we discovered that minimal longitudinal polar moment of inertia was desirable from a vehicle dynamics point of view and that the reservoir, when full of oil, represented about 40 pounds of weight cantilevered behind the rear axle, the Sanctioning Bodies discovered that the reservoirs were very vulnerable in case of accident and that this vulnerability resulted in large amounts of oil being spilled on race tracks and the occasional oil fire. The result of these simultaneous discoveries was that the Sanctioning Bodies barred the mounting of oil tanks outside the wheelbase at the same time that we all moved them behind the driver's seat for selfish reasons of our own. The basic design of an efficient reservoir has remained the same but the shape has changed from a simple cylinder to whatever is necessary to cram it in behind the seat along with the fuel surge tank, mechanical fuel pump, front drive package and most of the rest of the world. About the only serious disadvantage, other than difficulty of design and fabrication, is that we now have one more built in driver heater. This has not turned out to be the problem we feared so long as some air space is provided between the reservoir and the firewall and some insulation is provided. This location does, however, render inspection of the various cog belt drives more difficult than it was and results in an even more tortuous line of sight to the ignition timing marks.

THE OIL PAN

The design problem with the dry sump system lies almost wholly with the oil pan. The dry sump oil pan has only one function in life—to collect the oil from the cylinder heads, cylinders and crankshaft assembly in an area or areas where it will be picked up by the scavenge pumps before it has a chance to be whipped by the crankshaft. In order to be worth having, the dry sump pan must perform this function efficiently and be significantly less deep than a wet sump pan which will work equally well. This has proven difficult to achieve.

Present theory seems to run to the four basic designs illustrated in Figure (80):

(1) The rectangular box with scavenge pick ups in the two downwind corners (or in all four corners). This one is pretty primitive, has to be deep to work and requires a separate windage tray whose optimum shape and location takes a lot of experimentation to get right. Not recommended at all.

(2) The rectangular box with a pick up and collection trough at each side and pick ups in each corner. This is a big improvement as the collection troughs and scrapers control the oil much better than the plain box. It requires very little development and can be made about 3/4" deeper than the rod locus.

(3) The shaped pan whose sides follow the rod locus closely with a central collection trough and pick ups at each end (and at the

center if desired). This design can be made to work very well indeed. It is a favorite of the English but takes a lot of playing with to get right.

(4) My favorite—originally developed by either Brabham or REPCO. The upwind side of the pan follows the rod locus closely giving the oil nowhere to go but into the downwind collection box where the scavenge outlets are located. A couple of scrapers help out. This is the shallowest design of all, requiring only about .080" clearance from the rod locus. It is relatively easy to fabricate and, to my astonishment and pleasure, has required no development time at all.

Common features of all successful pans, regardless of design include:

(1) Use no spot welds. Everdur rod with a heliarc works best. (2) The pick up itself must be kept as close to the floor of the pan as possible so that the scavenge pumps will pick up oil, not air. The best method is a closed end tube with a slot in the bottom. It is important not to close the pick ups by jacking on the pan.

(3) Protect the pump by incorporating in-line screens in each scavenge line Figure (81). This is a better system than placing a screen directly over the pick up as it has more area and the pan does not have to be dropped to check or clean the screens.

(4) Use a pick up at the front for braking and one at the rear for acceleration. This is a minimum requirement.

(5) Do not use a cork pan gasket. It will crush or disintegrate.

(6) Don't try to force the oil to collect where you want it to—it will not. Instead figure out where the natural windage forces are going to send the oil and collect it there. It will always flow down hill and downwind.

EVALUATION

It is difficult to evaluate a dry sump system. Dynamometer comparisons cannot even approximate the lateral and longitudinal accelerations that occur on the track. A system that works well on the dyno may not work on the track. What is worse, you may not even realize that it isn't working. The driver is not likely to notice the loss of several horsepower coming out of a corner when the oil has piled up on the wall of the pan and been caught by the crank. So long as there is oil in the tank and the pressure pick up has not been uncovered, the pressure gauge will not dip. It is also true that under the conditions which lead to loss of oil control in the crankcase, the driver is too busy saving his life to look at gauges. If the system is really bad the oil temperature will be high and the engine will bail oil out the breather. Draining the oil after shutting the engine down immediately after exiting a corner is perhaps the best indication. There should be no more than a pint of oil in the pan (drain as quickly as possible because the hot oil will drain back through the pump and provide a false reading).

COOLING THE OIL

Opinion seems to be about equally divided between running scavenge oil through the coolers and running pressure oil through. From the plumbing convenience and pressure loss points of view it is preferable to cool scavenge oil. The rub is that scavenge oil, by its very nature, contains a fair amount of air in suspension which seriously reduces the thermal efficiency of the cooler. Mounting an aircraft screen filter in the scavenge line immediately before the cooler will break the big bubbles into tiny bubbles and will often result in a significant decrease in oil temperature. If you mount it where you can get at it easily without making a mess it will also allow you to very quickly check the state of

Figure (79): Typical Dry Sump Oil Tank

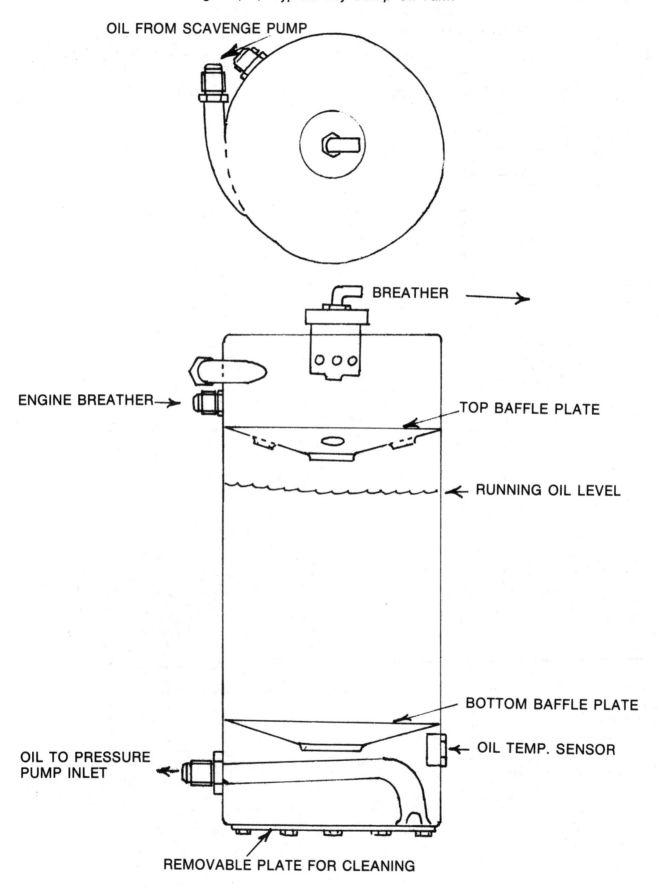

OIL FROM SCAVENGE PUMP

BREATHER →

ENGINE BREATHER →

TOP BAFFLE PLATE

RUNNING OIL LEVEL

BOTTOM BAFFLE PLATE

OIL TEMP. SENSOR

OIL TO PRESSURE
PUMP INLET

REMOVABLE PLATE FOR CLEANING

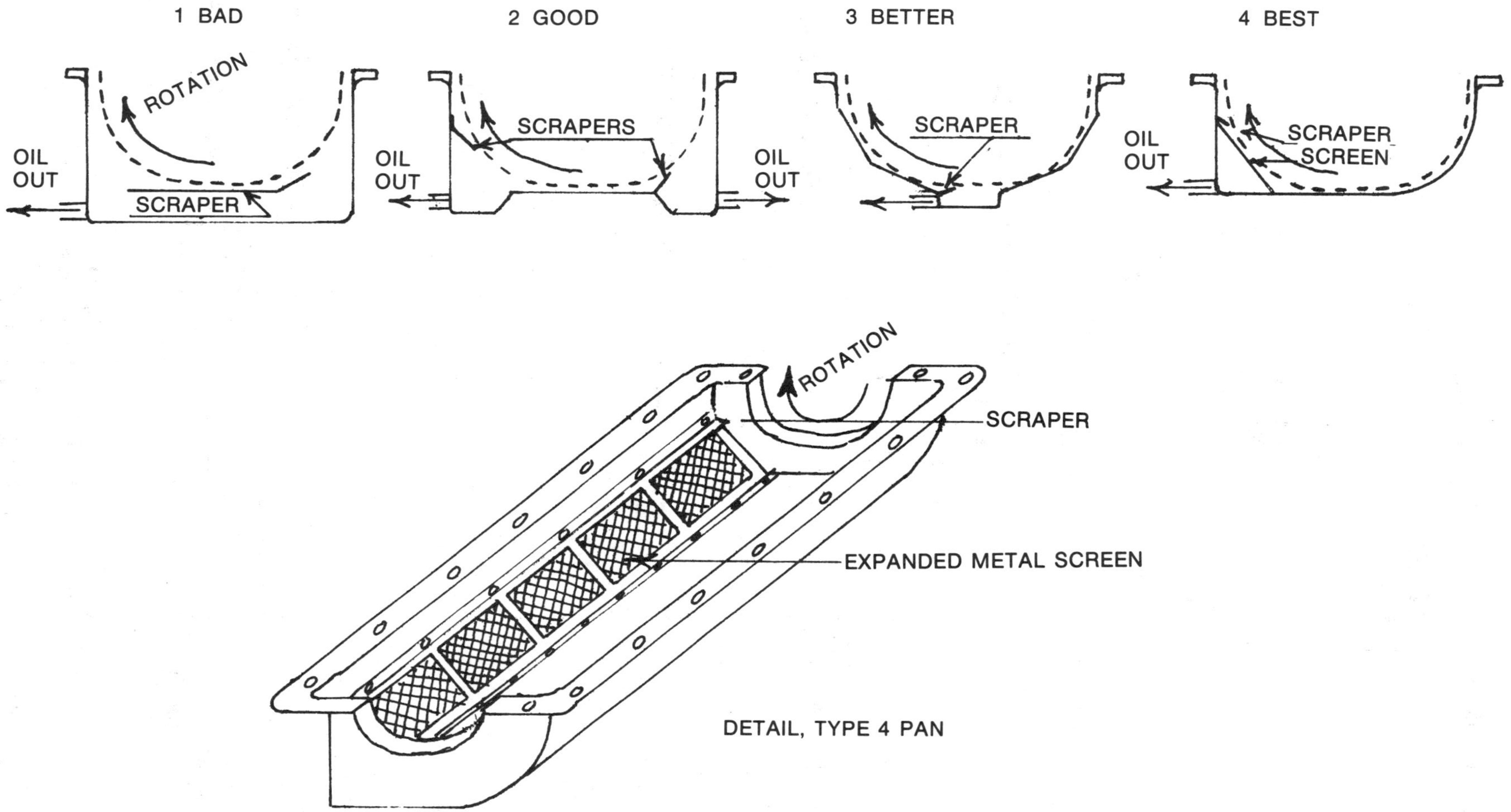

1 BAD

ROTATION

SCRAPER

OIL
OUT

2 GOOD

OIL
OUT

SCRAPERS

OIL
OUT

3 BETTER

SCRAPER

4 BEST

SCRAPER
SCREEN

OIL
OUT

ROTATION

SCRAPER

EXPANDED METAL SCREEN

DETAIL, TYPE 4 PAN

Figure (80): Types of Dry Sump Oil Pans

119

1. PROTECTS OIL PUMP, COOLER & TANK FROM ENGINE TRASH
2. PARTIALLY DE-AERATES SCAVENGE OIL

"O" RING SEAL

FLOW

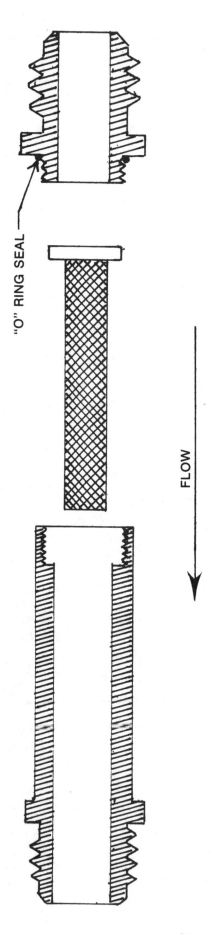

Figure (81): In-Line Finger Screen. Filter For Oil Scavenge Lines

the interior of the engine by inspecting the screen.

By and by large, however, I still prefer to cool pressure oil between the pressure pump outlet and entry into the engine. I do, however, still protect the coolers with the aircraft screen filter.

Oil coolers are not radiators; they are oil to air heat exchangers. In order to function they must be supplied with large amounts of the coolest air possible. This means ducting and it means that oil coolers should not be mounted in the exit ducts from the water radiators—no matter how convenient it may be. One last word—in cases where the designer fell off his drafting stool and has provided a totally inadequate water cooling system, it may be possible to drag the water temperature down by super cooling with oil. The most efficient oil coolers are made by Stewart Warner and are very expensive. The next best are the ubiquitous Coventry Pressings units supplied on all English race cars. Surplus coolers usually don't work well as they are designed for either aircraft or stationary installations.

THE OIL FILTER

Before leaving the oil system, mention should be made of the oil filter. Racing oil filters of the screw on type are better than stock ones, but they are not good. They bypass too much oil. The ones to use are the filters made by Fram and Purolator for the Indy cars. They are bulky, heavy, expensive and they filter the oil. The elements are usually available at Earls. By cutting apart the filter and reading its entrails you get a very good check on bearing condition.

ENGINE STARTING PROCEDURE

I am convinced that many racing engine failures are caused by poor installation and/or starting procedures. When installing the engine all lines, passages and fittings, both on the engine and on the auxiliaries must be protected by caps and plugs.

Fill the lubrication system (including a couple of quarts in the pan to avoid running the scavenge pumps dry). Remove the spark plugs and crank the engine over until you have lots of oil pressure on the gauge (some installations allow this to be done conveniently by turning the oil pump). Check the oil lines for leaks. Fill the water system, bleed the radiators and top water and leave the pressure cap off so that you can visually check the level while warming the engine up. Check the static ignition timing. Remove the fuel line from the metering unit or distribution block; turn on the electric pump and run a quart or so of gas into a can to clean and purge the fuel line. Disconnect the high pressure lines from the Lucas injectors, lead each into a can, open the shuttle all the way, turn on the high pressure pump and crank the engine over until all of the injector lines are bled (do this with the ignition off). Reconnect everything, gap the spark plugs, making sure that they are the right heat range (builders often ship engines with any old plugs just to fill the holes). Check the valve lash cold and make sure that the high tension leads are connected to the right spark plugs. Check the fuel injection timing, idle and full throttle stops and basic throttle synchronization. Make sure that the throttle return springs are connected. Turn on the fuel pumps and check for leaks. Before firing the engine, have

someone standing by with a large CO_2 fire extinguisher. This doubtless seems like a lot of wasted energy just to fire off a new engine—it isn't!

Fire the engine with minimum possible throttle and keep it running as slowly as possible while someone checks all lines and joints for leaks. Add water as necessary as the system bleeds itself and observe the water in the header tank looking for oil and telltale bubbles. Keep an eye on the oil pressure and water temperature gauges. After a couple of minutes running—or 160 degrees water temperature—shut it off, tighten the header tank cap and let it heat soak for five or ten minutes.

Thoroughly warm the engine up, check the ignition timing at full advance. Hot lash the valves and, if necessary, hot torque the cylinder heads. Synchronize the throttles (the uni-syn is as good a device as any) and adjust the idle speed. Install race plugs and you are ready to run the car.

Remember that although you have thawed out the engine, the oil is not hot enough for full throttle and the gearbox and final drive are stone cold—as are the brakes and tires. So do a few slow laps to get everything happy before you stand on it.

The surest giveaway of sheer bloody ignorance in motor racing is the soul who lights off his cold engine and instantly jazzes the throttle and keeps doing so. No surer way has been invented to spin a bearing, wipe the nose of a cam lobe or score a valve lifter. Cold engines should be run a minimum smooth running speed with as consitent a throttle opening as will keep the thing running. Revving the engine before shutting it off is of dubious value, but it sounds nice. The habit is hard to break and, in moderation, it doesn't hurt anything. In cold weather (below 60°F.) warm the Lucas metering unit before turning the engine over.

TRACK TUNING

Assuming that all of the prior steps have been done correctly, race tuning should consist of changing carburation/injection settings to compensate for changes in atmospheric conditions. Spark plug condition is still the best indication of full load mixture strength and I strongly advise long conversations with Champion's racing representatives. A pocket flashlight cum magnifying glass for about $4.00 is an invaluable aid to reading plugs. Remember that slightly too rich a mixture, slightly too little timing and slightly too cold a plug are vastly preferable to the other extreme.

Basic mixture strength is controlled by the main and air correction jets in a carb and by a mixture control adjustment that varies the starting position of the fuel control cam and must injection systems. Throttle response is controlled by the idle circuit, compensation circuit, emulsion tubes, float level, accelerator pump stroke and jets in carburetors and by the profile of the fuel control cam and the length of the idle rod in injection. Write down every change you make and its effect or you will become hopelessly muddled. Remember that unless the throttles are perfectly synchronized throughout their travel you will not achieve really good throttle response. Without instantaneous and consistent throttle response you are unlikely to go really fast. If this response is not forthcoming through your own efforts, consult (hire) an expert.

Do not flog around endlessly through a practice session with a misfiring or rough running engine. Come in and fix it. If you can't fix it—park it. All you are going to achieve on the track is a graphic advertisement of your ignorance and the annoyance of everyone who can hear you or who has to pass your moving chicane.

Moisture causes corrosion. Corrosion is one of the major causes of engine wear. After the race remove the plugs, crank the engine and spray a little WD 40 into each cylinder. By removing the plugs and cranking for awhile when next you want to fire it, you will remove the residual oil. Seal the intakes and exhaust and put it on the trailer.

CHECKING

A visual check of rod and main bearing condition at infrequent intervals will go a long way toward preventing bottom end failure. The best indication of the condition of rings, ring lands, valve seats and valves—short of a tear down—is a cylinder leak down test done when the engine is warm. Sun makes a very good cylinder leak rater (not to be confused with a compression gauge which is useless).

Your engine builder will give you a good idea of the expected life of self destructing components such as timing chains, pistons, distributor drive gears, valve lifters, valve springs, rod bolts, rods and the like. Check and replace these items on a schedule—it is cheaper and more convenient than ventilating an engine and losing a race.

Despite our best efforts and intents, every so often everyone scatters an engine. Unless you want to scatter the replacement, thoroughly clean all of the oil lines, fittings and coolers. Throw the filter away.

NOISE vs POWER

There apparently exists a large body of racers who confuse noise with power and who quite sincerely believe that the faster an engine is turned, the more power it puts out. There are legitimate cases of brute force and bloody ignorance triumphing over science and skill but this is not one of them. The rotational speed at which an engine produces its maximum power is determined by a multitude of factors including ratio of stroke to piston area, valve area, port configuration, valve timing, intake and exhaust system design, etc. Once upon a time metalurgy imposed limits that prevented some if not all engines from safely reaching the rpm at which they would produce peak power. This is no longer the case. Most racing engines are now reliable to several hundred rpm over their power peak. A quick look at your dyno sheet will convince you that once the power stops going up, it comes down—in a hurry. A close inspection of the dyno sheet will show you at what point you want to shift and to what rpm you want to run the engine in top gear. Shift a couple of hundred rpm over the power peak so as to retain the greatest area under the curve and run to the power peak in top.

FEEDING THE ENGINE—FUEL

That pretty much covers the care of the engine—now for the feeding. Basically we feed our engines with gasoline, which tends to vary in octane rating, moisture content and revapour pressure—a lot. The best commercially available automotive gasoline is Sunoco 260. If you live in an area where it is available you are looking good. Buy from a dealer who does a large volume and try to buy right after he has had a delivery. How you store and transport it is up to you. If you discover a safe, economical and legal way, let me know.

Pure or Union race gas is slightly better and is available in some locations—mainly major race tracks and usually to professionals only.

Except for Pure and Union, track gas is almost guaranteed to be stale and contaminated and is suitable for tow cars only. If you cannot obtain Sunoco, Pure or Union, then go to your local airport and find a lineboy who will sell you 110/130 AvGas. This is not strictly legal, but except for its light green color (yes, that's what they make red analine dye for) it is undetectable. It is about 104 octane and is pretty highly aromatic which means that you are going to lose about 5% of your fuel mileage. It is not notably more expensive than the trash that you can buy at your service station since the Energy Crisis was invented. Storing and transporting fuel is no fun at all but it is preferable to spending the weekend trying to tune on bad gas—or burning your engine down.

Whatever gas you use, chamois it into the car (through a real chamois skin which will remove all of the sediment and most of the water) and don't store it for more than a month.

FEEDING THE ENGINE — OIL

We also feed the engine with oil. No street oil will get the job done simply because the service conditions are totally different. The same goes for the aircraft oils. I personally do not believe—yet—in the multi grade racing oils—but I am anxious to be proven wrong. So far the oil gauges and the engine bearings have proven me right every time I have tried the multi-grades. Do not be mislead by claims. Use what your engine builder recommends or what the good guys are actually using (which may not be the same stuff they claim to be using). Unless you are getting a lot of blow by there is no need to change racing oil more than every 1000 miles or so. Free oil is not going to save you money unless it is also good oil. Any and all additives are a No No!

FEEDING THE ENGINE — WATER

We also feed the engine with water. Water system schematics are show in Figures (82) and (83). Hopefully the engine will not consume any water at all. It will, however, regurgitate some. If it regurgitates enough water we will get an air lock in the system and instant overheating will result. The reason for all this is a combination of thermal expansion and the phenomenon known as "heat soaking".

We set out from the pits with the water system bled and full. We have pressure checked the system and it has no leaks. The pressure cap is in place and wired. As the engine heats up the coolant water expands and pressurizes the system. When the pressure within the system reaches the limiting pressure of the relief cap, the excess water with which we filled the system is bled past the cap and into the catch tank or onto the track. The system is now full at operating temperature and everything is fine. Now we come into the pits with a hot engine and shut it down. Or we don't shut it

Figure (82): Water System Schematic—Single Radiator

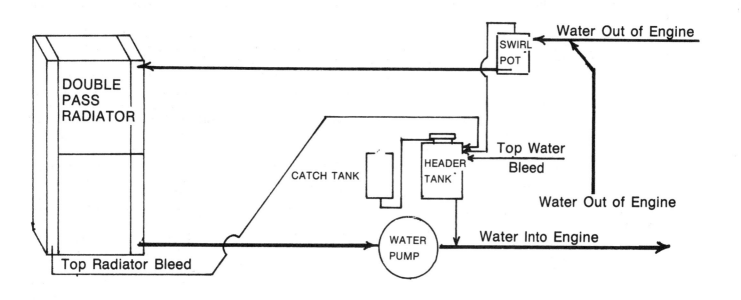

Figure (83): Water System Schematic—Twin Radiators

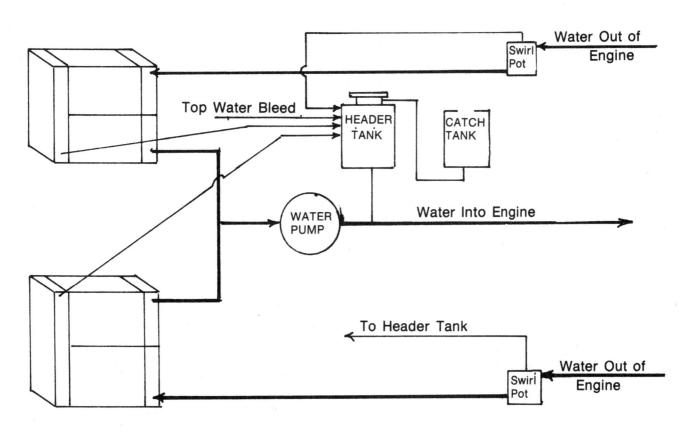

down. In either event, air is no longer passing through the radiator which is now a radiator rather than a water to air heat exchanger. If we shut the engine down, water is no longer circulating. Engine temperature goes up due to lack of cooling, the coolant expands, the pressure cap kicks and more coolant is lost. Eventually we go back out, the coolant circulates, the radiator starts to function again and the water temperature returns to normal. But we lost some water in the pits and the header tank is no longer full of water—now it has some air. If the header tank is too small—or even if it is marginal—the water level is too low and the coolant system gulps air. Instant air lock followed by instant overheat.

The solution is simple. Use a big header tank and mount it high. Better yet use a moderately sized header tank and a commercial water recovery system. You have to have a catch tank anyway so it costs nothing in weight to run the closed system. It is necessary to start with some water in the overflow bottle, however, and the bleed from the header must enter the bottom of the recovery tank.

STEAM POCKETS

If your engine makes its own air locks—usually by forming steam pockets in the heads—you may have to bleed the rear of the heads to the header tank as well as top water. If the engine persists in this behavior, a swirl pot as illustrated in Figure (84) will usually solve the problem.

FEEDING THE ENGINE — DIRT

We do not wish to feed dirt and dust to the engine. At best this will accelerate bore and valve wear, dent the valve seats and put abrasives in the oil. At worst a stone may hang the throttle open. However, race tracks are traditionally dusty places and other drivers are forever running off the road and forcing you to drive through dust clouds as well as showering you with rocks.

Step one is to incorporate a stone screen in your air intake system. This will keep the boulders out. It must be located at least 1-1/2 intake trumpet diameters above the intakes themselves or it may interfere with airflow.

Step two is a thin layer of plastic foam to keep most of the grit out. "Filtron" filter material is the best that I have found. All this will take some playing with to make sure that you are not robbing the engine of much needed air. It will also require frequent cleaning. It will also save your engine.

Slide throttles are especially susceptible to sticking because of dirt. The Formula One teams have now taken to starting the race with a nylon stocking (source not revealed) over the cold air box inlet. This ingenious device is secured by a piece of string leading to the cockpit. After 4 or 5 laps, when most of the dust has been blown off the track and the early off course excursions have mainly happened, the driver pulls on the string and the stocking is discarded. Very clever—and very cheap. What happens when the driver immediately behind wears the stocking around his Bell Star or in one of his air intakes, I don't know.

Figure (84): Water Swirl Pot for De-Aeration

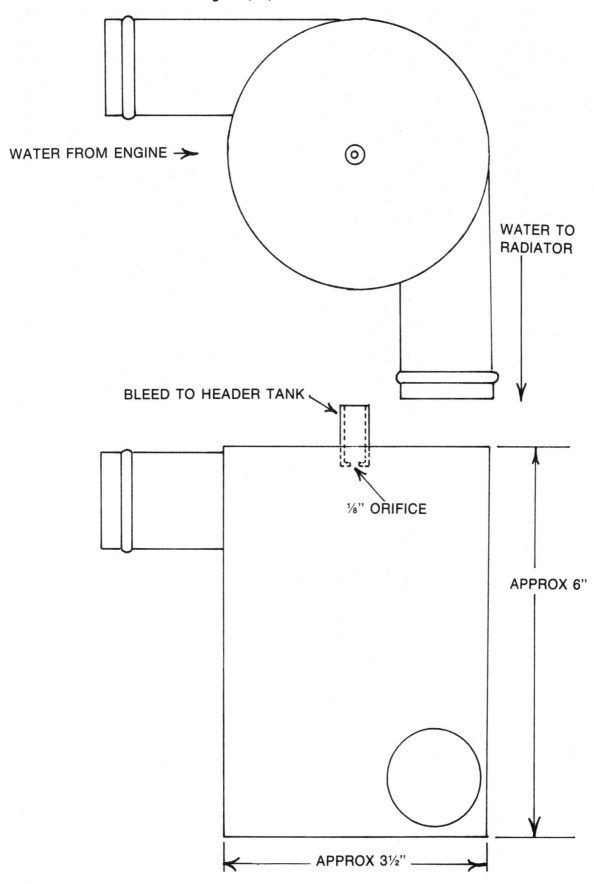

WATER FROM ENGINE →

WATER TO RADIATOR

BLEED TO HEADER TANK

⅛" ORIFICE

APPROX 6"

APPROX 3½"

CHAPTER NINE

THE GEARBOX AND THE FINAL DRIVE

Thanks to Mike Hewland, with an assist from Carl Haas, most serious racing cars can now be geared to take maximum advantage of the engine's power curve characteristics on each circuit. Thanks to these same gentlemen, not only can we do this very quickly but we are also able to inspect the gear trains with a minimum of fuss, bother and effort. We can inspect the ring and pinion with rather more of the same. This is just as well as we mainly insist on using transaxles that are a bit too small for the job.

About 98% of the present generation of racing cars use one of the Hewland transaxles. The other 2% are the really fast Indy cars which use Pete Weismann's new transaxle because the Hewland LG is not reliable enough for serious USAC types. I hope that that this 2% will increase as people start to use Weismann's very new Formula 5000 box. The basic differences between the two brands are that Weismann does all of his shifting on the constant motion shaft rather than on the pinion shaft. This considerably reduces the inertial forces involved, makes the shift notably quicker and increases the life span of the engaging dogs by a notable margin. Weismann also features full dry sump lubrication, a man sized inspection hole for the ring and pinion, a much stronger (and cheaper—it's a Chevy) ring and pinion and cases designed to accept suspension and wing loads. Since virtually everyone in racing owns a whole load of Hewland parts and since all English cars come with Hewlands, the Weismanns will probably remain relatively rare until the Hewland DG 300 loses its borderline reliability as engines get more powerful and tires get stickier. I reckon that this will happen about mid 1975.

All of the comments in this chapter relate directly to the Hewland Units. Gears and bearings being what they are, the comments apply to any other make.

Step one is to obtain the Hewland manual pertaining to your transaxle from Carl Haas or one of his distributors. Step two is to commit it to memory. Having memorized it, take it with you wherever you go with your racer. This is as good a time as any to point out that in all of racing there are only two pieces of equipment for which there are comprehensive manuals with exploded diagrams, parts lists and detailed instructions. They are Lola cars and Hewland transaxles. They also happen to be the only two items for which full spares are available in this country. It is probably not coincidence that both are exclusively imported into this country by Carl Haas who just happens to be the only man around making anything that resembles a good living by selling racing cars and parts. There must be a message there somewhere.

THE TRANSAXLE—INITIAL STRIPPING AND RE-ASSEMBLY

Like chassis, transaxles are shipped in one piece for reasons of convenience—although they are getting better. Whether your unit is new or used, strip it entirely and start over. First remove all of the studs from the cases, clean both male and female threads and re-install them with red loctite. Then forget about them.

Remove the selector finger housing and dowel it to the gearbox case with 1/4" dowel pins. (This is because we insist on hanging wings on the back of the gearbox which causes relative motion between the selector housing and the gearcase. This in turn screws up the rail alignment and beats out the gasket.) Lap the shift finger and the shift rails into their respective bores with fine lapping compound until they are perfectly free. Then make sure that you get all of the lapping compound off the rails and out of the bores. Before re-assembling, coat the rails and the finger with vortex or one of the moly assembly lubes. If you happen to live in L.A. have them Microsealed and do the shift forks, gear hubs and dog rings as well. Adjust the neutral detent spring pressure until you can just positively feel the detent on each rail. You should be able to shift the box into any gear with the pressure of your thumb without causing undue discomfort. Adjust the reverse lock out plunger spring until it is possible to get the finger into the reverse gate without twisting the linkage in half. Do not, however, make it very loose or the driver will get into this gate when downshifting into third and big trouble will result.

FORK ADJUSTMENT

The only difficult part in setting up the gearbox end of a Hewland is the adjustment of the shift forks and rails. It is not so much difficult as time consuming. There are three adjustments.

To prevent over travelling of the shift rail and its fork and eventual bending of the fork, the shift rails are positively stopped in both directions of travel by the gearbox casing. Forward travel is stopped by contact between the slotted shift rail head and the rear face of the casing. Rearward travel is stopped by contact between the rearmost face of each shift fork and the casing. Machining tolerances here are very close indeed and whatever adjustment is necessary is provided by shim rings which slip over the shift rails inside the gearbox and which decrease the rearward travel of the rails.

The position of the neutral detent on the rails (non adjustable) determines the neutral position of each shift fork. The actual dimensions of the gear stack on the pinion shaft (also non adjustable but very closely controlled so that all gears and gear hubs are interchangeable) determines the axial location of the gears on the pinion shaft. Shim adjustment is provided between the shift forks and their rails so that the neutral position of each fork can be adjusted to optimum.

The fork adjusting shims are cunningly hidden away inside the shift forks and many people who should know better are not even aware of their existence. These mild steel shims are impossible to buy but quick and easy to make on a lathe so I make up a batch every so often in .002" increments. I then end up giving them away to my friends at the track.

When properly positioned each fork will be located (when in neutral) midway between the two gears which it selects, will engage fully with each gear and will still have some clearance between the face of the dog and the face of the gear when the gear is engaged. It is also essential that some clearance be present between the thrust face of the shift fork and the dog ring when each gear is engaged. If the dog does not fully engage either of the gears, it may jump out of gear and excessive wear will surely result. If there is no clearance when the gear is engaged you will eventually bend a shift fork. You will also bend a shift fork if there is no clearance between the shift fork thrust face and the dog ring with the gear engaged—although in this case you may well burn out the fork before it bends. Further, the forks and rails must be correctly aligned in the rotational sense as well as in the axial sense so that the dog rings will not bind on their hub and the shift rail heads will not rub against each other.

This sounds a lot more complicated than it actually is. If you happen to have access to a Hewland fork setting jig, consider yourself fortunate and use it according to directions. If, like most of us, you do not, obtain a ruined pinion (they are in plentiful supply) and an old pinion bearing. Weld a chunk of 1/4" steel across the nose of the pinion so that it can be securely held in the horizontal position in a large vise and you have a poor man's fork setting jig. The pinion bearings must be installed on the shaft.

Step one is to make sure that the pinion gear stack has the correct clearance. This is called out in the manual. (.008" to .010" for most models) and is adjusted by grinding the thrust washer which rides in the gear case behind top gear. To check it I use plastigauge and merely assemble the whole mess, torque everything down, take it apart and read the plastigauge. If you are particularly dextrous it can also be checked by inserting bent feeler gauges through the layshaft bearing bore with the layshaft removed. Once adjusted, this will not have to be checked again until, for whatever reason, you find it necessary to change the differential case or the gear case. If you change a gear hub, check the clearance, but it will not have changed. Gear thickness and gear hub tolerances as near as I can tell are plus or minus zero.

Having done all this, assemble the pinion shaft gear stack with all of the hubs, bearings, gears, forks and the dummy pinion shaft. Clamp the shaft in a large vise so that the whole assembly is horizontal and tighten the pinion shaft nut. Make sure that the fork retaining nuts are tight but do not lock them yet. Check that each dog ring is approximately centered between its respective gears when in the neutral

position. Don't change anything yet if it is not. Next shift the box into each gear in turn and check to make sure that you are getting full dog engagement while maintaining .002"/.006" clearance between the face of the dogs and the face of the gear when fully engaged. You must also double check to see that clearance exists between the thrust face of the shift fork and the dog ring with the gear engaged. Write down all of the clearance figures that you come up with. Selection of fork shims to obtain proper axial spacing is now a matter of common sense and simple arithmetic. You will almost always find a new Hewland box to be properly spaced and aligned. When replacing shift forks you will have to adjust the spacing. Remember that the only way that you have of adjusting total shift rail travel is by shimming under the rearward face of the fork between the fork and the case. You will not have to change this shim unless you change a shift rail. It is, however, important not to lose or misplace any shims that Mssrs. Hewland may have installed on the rails. Shift forks should be checked for cracks and burned grooves frequently and should be replaced at the end of each season. When installing a new fork it is necessary to grind or file a flat on the circumference of the shaft portion of the fork in order to provide a register for the lock tab.

When you are satisfied with the axial spacing, take the unit out of the vise, assemble the constant motion shaft and gears and tighten the constant motion shaft nut. Loosen the shift fork retaining nuts just a little and lay the unit on a bench so that you can get at the shift rail heads. Obtain correct axial spacing and clearance of the rails by jamming the thickest feeler gauge that will fit between the First/Reverse rail head and the Second/Third rail head. Repeat the action between the Second/Third and Fourth/Fifth rail heads. This should lock the rails axially with clearance between the heads so that they cannot rub against each other as you shift the box. Required feeler gauge thickness will vary a bit but will be in the .010" to .015" range.

Now place the assembly on a bench with the gears facing up and tighten all of the fork retaining nuts while you hold the forks centered. Usually the First/Reverse fork has to be held pretty firmly toward the gears to obtain proper alignment. With everything tight, remove the feeler gauges from the shift rail heads and make sure that each fork is still centered (you should have a little axial play in each direction) and that the First/Reverse fork is so positioned that it doesn't have a tendency to spring away from the gear stack. Lock the fork retaining nuts and you are done.

Some people believe in grinding .010" or so from the face of every other engaging dog in the belief that it makes gear selection easier. I do not agree and I don't do it. Some people do and it is necessary to make sure that this has not been done to the gears or dog rings that you are using to space the shift forks. If it has been done and you don't know it you are going to end up at the funny farm!

MAINTENANCE

Maintenance of the gearbox is ridiculously simple. Gear failure occurs only with Indy cars and Can Am cars and then, usually, only with gears which feature lightening holes. Can Am and Indy gears must be the latest pattern "S" gears or Marv Webster's super gears and must be magnafluxed every time the car stops. It all has to do with torque. Lightening holes are a distinct No No in these cars.

Not so with the rest. I magnaflux Formula 5000 gears twice a season and visually inspect them every time I change a gear. I replace bearings and seals at the end of the season except for the pinion bearing which I replace every 1000 miles. I replace shift forks at the end of the season or when they get loose, which should take a season. If a fork is showing heavy wear or burning on a thrust face it is improperly spaced and is over travelling in the direction of the wear. If the end faces of the gear hubs show fretting, you are losing the pinion thrust bearing.

When assembling the box, every time, oil the hubs, the hub bearings and the dog rings. Make sure that all of the needles are present in the hub bearings. Clean the gears that you take out before you put them away.

Store your gears in such a way that they cannot bang against each other; don't let them rust and keep them in pairs so that you can find what you want without digging around. The best way is in an egg crated box or on a wooden board with dowels to hold the gears. In either case store the gears—in matched pairs—in ascending or descending order of numerical ratio and mark the position of each gear. It will save you many hours during the course of a season. Besides, it makes you look as if you know what you are doing.

The only wear that normally takes place in the gearbox end of a Hewland is that of the selector dogs. Depending on the expertise of the driver involved dog wear can vary from virtually none to utterly ridiculous. This expertise has nothing to do with speed of shifting—it is entirely a matter of technique (assuming, of course, that the gear box and shift linkage are properly set up). It also has nothing to do with the reputation and/or record of the driver. I know world champions who regularly destroy two dog rings per practice session. If you are a world champion and the box will still shift at the end of the race, then the dog rings don't matter and no one is going to mention them (if you drop out of the race or lose a place because the dog rings that you wore out gave up the fight—then someone is damned well going to mention it).

As wear takes place on the dogs of both the dog rings and the gears and as both tend to be horribly expensive, it pays to learn how to shift. I have always felt that the drivers ought to be allowed to pay for prematurely worn out dog rings and gears. The rule of thumb is dogs whose corners are rounded more than 1/32" are not useable. Refacing with a hard stone will restore mild damage. The only trick is to judiciously change the position in the box of the dog rings as they start to wear. Normally the least wear will be shown on the side of the Fourth/Fifth dog ring that is towards Fifth. The downshift side of this dog gets no wear at all. Conversely the upshift side of the second gear dog gets no wear and the downshift side of that one gets the most punishment of all. So, by turning the Second/Third dog ring around and putting it in the Fourth/Fifth slot, what was the downshift side of second gear is now the downshift side of fifth and the fact that it is worn out doesn't matter. This assumes that the rest of the dog ring is still serviceable. If the box starts to jump out of gear, or is difficult to get into one or more gears, it is invariably worn out selector dogs or mis-adjusted

gear linkage. Worn dog rings and gears can be reground at very nominal cost by Pete Weismann at Traction Products.

GEARSHIFT LINKAGE

Far too many cars come with totally inadequate shift linkage. Usually the layout is adequate (laying out a good linkage is a real bitch) but the bearings are tight and/or the universal joints are junk. The bearings should be real cheapies (bronze races are the best in this application) and the linkage shafts should be pretty loose in the bearings. The brackets which hold the bearings in place are usually junk and must be beefed up. The only good universal joints are the "Apex heavy duty" units (MS 20271 series) available from Earl's Supply or direct from Apex. Bolts that hold the linkage together must be in reamed holes with no slop at all (I use taper pins with a thread on the small end and elastic stop nuts). It is also necessary to make very sure that the linkage cannot bottom against anything—brake discs, linkage bearings, etc. Time spent in this department will result in time and money saved during the season. The linkage tubes must be a free fit in their bearings and should have an excellent surface finish.

CHANGING GEAR RATIOS

The first tip in changing gear ratios is to make sure that the gears are assembled in correct pairs and in the right order (it is indeed possible to assemble the box with either the pinion shaft or constant motion shaft gears installed either out of sequence or backwards). If a pinion shaft gear is in backwards you will not be able to select that gear (dogs are facing the wrong way). If a constant motion shaft is in backwards (i.e. with the chamber facing the wrong way) it will contact the next adjacent pinion shaft gear and make a really nasty noise as the gears destroy each other. If the gears are not installed in matched pairs you are going to shuck gear teeth. The prevalent notion that you can get away with using the 28 tooth gear from a 28/28 to make up a 27/28 etc. is just not true—it has to do with gear center distance and tooth contact patterns.

The second tip is to be very sure that you have all gears in neutral and the selector finger in the slots on the shift rail heads before you replace the back cover. You can make two mistakes here—leaving the box in fourth and reverse after you have torqued the pinion and constant motion shaft nuts or leaving the box in any gear with the selector finger not engaged in that shift rail. In either case the box cannot be shifted.

The third tip is to replace the oil. My system, which works very well for me, is that a box which has the filler plugs safety wired has oil in it and, conversely, if the filler plug is not wired there is no oil in that section of the box.

The fourth tip is that when you are re-assembling the box and the gear case doesn't want to go that last 3/8" onto the differential case, tap the starter and it will slide right on. If you cannot hit the starter then install the constant motion shaft nut and turn the engine over with the constant motion shaft—same result.

The last tip is to engage each gear in turn before putting on the rear cover and also to turn the box over in neutral as fast as you can (socket and bar on the pinion shaft nut) while listening for strange noises from the inside that indicate a foreign object, a backwards constant motion shaft gear, a leftout bearing or whatever.

THE RING AND PINION

If the gearbox end of the Hewland is simple and trouble free, it is more than made up for by the ring and pinion. The basic problems here are threefold. First is the fact that every time that Mike Hewland designs a unit for a specific purpose, we the racers either succeed in coaxing another 100 horsepower out of the engine, or we put bigger and stickier tires on the thing, or we make a big breakthrough in wings or we decide that the nice light 3 litre box is so reliable in Formula One and shifts so fast that it'll do just fine as a Formula 5000 box. The trouble is that it always works—just. This has to be a tribute to Hewland's design genius and an indication of the safety margins that he uses. I guess he understands us pretty well!

None of this was too awful in the days of outboard rear brakes when we could get at the ring and pinion without much bother. At the moment, with inboard rear brakes and all of the rear suspension firmly attached to the final drive casing, removal of the ring and pinion tends to be a bit of a drama. Luckily the good Mr. Hewland has provided a convenient if rather small inspection hole at the top of the casing where the oil return from the pump lives (not the filler plug—you can't see the pinion teeth from there). With any kind of an eyeball on a stalk (medical ophthalmoscope looks trick and costs a lot and a flashlight bulb soldered to some wire and a couple of batteries does just as well) we can closely inspect the teeth for wear, pitting and cracks every night—and we had better!

The units used on Formula Ford, Formula B, Formula Atlantic and up to two litre sports racing cars are reliable to the point of boredom while the Formula 5000 (DG 300), Can Am and Indy (LG 500) boxes require frequent inspection and parts replacement. In both the DG and the LG the pinion bearing is the weak link—followed closely by the pinion itself. The ring gear will live forever but each ring and pinion is a matched and lapped set so you can't just change the pinion.

The DG uses a combination of a straight roller bearing to take the pinion radial load and a split inner race ball bearing to take the thrust loads. This is an excellent system but the bearings are just a shade too small for Formula 5000 use (the box was designed for Formula One—a long time ago). They will run 600 to 1000 miles which is not as far as the pinion will go (if it is a good one and is correctly set up). So you get to replace the bearings more often than the pinion. Never install a new pinion with old bearings if you can help it. The split inner race thrust bearing is available only from your Hewland distributor. The roller is available from any good bearing house but make sure that you get one with a bronze cage vs a pressed steel cage which is a bit marginal for this application. Both of these bearings live in a steel housing and should have .002" to .003" axial preload in the housing. The steel housing itself used to fail fairly frequently (the rear retaining lip fell off which was pretty bad) so that I got to make a fair few of them from big bar stock which was no fun at all. Apparently this has now been rectified as I

haven't heard of a failure this year (1974). The roller bearing goes to the front of the assembly and the preload is adjusted by means of a shim between the two bearings. The bolts which hold the housing in place must be safety wired which is a real pain. In an emergency the life of the thrust bearing can be prolonged by turning it around in the housing.

With the LG units, replacement of the stock pinion bearing with the directly interchangeable FAG 3309A split inner race bearing (available from your bearing house or from Webster Racing) solves the problem. However the serious Can Am and Indy types replace ring, pinion and bearing every race no matter how good it looks. Several of the Formula 5000 teams do the same with the DG. This means that a supply of perfectly useable gear is available to the club racer at vastly reduced cost if he knows who to contact.

Setting up the ring and pinion is perfectly straightforward, although the use of Hewland's pinion depth setting jig does make it a lot easier. The fixture works on either Hewland or Webster ring and pinion sets. Step one is to make sure that the serial numbers of the ring and the pinion match so that you do indeed have a matched set. Step two is to make a set of dummy side carrier and pinion bearings so that you don't have to spend hours shrinking bearings in and out of cases while you are setting up a ring and pinion. This can be done by taking old bearings and rotating them against a belt sander for a long time. What you are looking for is an outer race that will just drop into the housing at room temperature. When you get them done color them with dychem or something to identify them as set up bearings only.

The procedure outlined in the Hewland Manual works just fine. The only deviation that I practice is that I use more side carrier preload than recommended. With the LG I am using .015" to .020" and with the DG I use .010" to .012", both measured cold. I measure by bolting up the side covers (no gasket sealant, diff in place and less the output shafts) and then loosening off all of the nuts on one side and measuring the resultant gap with a feeler gauge. In no case should you run so much preload that you cannot turn the pinion shaft by hand when the box is cold. Increasing the preload from stock keeps the pinion in constant mesh with the ring gear at operating temperatures when the differential case expands.

With the Hewland ring and pinion my experience has been that the pinion depth marked on the pinion head has given a perfect pattern every time. I still check it with red lead or white lead. With the Webster unit for the LG I have found the odd set where the marking was .004" or so off. In all cases it is best to have a bunch of pinion depth adjusting washers in stock. It is also best to buy all of your ring and pinion sets with the same depth marking so you don't have to have so many washers. Comparing the depth marked on the pinion you take out with that marked on the new one and then measuring the shim used with the old one will tell you what thickness shim you need for the new pinion. Do not try to use thin shims for pinion spacing as they will beat out instantly. The same is true of trying to shim the pinion and constant motion shaft nuts so that the cotter pin holes will line up. Buy some spare nuts and machine them.

Occasionally (very rarely in the past couple of years) you will find a ring and pinion that will just not set up. The clue is a large variation in back lash. Assuming that the ring gear is securely bolted to the carrier with no burrs or dings and that the carrier face is true, send the ring and pinion back. Maximum backlash variation should be .004".

Backlash is adjusted by moving the thin shims under the carrier bearing races from one side of the box to the other. Once the preload is established you cannot add or subtract shims—you can only shift them from side to side.

There are virtually no tips for the ring and pinion set up. It is all in the manual. I don't use the stock lock tabs to lock the ring gear bolts because they are soft iron and will beat out resulting in a loose ring gear. I use Chevrolet flywheel bolgs for ring gear bolts, drill the heads and safety wire them. I do not use washers unless the bolts are too long in which case I use hardened and ground washers from the machine shop supply house. I also use red loc-tite. The AN Bolt number is AN-7H-7A but the area under the head is not sufficient for absolute safety.

You are looking for a contact pattern on the load side of the pinion that is quite heavy towards the toe, but not running off the toe. It should be quite even in depth although it will taper towards the heel, being thinner at that end. The taper will be away from the tooth root. The pattern should extend 2/3 to 3/4 of the distance from the nose of the tooth toward the heel. The cold pattern must not extend to the root of the tooth or the tooth will fail at the root under load. You need from .060" to .080" clearance from the root of the tooth. Under load this rather strange contact pattern will cover almost the entire tooth except for the required clearance at the root (.030" minimum under load). The load pattern may run off at the heel, but it should not at the nose. Don't worry too much about the pattern on the coast side of the pinion. In the unlikely event that the pinion lasts long enough to gain as much as .004" backlash, reset it.

Break in a new ring and pinion by loading it heavily for short periods of time. Avoid constant loads and long time loads. The object is to get heat into the gears quickly and then give them time to cool off. You will be able to see the load pattern through the inspection hole after 5 or 6 laps.

The best protection for a new ring and pinion is Micro-Seal—if you live in L.A. Otherwise after you have finished setting up (take a final check of both lash and pattern after the real bearings have been installed) use a sparing coat of any of the assembly lubes—I use Vortex.

Frequent visual checking of the pinion teeth for pitting, spalling, or wiping is a necessity. Small pits are usually the first sign of distress and, so long as they remain small, are not cause for worry. If metal starts to pull away from the pit, replace the unit. I don't let pits get any larger than about .040". Spalling or wiping is caused by either a bad set up or unsuitable oil. Suitable oils include Shell SL 7923 which is almost impossible to obtain and Valvoline's new 90/140 high performance gear oil. We do not need any additives at all and we do not need any trick oils.

After practice I visually check the ring and pinion first thing because replacing it is a long job and I don't want to find out about it at midnight.

You can save yourself a lot of unpleasant night time activity at the race track by setting up your spare rings and pinions at the shop and carrying them around complete with their shims so that you can just plug them in without going through the set up bit. It is also wise to machine each of your differentials so that they are all dimensionally exact and directly interchangesble.

THE DIFFERENTIAL

Three types of "self locking" differentials are in common use. First is the clutch or Salisbury tupe about which I know nothing except that I have tried them a few times, didn't like them and don't use them, the cam and pawl or ZF type and the Weismann locker.

The cam and pawl is the most common so we will discuss it first. It is a very straightforward device and, as you would expect when you first look inside of one, it is subject to wear—lots of wear. When the inner and outer cams and the pawls are all new it works fine. The pawls and the inner cam engage in a race to see who is going to wear out first. The race is usually won by the pawls—by a nose. The visual symptoms of excessive wear are wear marks on the high surfaces of the cams and on the operating faces of the pawls. The dynamic symptoms increasing and unpredictable oversteer under power. With a good driver in professional Formula 5000 racing (when I must run a cam and pawl unit) I run the parts from the last race (if they look reasonable) for whatever testing is done and for the first day's practice. Then I give it a new inner cam and a set of pawls. Every second race it gets a new outer cam. If it is run in the rain you junk the whole thing. Pack the unit with lots of moly based assembly lube.

The Weismann unit which works a lot better and costs a lot more (although not over the course of a season) requires very little maintenance. Every couple of races I check the rollers for cracks and the drag springs for distortion. If a drag spring breaks, you will know about it—the car gets really squirrelly. If the "C" spring breaks (I've heard of it happening but have never seen it) you will have a locked rear end and you will also know about it. The preload or bias of the Weismann is adjustable by shimming behind the paper clutches at the ends of the unit and is a matter of driver performance. Decals and newspaper make perfectly good shims. About 20 lbs. of breakaway torque is a pretty good setting for most drivers. This can be measured without disassembling anything by jamming a screwdriver in one brake disc and turning the other wheel with a torque wrench. The giant No No with the Weismann is the use of graphite or moly. The device works by friction and the car is absolutely undrivable if any moly or graphite gets into the locker. It is also very sensitive to the right oil—the previously mentioned Shell and Valvoline are the only oils that I know that work. If you must run another oil, seal all of the holes in the diff with silicon bathtub caulk and assemble it with 90 weight E.P. oil.

I replace the drag springs and rollers at midseason just on speculation.

INPUT AND OUTPUT SHAFTS

Input and output shafts take a lot of abuse and should be magna-fluxed every 1000 miles. Examine the output shafts for twisting at the end of the splines every race. The bearings and seals will last a season. The bolts which hold the input shaft bearing housing to the differential case have a habit of working loose. Either safety wire them or use longer bolts and elastic stop nuts on the inside of the housing.

INSTALLATION

Installing the transaxle is simplicity itself—except for stabbing the input shaft onto the clutch. Everyone has their own system. Mine is to get the unit to the right height on a jack or a cherry picker and install some dummy bell housing bolts (way too long) to act as guides. The long bolts (2 at the top and 2 at the bottom) will hold the transaxle in alignment while you slowly turn the wheels (via the constant motion shaft or the brake discs) to align the clutch splines and push the whole mess into place.

Make sure that the transaxle is very rigidly attached to the engine. This sometimes requires some sort of connection to very generous ears on the oil pan. This last is especially true of the LGs which were never designed to accept suspension loads.

Gear oil is reusable for a long time—particularly if you are paying for it. It is important, however, to keep the screen filter which protects the oil pump clean or oil will not circulate and everhthing will go to hell. The oil pump will work just fine with its housing terribly scored. It will not function at all if you forget to put its drive gear on the input shaft or if you leave any of the gear circlips off. Run a magnet in the diff case and one in the gear case. The drain plugs are good locations and the magnets should be integral or bolted in place rather than epoxied.

You can use virtually any sealant on the mating faces of the box. I use either Hylomar or G.E. silicon gasket sealer because they are both easily removable. I do not use a gasket on the gear cover plate although I usually have to grind clearance or the shift finger into the cover plate. I also do not run a breather line. Instead I drill a #60 hole in the top of the rear cover plate. No oil comes out and the whole box is open to atmosphere.

Money saving tips are virtually non existent. Most of the bearings and seals are available at your local bearing house. If you, or a friend, happen to be going to England, Hewland will not sell to you. The Racing Gearbox Center will and will save you money. The biggest money saver in the transaxle department comes from preventing failure by correct setup, shifting technique and maintenance.

Last word on the subject—the familiar great clunk as the driver engages a gear to leave the pits can be totally eliminated by pushing the car slowly while the driver "feels" the gear in. It's easy, no trouble at all and it sounds so nice.

DRIVE SHAFTS

From the final drive unit power goes to the wheels by means of the drive shafts. Construction and design varies a lot. Most of the new generation of smaller cars are now using constant velocity joints of the Rzeppa type which are lovely devices indeed. They achieve true constant velocity under all conditions, have virtually frictionless plunge provision and are made possible in small racing cars only because Volkswagen and Fiat are making them in giant quantities. They are also found on BMWs, Porsche 911Ts and Carrera

(the Porsche units are beefy enough for Formula 5000) and on Indy cars because nothing else will do the job. The Indy units are particularly nice and are made by the ConVel division of Dana Corp. in very limited quantities at prices which would allow you to run a Formula Ford for a season. The Porsche units are pretty inexpensive. These joints require precious little maintenance. You have to make sure that the shaft doesn't run out of plunge (in either direction) as the wheel travels, you have to keep them lubed with a good grade of moly grease and you have to look at the balls, slots and retainers every so often. As the shafts themselves tend to be a bit on the small side in the diameter department it is a good idea to paint a thin line the length of the shaft to provide a quick visual indication of twisting beyond the elastic limit of the material. Polishing and shot peening the production shafts should help a lot.

Weismann markets an excellent half shaft kit made from Porsche parts which directly substitutes for the trouble-prone BRP units on Lola Formula 5000 cars.

Before the industrial giants started to make Rzeppa joints in vast quantities, many smaller race cars used a combination of a standard Hooke type universal joint at one end of the drive shaft and a rubber doughnut at the other to take plunge. These worked just fine and they still do. Replacements are hard to find. Keeping the doughnut wet with a silicon based grease increases the life as does not washing them with solvents. Assembling the rubber doughnuts tends to get a bit frustrating. Tightening a giant hose clamp around the O.D. helps a lot.

Most race cars, however, still have driveshafts consisting of a Hooke joint at each end with a male and female spined shaft to provide the necessary plunge. The splines may be either of the roller or the ball variety (ball splines are better). They had better not be of the straight spline with no bearings variety or the car will not handle. A certain amount of track change is inevitable and if this is not accomplished smoothly and with no binding of the splines, the behavior of the rear suspension under power will be unpredictable at best.

The rollers or balls which make the splines "frictionless" are assembled onto the male spline and located by little pressed steel cages. Rollers should be arranged so that alternate rollers face opposite directions. They are lubed with any good grade of grease, the cages are slipped on and you then try to feed the male assembly into the previously greased female part without cocking or losing the bearings. Make very sure that you have the universal joint yokes correctly aligned the first time or you are going to get to do it all over again. Patience helps a lot.

The male shaft is prone to cracking where the machined groove in which the bearing live ends. The cracking can be considerably delayed by radiusing the end of the grooves with a carbide ball end mill or a rotary hard stone. If cracking does occur, the cracks will propogate from the end of the groove at about 45 degrees to the axis of the shaft in the direction of driving torque. If detected early enough they can be ground out.

The automotive industry has been making Hooke type universal joints, yokes, flanges and replacement cross kits for a long time. Original equipment is of unvarying excellent quality. The laws of economics tell us that if a replacement part can be made cheaper, lots of parts houses are going to stock it and lots of repair shops are going to use it—regardless of quality. For our purposes original equipment means Dana, Rockwell International, General Motors and no one else. All three of these concerns market cross kits which are directly interchangeable with the BRD units supplied on English race cars. Most Formula 5000 cars use the 1315 series joints. The Dana Spicer part number is 5-178-X. The GM part is superior part in that it has no grease nipple hole to act as a stress raiser.

Universal joints go through hell! I don't run them more than 1000 miles. I also don't much enjoy changing them. It helps to do it right. The first spot of trouble that you will run into is that whoever put the last set in assembled them dry and the cups are probably corroded solid. Lost of penetrating oil is the only answer followed by assembly with any good anti sieze compound. Assuming that you don't feel like taking the whole car apart, the cross will have to be removed from the outboard yoke without a press (or a vise, which is really all the press you need for U-joints). Remove the retaining clips and, using a large copper hammer and an adaptor, knock the cross as far one way in the yoke as it will go. This will push the cup about 1/4" outside the yoke. Grab the cup with a pair of vice-grips (don't worry about ruining the cup as you are going to throw it away) and wiggle it out. If it won't come, beat on the vice-grips with a big punch while you rotate them. Eventually it will come, probably scattering rollers all over the place. Knock the cross back the other way and repeat the operation with the opposite cup.

Next undo the inboard drive shaft flange bolts so that you can take the drive shaft off the car. In all probability you will have to undo the rear upper suspension link and tilt the hub carrier to get the shaft out. With the cups out of the outboard yoke you can turn and wiggle the cross to withdraw it from the yoke.

With the shaft off the car the whole performance is repeated three more times and the universals are disassembled. If the cross journals don't show any signs of brinelling and there is no roller dust or thin or broken rollers, it is worth magnafluxing the crosses and saving them for emergency spares. Assembly is a reverse of disassembly. Assemble the shafts so that the inboard yokes (with respect to the shaft) are in line with each other or you will not achieve constant velocity and binding will result. For reasons which escape me the crosses will last longer if the grease nipples (if any) both face inboard with respect to the shaft. Do not overtighten the grease fittings.

The easiest assembly procedure for me is:

(1) Deburr the cup bores in the yokes and flanges and thinly coat with anti-sieze. It is a good idea to ensure that the cup bores are in line with each other. To do this you make a go-no go gauge about .0005" undersize and long enough to pass through the yoke.

(2) Pack the new cups with grease and make sure that each has its full compliment of rollers. Make equally certain that the rollers are properly aligned. Coat the O.D. of the cups with anti-sieze. Insert a cross journal into each cup to make very sure that the rollers are aligned and visually check to make sure that they are still there when you withdraw the journal. Remove the grease fittings from the crosses so that they are vented for assembly.

(3) Insert a cross into one of the shaft yokes and then start both cups squarely into their bores by hand.

(4) Move to a large vise with soft jaws, and, making sure that the yoke is square in the vise and the cups are square in the yoke, start squeezing. One cup will start easily. Press that cup in slowly, inserting the cross into that cup as soon as it will reach. About now a second person would be a big help.

(5) As soon as the cup that is moving is in far enough, wiggle the cross around until it is started in both cups. This will prevent cocking a roller which will cause you to say bad words when you discover it. When you are very sure that the cross is well started in both cups, stop being gentle and squeeze both cups as far as they will go which isn't very far as they will end up flush with the ends of the yoke.

(6) Remove the shaft from the vise and place an adaptor against one cup. Put it back in the vise and shove that cup in far enough to insert the retaining clip. I don't use the stock clips but substitute a 5000-118 Tru Arc retainer which offers more positive retention.

(7) Remove the shaft from the vise; place the adaptor against the opposite cup; press it into place and install the retainer. If the cup squeezes to about .050" short of going into place and stops, you have cocked a roller and it now reposes in the base of the cup. You may now say bad words and start over. Do not try to force the cup if it won't go that last .050". You will not succeed and you will break something.

(8) Repeat the process until you are done. Install the crosses in the shaft yokes first and the drive flanges last as it is easier to hold the shaft in a vise and the flange in your hand than vice-versa.

(9) Replace the grease fittings, but not very tightly.

(10) Fiddle the shaft into position on the car and insert the outboard cross into the outboard yoke.

(11) Bolt everything solid and repeat the whole procedure on the other side of the car.

INSPECTION OF DRIVE SHAFTS

Visual inspection of drive shafts is difficult. About all that you can do is to make sure that the bolts fastening the inboard drive flange to the output shaft are tight (they tend to loosen a lot, particularly the left side ones, and the only solution is red loc-tite and frequent checking), that the shafts have not twisted and that there is no relative motion between the universal joint crosses and their yokes or flanges.

By breaking one end of the upper link loose and removing the end cap from the sliding spline you can usually withdraw the male shaft far enough to check for cracks with spray cans of dye penetrant.

It is worth replacing U-joints and magnafluxing stuff on a pretty strict and conservative schedule because a broken drive shaft not only results in instant loss of control and a rather sharp turn, but the shaft tends to flail around like a mad thing and it will remove anything in its path—like suspension links, shock adsorbers and the like. If you break one drive shaft, or one universal joint and the car is fixable, replace the others without question.

CHAPTER TEN

SUSPENSION ALIGNMENT

The best designed and constructed chassis, suspension and tires won't do you a bit of good unless the chassis is precisely and correctly aligned. Additionally, unless you know exactly how your suspension is set, it is unlikely that you are going to make successful adjustments at the race track. Nor will you be able to return the chassis to its starting point if, as frequently happens, an adjustment or a series of adjustments turns out to have been a step in the wrong direction.

Suspension alignment can be conveniently divided into two broad categories—"static alignment" and "bump steer". Static alignment consists of setting ride height, castor, camber, toe in, track, wheelbase, rear upright inclination and corner weight to the designer's specifications or to those settings which you have determined to be best. Bump steering a car (also called "toe steering") consists of moving each wheel through its range of vertical travel, measuring the wheel's deviation from its static toe in setting as it rises and falls and then correcting the deviation. For no very good reason the whole process is obscured by clouds of fear and superstition.

EQUIPMENT

In order to do a good job of alignment a few simple pieces of equipment are necessary. Most can be made rather than bought. The equipment chosen must be simple, portable and sufficiently accurate to establish a repeatable system. Minimum needs are:

(1) Some sort of camber gauge which can be read in increments of five minutes of arc (there are sixty minutes of arc in one degree of angle so that five minutes of arc is equal to 1/12 degree).

(2) Some sort of castor gauge which can be read in increments of ten minutes of arc.

(3) A good 18 inch machinist's rule with both 1/32" and 1/64" divisions.

(4) A good ten foot steel tape measure.

(5) A ball of strong string. It should be both fine and dark in color. Cheap fishing line works well but don't buy the newfangled monofilament line as you can't easily see it well enough to accurately read the measurements.

(6) A flat plate of metal about 18" by 8" with provision for rigid attachment to either the wheels, brake discs, or hub carriers.

(7) An accurate carpenter's level.

(8) A straight piece of some sort of tubing or angle stock heavy enough to be reasonably rigid and long enough to extend across the tops of both front and rear wheels normal to the centerline of the vehicle.

(9) A bunch of floor shims about 18" square and about 1/8" thick. Masonite is fine and old magazines will do in a pinch.

(10) A set of trammel pins made from scrap Figure (85).

(11) Access to four accurate scales capable of weighing the wheels of the car individually and simultaneously. These can be grain scales, Lo Boy race car scales, bathroom scales (if the car is light enough) or one of the proprietary (or home made) lever devices. Two scales will do the job, but four makes it much easier.

STATIC ALIGNMENT

The best starting point is to take all of the suspension links off the car and assemble them on a bench to designed dimensions. It is true that this process will consume at least half a working day. It is equally true that it is the only way to achieve an optimum job and that it will save more time than it consumes. The idea is to start out with the left side of the car dimensionally exact to the right side with respect to link lengths and outboard pivot point locations, both longitudinally and laterally. Since virtually no manufacturer provides this information with the car, a certain amount of initial guess work followed by later adjustment is inevitable.

If the design dimensions are unknown I usually do a rough static alignment, at least on one side of the car and make sure that the suspension will swing freely with no interference from brake lines, ducts, sway bar links and the like. Then I take it apart and start from there.

At the front the essential thing is to make sure that the front outer ball joint locations, upper and lower, are the same lateral distance from the vehicle centerline and the same longitudinal distance from the front bulkhead. This is accomplished by making the lower wishbones, upper transverse links and upper leading arms dimensionally exact on either side of the vehicle. Figure (86) illustrates the use of trammel pins to determine link length.

Now is also the time to ensure that the steering rack is level and centered relative to the chassis, that the steering track rods are of equal length and to make some sort of rack stops to hold the rack centered while you are aligning the car. On most cars rack stops can be made from half tubes cut to exact length and slipped over the rack itself outboard of the rack housing. It is a very good idea to equip the rack stops with some sort of brightly colored and highly visible flag to indicate that they are installed (surplus "REMOVE BEFORE FLIGHT" flags are fine). I have seen cars attempt to leave the pits with the rack stops installed.

At the rear the lower rear wishbones (or parallel links), upper links and upper and lower radius rods are assembled to equal length left and right. With parallel links a very quick calculation will allow you to build in the desired amount of toe at this stage. The same is true of rear upright inclination and radius rod length.

Assuming that the chassis itself is accurate and square, when everything is reassembled we can be certain that the wheelbase, track, camber, castor, pin inclination and suspension curves are now equal on both sides of the car. We also know that, so long as we duplicate the adjustments made on one side of the car on the other side, everything will remain so. Further, if we keep track of every adjustment

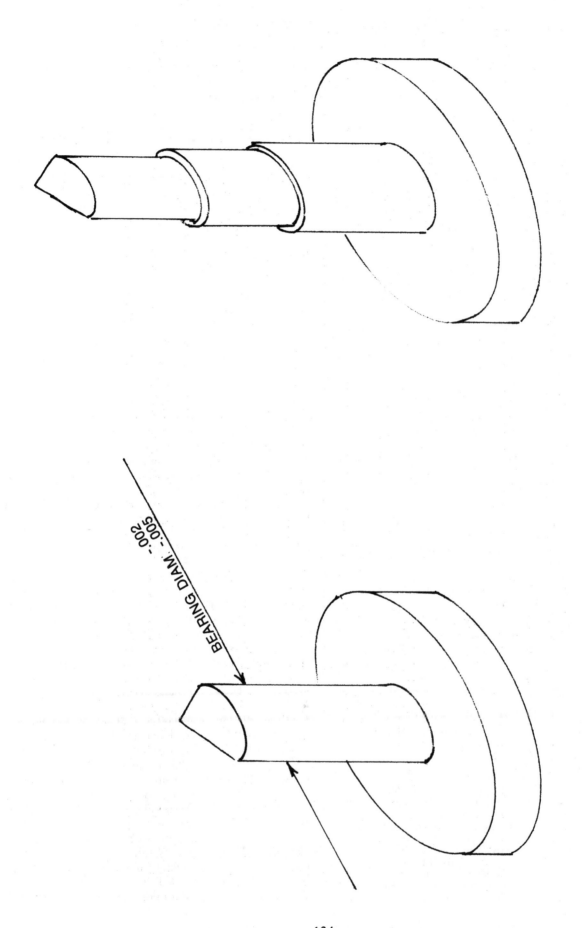

BEARING DIAM. -.002
                 -.005

Figure (85): Trammel Pins for Suspension Link Measurement

134

Figure (86): Use of Trammel Pins

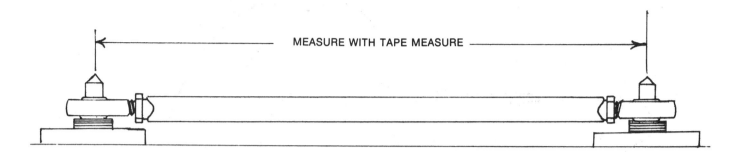

MEASURE WITH TAPE MEASURE

made while aligning the vehicle, by calculating the linear change made by turning threaded adjustments, we can arrive at an exact length for every link installed on the vehicle. This will enable us to set up any spares that we may have so that trackside replacement of damaged items can be made without the necessity for re-alignment. What we have done is to establish a valid reference from which to start our chassis alignment.

ESTABLISHING A LEVEL SURFACE

Step one in the actual alignment procedure is the establishment of a level surface from which to work. To do this we use floor shims. Any number of methods can be used to measure. Don't bother trying to use your camber gauge or carpenter's level as it is unlikely that you will find an entirely level floor—especially in California earthquake country. The water manometer supplied with Lo Boy scales or made from a length of clear plastic tubing works well. My usual system, less scientific but easier and plenty good enough, is to make sure that the tires are equal in diameter left to right (and free of rocks), place a rigid straight edge across the tops of each pair of tires—normal to the vehicle centerline—place a carpenter's level on the straightedge and shim the low wheel until the level reads zero. Figure (87) illustrates. Unless you are parked on a hill, any unevenness in the longitudinal plane is going to be so minor that it won't bother you. With paint or tape outline the positions of the shims on the floor and write down how much shim is required in each position. You have now constructed a poor man's surface plate from which you can set your suspension with confidence and repeatability. What's more you can re-establish it in minutes and you can take it with you.

REQUIRED INFORMATION

The manufacturer of your racer will supply you with the recommended suspension data and settings. I strongly suggest that you start there. With older cars the previous owner will probably give you a lot of information. How much credence you place in his recommendations is a question of your opinion of his competence and of his track record. You need to know:

(1) Front and rear ride height with 50% fuel and driver.
(2) Front and rear static camber at ride height.
(3) Front and rear toe in.

(4) Front castor and rear hub carrier inclination.
(5) Wheelbase.
(6) Front and rear track.
(7) Front and rear spring rate and initial shock absorber setting.
(8) Front and rear sway bar diameter and lever arm length.
(9) Front and rear wing angle of attack.

Don't delude yourself for an instant by believing that anyone carefully aligned the car before you took delivery.

RIDE HEIGHT

Ride height is defined as the height of a reference point at each corner of the chassis above the ground plane. It is critical from several aspects: if it is too low, the car will bottom; if it is too high the vehicle's center of gravity will be high. Further, ride height determines the static inclination of the suspension links and therefore the static location of the insantaneous centers and roll centers as well as the nature of the camber curves. Relative front to rear ride height has a profound effect on both suspension and aerodynamic characteristics (most race cars are designed with front ride height from 1/2" to 3/4" lower than rear ride height). Ride height also determines the effective amount of suspension travel—the lower the ride height, the less suspension travel is available in bump.

The static ride height at which you adjust your suspension is unlikely to be the ride height at which the car runs—even on a smooth track. If your car features wings, the downforce is going to progressively lower the car with increasing road speed. Downforce varies as a square function of road speed and so has a profound effect on dynamic ride height—hence one reason for the progressive rate suspension systems featured on the present generation of Formula One cars.

If your vehicle doesn't feature downforce devices, then it will probably run higher than you set it—at least at one end. The ride height will also vary during braking, acceleration, negotiations of bumps, banks and hills. Due to the jacking effect of the suspension while cornering it will also vary in corners. However, we have to have some reference height from which to set the suspension and static ride height is all that is available.

I set ride height and cross weight before doing the static alignment and bump steer. While adjusting cross weight, the ride height may vary slightly from side to side (very slightly unless something is bent). Due to the nature of shock absorbers it is almost impossible to get ride height

Figure (87): Use of Carpenter's Level & Shims to Establish a Level Alignment Surface

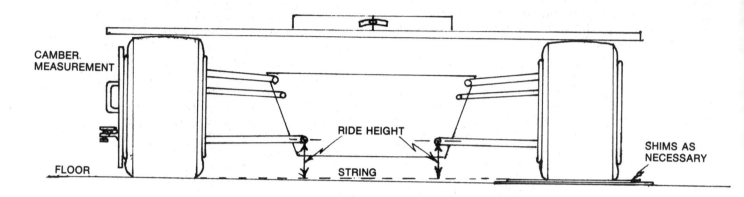

measurements to repeat closer than 1/16". By doing ride height and cross weight first you will make all of your adjustments at final ride height, will avoid some confusion and won't have to do it all over again. Before starting, back the shock absorber adjustments all the way off, clean and oil the spring adjusting threads, disconnect both sway bars and inflate the tires to hot running pressure. Life will be more pleasant if you convert the usual ride height reference distance from the bottom of the tub to the floor to some easily reached point such as an inboard suspension pivot bolt. We spend enough time grovelling on the floor as it is.

SPRINGS

Since we adjust both ride height and cross weight by moving spring perches up and down, this is a good place to discuss those properties of the springs which effect chassis alignment. Comments will relate directly to the common coil spring. Since a spring is a spring is a spring, the concept is the same for torsion bars and leaf springs.

Any spring is designed to provide a certain resistance per unit of deflection. For suspension springs this is usually expressed as so many pounds per inch of spring compression and referred to as the "spring rate". It is important to differentiate between "spring rate" and "wheel rate". Spring rate is the amount of force necessary to compress the spring itself one inch while wheel rate is the amount of force necessary to move the wheel one inch into bump. Because the wheels are located outboard of the springs (and may also be inclined), the laws of leverage ensure us that wheel rate will always be less than spring rate.

In addition to being designed to achieve a given rate, each spring is designed to compress to a certain height under a given load. This is actually the starting point for spring design and can make life a lot easier for the racer who is acquainted with the basics of spring design. For example, the front spring of the 1973 McRae GM 1 Formula 5000 car has a rate of 390 pounds per inch. At its installed height of 7.50" it supports a load of 280 pounds to achieve equal ride height on the left front and the right front, by definition, the distance between the upper and lower spring attachments must be equal, so all that we have to do is adjust each spring perch on the shock absorber so that the distance from the

center of the lower mounting bolt and the bottom of the spring perch is equal. Measure from the center of the mounting bolt, not from any reference on the shock absorber body as the locations of adjusting knobs and the start of spring perch threads tend to vary. Having done this, we can adjust ride height to the desired dimension by moving the left and right spring perches an equal number of turns. In achieving equal ride height (within the manufacturing tolerances of spring mounting points and spring loaded heights) we are also achieving equal cross weight within the same tolerances. This only works when left and right springs are designed to the same loaded height. Lately most of the springs supplied by the manufacturers have been very close. If all of the front springs for a given car are designed and manufactured to the same load at height but with varying rates and free lengths (and the same is true of the rears), spring changes can be made by carefully measuring the platform height and the car will return to its original ride height and cross weight without the necessity of going back on the scales. This can be a real god-send during testing. This is also a good time to lay away the prevalent myth that varying the spring rate will vary the static corner weight. It will not unless ride height is changed at one corner.

ADJUSTING THE RIDE HEIGHT

To set the ride height, install the driver and a half load of fuel, roll the car onto your level area and start measuring to a string stretched across the shims with which you established the level area—not to the floor. Since you started with the spring perches equalized, adjust left and right sides in equal increments to keep things level. It helps to mark one point on each spring adjustor with a felt pen so that you can keep track of where you are going. Count the turns of the spring perch, not the spring. Since you will have to jack the car up to rotate the spring perch, you must roll the car at least eight feet in one direction or the other and jounce it before you measure again. Otherwise the track change will get to you and your measurements will not be accurate.

When you jack the car up the wheels move into droop and the track decreases. When you let it down again the wheels hit the ground before ride height is reached and the friction of the rubber with the ground prevents the tire from

136

moving all the way sideways to its original position. Rolling the car while jouncing it will return everything to normal (including the shocks). This is also necessary when adjusting camber. If you must change the ride height a lot it will effect the static camber which should be kept within 15 minutes of arc as you go along.

CORNER WEIGHT

Whatever method you use to determine corner weight, make sure that the scales are zeroed before you start. I use my own weight to check the fronts and that plus a friend to check the rears. With the various lever devices, which operate on the principle that the amount of torque required to lift a wheel just clear of the ground is directly proportional to the weight of that wheel, the "just clear" point is usually measured with some sort of feeler gauge. The tires must be clean and smooth. Don't try to use the feeler gauge on a concrete or black top surface—use masonite or metal shims.

If the loaded heights of the springs are right on and if you have kept the adjustments ever—and if the chassis is straight— and if the design doesn't contain too much offset weight, the corner weight should be very close. If it isn't, now you get to adjust it.

The basic rules here are that weight transfers diagonally and that you compress a spring (raise a spring perch) to jack weight into that corner of the car and into the corner diagonally opposite. Naturally the weight which is transferred comes from the other two wheels. If you wish to transfer weight from one side of the car at both front and rear to the other, then you must raise the light side of the car at both ends (or lower the heavy side). Equal turns won't work in this case as spring inclination is never the same at the front and the rear. While adjusting corner weight note what effect on turn on each spring has and write it down—it will come in handy.

For road racing we are trying to achieve a square car—i.e. you want the weight of the left front wheel to equal that of the right front wheel and the weight of the left rear wheel to equal that of the right rear wheel. With single seaters you should be able to get it to about five pounds. With cars in which the driver's weight is offset from the centerline things are somewhat more difficult. Normally it is more important to have the front wheel weight equal and to accept a discrepancy at the rear.

Intentional weight jacking is for oval tracks (mainly) and for people who know what they are doing (always). Depending on how hard and how deep your driver brakes, you may want to carry a few extra pounds in the inside front wheel to prevent locking it.

Variations in wheel weight are due to: offset weight in the design of the vehicle, constructional variation in spring and suspension link attachments, chassis twist or to variations in spring loaded height—not to variations in spring rate. From now on, if ride height variations are made by equal adjustments at each side of the car, corner weight will remain close. Lock the spring perches and tape the threads to prevent stone damage. Reconnect both front and rear sway bars making sure that there is no pre-load in them.

RIDE HEIGHT BLOCKS AND DUMMY SHOCK ADSORBERS

This is a good time to construct a set of ride height blocks so that you can support the car at ride height with the springs and shocks removed while bump steering. Sawed off 4x4s are cheap and effective. You will need four at whatever dimensions it takes to hold the car at ride height. Paint them red and store them somewhere so that they will not be used for drill press blocks or firewood. It is also a good time to construct a set of dummy shocks from bar stock, telescoping tube or whatever. These should have three positions allowing you to set the wheels at full droop, ride height and full bump with the car on jack stands. They will come in very handy when you have to make exhaust systems, body parts, ducts, plumbing runs, etc. Paint and store them as well.

CASTOR

Begin the static alignment procedure by setting the front castor. Castor is designed into the front suspension to provide a self-centering effect into the steerable wheels by ensuring that the line projected through the upper and lower outboard ball joint centers is always ahead of the tire contact patch. It also promotes straight line stability and provides steering feel to the driver.

Most racing cars are designed with between 2½ and 4½ degrees of positive castor. Not enough leads to very light steering, insufficient self return action and straight line instability. Too much makes the steering heavy, gives excessive wheel camber while steering and makes the steering response slow. Getting the castor even from left to right is more important than getting it exact.

MEASURING CASTOR

There are two ways of measuring castor. The classic method involves mounting a castor gauge on the wheel or hub, placing the front wheels on swivel pads, turning the wheel twenty degrees toward the opposite side of the car, zeroing the gauge, turning the wheel back through center and twenty degrees the other way, re-zeroing the gauge and reading the castor. In the absence of castor pads, twenty degree chalk lines on the floor will do just as well. In the absence of swivel pads, apply the brakes while turning the wheels and you'll never know the difference. It is worth noting that most race cars have about eighteen degrees of steering lock and that is plenty close enough to twenty for our purposes.

The alternative is to use a bubble level to directly measure the angle of inclination of the ball joint axis. On some cars this is a simple matter of laying the level across a convenient machined surface (the surface must be normal to the ball joint axis) and reading the number. Needless to say, the wheel must be in the straight ahead position. On other cars, some sort of fixture must be made.

ADJUSTING CASTOR

Castor is normally adjusted by varying the length of the front upper leading arm which is provided with a rod end bearing for the purpose. On cars which feature inboard suspension, the top rocker arm can often be shimmed back and forth to adjust castor. Alternatively castor adjustment is provided on the lower wishbone. Some designers have now decided that there is no need to adjust castor and no adjustment is provided. I think that they are probably close to being right—until the car gets crunched.

Every time that you change the castor you will also, due to the laws of geometry, change the camber and the toe in so that a certain amount of chasing one's tail is inevitable. Again, measuring the effect that one turn of castor adjustment will have on castor, camber and toe will eventually enable you to develop a feel for what compensations are necessary.

CAMBER

Camber is used to achieve the best compromise for the size, shape and pressure distribution of the tire's contact area with the road under the varying dynamic conditions that exist on the race track. It is measured with some sort of spirit level capable of being read to five minutes of arc (see Figure 89). The best gauge available is the Dunlop unit but a good one is very easy to make. Camber is adjusted on the upper transverse link at both the front and rear of most race cars and on the front lower wishbone on most cars with inboard front suspension. Depending on the configuration of the individual vehicle the actual mechanics of adjustment vary quite a lot.

It is vital to make sure that you are getting a true reading and have not placed the gauge on a bent portion of the wheel rim or against the tape that holds the wheel weight on. If your wheels are bent to the point where they do not provide a good reference, or if your gauge will not fit onto the wheel place it against the tire either far enough forward or far enough back to miss the bulge at the bottom of the tire and make sure that you do not have one end of the gauge on the raised letters that say Goodyear or Firestone. Usually the adjustment provided at the front will be in increments of 1/2 turn of a rod end bearing (about .025" in linear measurement) so that you won't get any closer than five minutes of arc and the left and right won't come out exactly even. Don't worry about it.

TOE-IN

The classic reason for toe-in at the front of the vehicle is to ensure that the wheels cannot toe out under braking loads. This reason went away with rubber suspension bushings and narrow based wishbones.

Front toe-in (or toe-out) is now provided to promote straight line stability and/or to influence corner entry characteristics during the transition period when weight is being transferred. In order to minimize scrub and rolling resistance it should be very close to zero on present generation racing cars (1/32" one way or the other covers the range).

Rear toe-in (never toe-out) is used to promote stability under acceleration loads and is basically a function of available torque. It can be as little as 1/32" per wheel on a Formula Ford and as much as 1/8" per wheel on a Can-Am car.

MEASURING TOE-IN

In order to accurately measure toe-in it is necessary to construct some sort of rectangle with sides parallel to and equi-distant from the centerline of the vehicle. Optical alignment gauges or trammel bars are perfectly satisfactory for measuring front toe. As they are capable of determining only the total convergence of a pair of wheels it is possible and probable that their use at the rear may result in correct total toe-in with unequal results at each side of the vehicle. This will cause the vehicle to crab down the track at an angle to its path of motion—an undesirable state of affairs. Besides, both optical gauges and trammel bars are hard to carry and lead to a certain amount of grovelling in the dirt. The optical gauges are also expensive.

A pair of aluminum I beams don't cost much and fit nicely on the trailer. String is even cheaper and more portable.

To find the centerline, carefully measure the centerpoint between the front lower control arm pivots on the chassis and mark the exact center on the lower crossmember. Repeat the operation at the rear (which may require some ingenuity) and you have found the effective vehicle centerline, referenced to the suspension pick ups. Extend a tight string beneath the level car, exactly under the two center points (use a plumb bob) and you have a reference from which you can construct your rectangle.

All that is necessary is to establish two reference lines, one on either side of the vehicle, which are parallel to and equi-distant from the already established centerline. There are many equally satisfactory ways of doing this. Aluminum I beams are my favorite method in the shop but string is more satisfactory on the road (the I beams get bent in transport and people are always borrowing—and damaging—them). The best string system consists of attaching a couple lengths of square tubing to the chassis with pip pins and drilling small holes for the string at the proper locations so that to set up the parallelogram you have only to pin the tubes in place, stretch the string through the holes and go. A certain amount of ingenuity is required to find a place for the tubes and a high degree of accuracy is called for in laying out the holes but you only have to do it once for each car. The height of the strings should be at or near hub centers at each end of the vehicle. The lateral distance from centerline should be great enough to allow the insertion of a camber gauge without dismantling the parallelogram. If you are going to construct your parallelogram by stretching string between jackstands or whatever, after you have it done re-measure the whole thing referencing the brake discs or the hub ends so that you can quickly reconstruct your reference in the field. The same holds true of the aluminum I beams. Figure (88) shows the parallelogram referenced to centerline and Figure (89) shows it referenced to hub ends. When one is in a great rush with an unfamiliar car, the parallelogram can be set up by referencing directly off the discs or hub ends to start with. Assuming that the suspension links were bench built to dimensions as previously described, the only errors will be in the machining tolerances of the hubs and uprights which will be closer than we can measure.

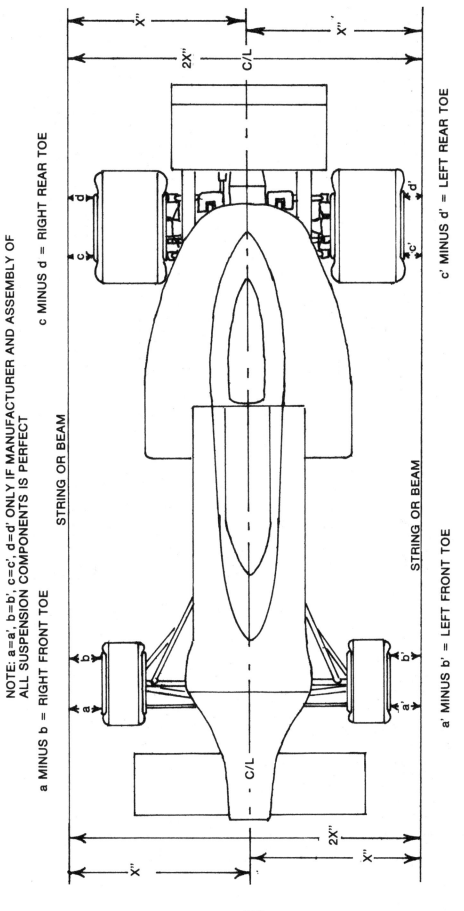

NOTE: a=a', b=b', c=c', d=d' ONLY IF MANUFACTURER AND ASSEMBLY OF
ALL SUSPENSION COMPONENTS IS PERFECT

c MINUS d = RIGHT REAR TOE

a MINUS b = RIGHT FRONT TOE

STRING OR BEAM

STRING OR BEAM

c' MINUS d' = LEFT REAR TOE

a' MINUS b' = LEFT FRONT TOE

Figure (88): Toe-In Parallelogram Referenced From Vehicle Centerline

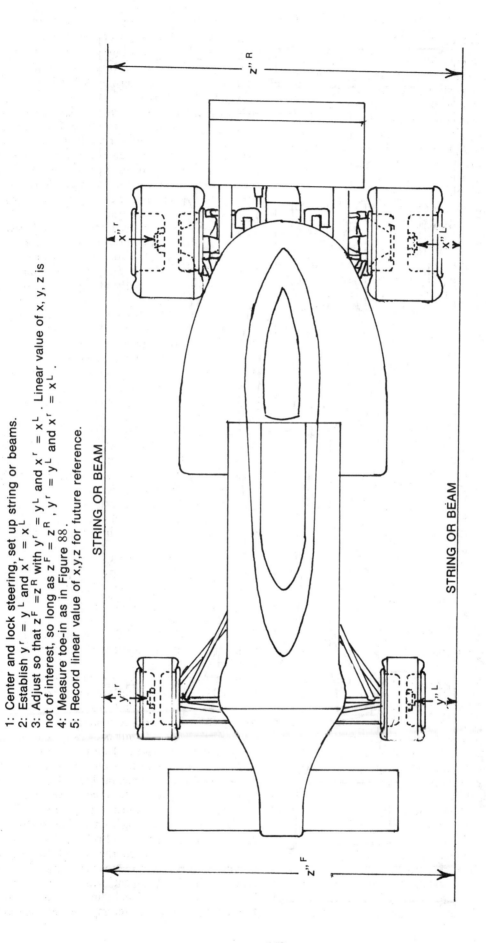

1: Center and lock steering, set up string or beams.
2: Establish $y^r = y^L$ and $x^r = x^L$
3: Adjust so that $z^F = z^R$ with $y^r = y^L$ and $x^r = x^L$. Linear value of x, y, z is not of interest, so long as $z^F = z^R$, $y^r = y^L$ and $x^r = x^L$.
4: Measure toe-in as in Figure 88.
5: Record linear value of x,y,z for future reference.

STRING OR BEAM

STRING OR BEAM

Figure (89): Toe-In Parallelogram Referenced From Axle Ends or Brake Discs

140

ADJUSTING TOE-IN

Before setting front toe-in, make sure that the steering rack is still centered and that the track rods are of equal length. Determine toe by measuring from the reference line to a machined surface on the wheel rim as close to the O.D. of the rim as possible. Make sure that the wheels are tight. A machinist's rule or a vernier caliper is the best measuring device. Keeping the track rods equal in length, adjust the front toe-in to specification. When you have finished, remove the steering column from the spline on the pinion and center the steering wheel.

If we have assembled the suspension links properly to specified lengths, the wheelbase will now be equal on each side of the car. Check it anyway and make whatever adjustments might be necessary by shortening or lengthening the rear upper and lower radius rods together—maintaining the rear hub carrier inclination. Plus or minus 1/8" is plenty close enough for wheelbase and I would rather see the drive shafts in line with each other and normal to the centerline with the wheelbase slightly off than see the wheelbase exact and the driveshaft askew.

Rear toe-in is measured exactly as is the front. If you are lucky it will be adjustable by left and right hand threaded rod end bearings with parallel link systems or by means of a rod end bearing at the rear outboard end of the lower wishbone. If you are not lucky, rear toe-in is adjusted by varying the length of the lower radius rods which screws up everything else.

Again, as at the front, changes in toe effect camber and upright inclination so we will once again chase our tail for awhile. It should be noted that once the final static alignment is completed, the changes normally made in track tuning will be of small enough magnitude so that we can safely ignore this inter-relationship—i.e. you can change camber at the track without rechecking castor and toe.

When you finish with the rear toe-in adjustment, go back and check all of the static alignment before proceeding with the bump steer. Also make sure that all attachment bolts and rod end bearing check nuts are tight.

BUMP STEER

With the static alignment complete, it is time to worry about bump steer. There are at least as many ways of measuring bump steer as there are racers who know about bump steer. Some are valid and some are not. I will describe the methods I have found best. First I will attempt to explain what bump steer is all about.

Visualize the front suspension in end elevation with the steering rack positioned ahead of wheel centerline. If the steering track rod is in line with and of equal length to the upper control arm (this is usually not practical due to constructional limitations), then the wheel can move up in bump and down in droop without changing the relative length of the steering track rod and toeing the wheel in or out. However, if we move the rack mounting on the chassis up (or the steering arm on the upright down), then when the wheel moves up in bump, the track rod moves in a relatively longer arc than the upper control arm toeing the wheel out in bump and in in droop. The reverse is true if we move the rack mounting down or the steering arm up. This is front

bump steer (or toe steer) and can cause instability under braking, under diagonal bump situations and in the transition stage of corner entry. It is adjusted out by changing the relative height of the steering track rod joints. Figures (90), (91) and (92) illustrate.

The situation is similar at the rear. Once again visualize the standard rear suspension layout. If the forward pivots of the upper and lower radius rods are the same transverse distance from the vehicle centerline as the inboard pivots of their corresponding transverse links and if the rear hub carrier is vertical and if the upper and lower radius rods are parallel to the ground, then, as the wheel moves up and down, the law of similar triangles prevails and no change in toe-in occurs. For structural reasons the forward pivots of the radius rods, particularly the lower radius rod, are often located well outboard of the onboard pivots of the transverse links. Additionally either squat or anti-squat provisions in the geometry angle one or both of the radius rods from the horizontal. In these cases the triangles are no longer similar and the toe-in will change with vertical wheel movement. The widely held theory that the use of parallel links for the lower rear transverse links will prevent rear toe steer is not true. Rear bump steer is adjusted out by varying the inclination of the rear hub carrier with relative upper and lower radius rod length.

Bump steer occurs when one or more wheels move up or down and the toe-in of that wheel changes. Roll steer is a similar and related phenomenon which occurs when the vehicle rolls due to the centrifugal forces generated when cornering. To state that under roll conditions the outside wheel (relative to the corner involved) moves into bump while the inside wheel moves into droop is an oversimplification. However this statement is valid enough for our present purposes and so we are going to make it. If, in the case of the rear suspension, the bump steer is such that each rear wheel toes in in bump and out in rebound, then as the car rolls, both rear wheels will point into the center of the corner which will increase rear wheel adhesion to some degree. This is called "roll understeer". Should the opposite condition occur—i.e. the rear wheels toe out in bump and toe in in droop, then as the vehicle rolls both rear wheels will point out from the center of the corner decreasing rear wheel adhesion. This is the dreaded "roll oversteer" and must be avoided.

Some contention exists among designers as to the desirability of some slight amount of roll understeer in the racing vehicle. Those who favor it hold that by allowing (or forcing) the rear wheels to point into the corner as the vehicle rolls, rear wheels adhesion will be increased thus increasing total adhesion and cornering speed. They also point out that roll understeer is an automatic correction factor when the vehicle is momentarily displaced from straight line travel by wind gusts, one wheel bumps and the like.

Those who are against the incorporation of roll understeer in circuit racing cars design point out that a car with a significant amount of roll understeer has some fairly unusual corner entry characteristics (when the vehicle is steered into the corner the rear wheels are also steered in instead of following the fronts with the result that the driver is liable to have some difficulty in following the intended line). Further the rear wheel steering tendency increases with roll

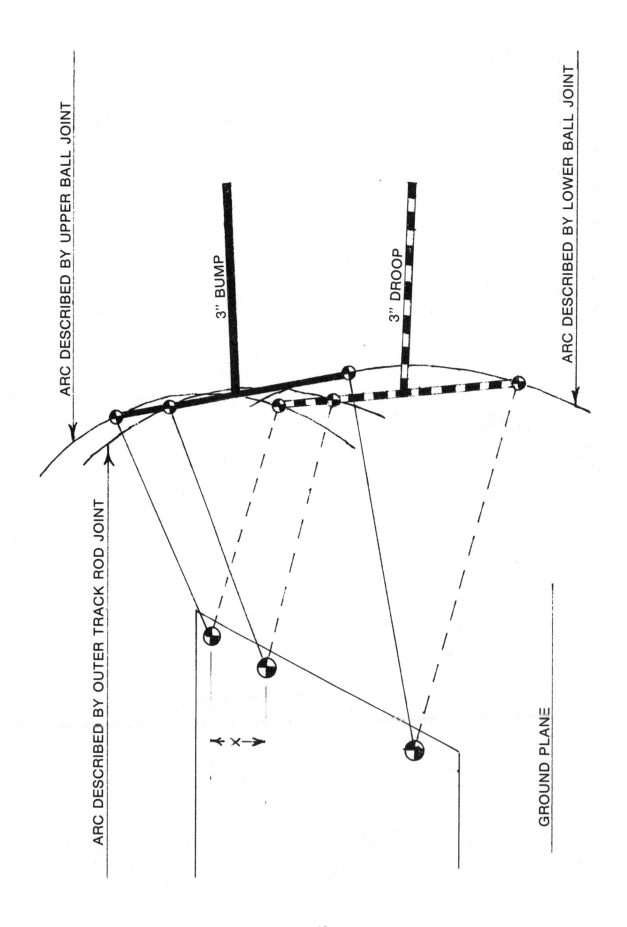

Figure (90): Steering Geometry Correct Resulting in Zero Bump Steer (Rack is Forward of Wheel Center)

142

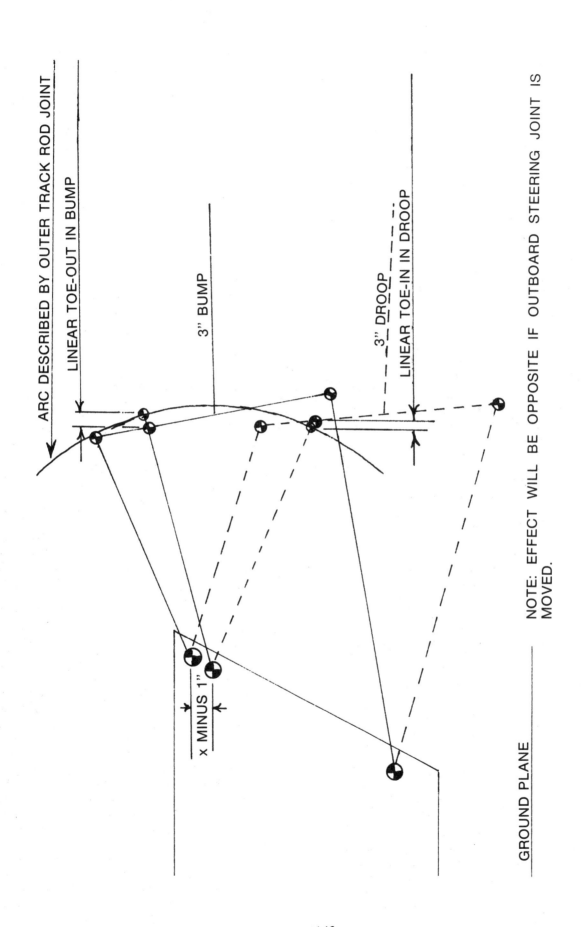

Figure (91): *Steering Rack Moved Up 1" From Correct Position Resulting in Toe-Out in Bump and Toe-In in Droop Caused by Dissimilar Arcs of Motion*

143

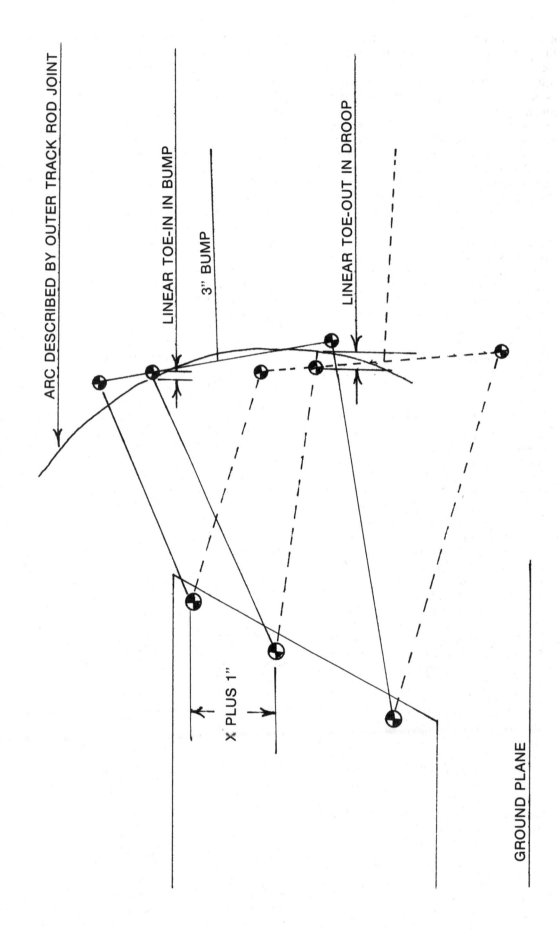

Figure (92): Steering Rack Moved Down 1" From Correct Position Resulting in Toe-In in Bump and Toe-Out in Droop

144

(and bump) making the period when the car is assuming its roll attitude a little unpredictable—as well as the period when the roll is decreasing as the car exits the corner under acceleration. Additionally, should it be necessary to quickly change direction—as in a series of "S" bends—the car can become quite unmanageable.

My own opinion is that anything that tends to decrease the driver's direct control over the vehicle is bad. I am willing to admit that a certain amount of roll understeer can increase a car's total adhesion and therefore its speed through long, smooth and fast corners. However, I feel (and test results have confirmed my opinion) that on most road circuits roll understeer is an overall detriment to lap time and to driveability.

To my knowledge no one has ever said one kind word about roll oversteer. This is a violently unstable condition and must be avoided. My own method is to put in just enough roll understeer to ensure that suspension compliance and normal wear cannot result in roll oversteer. This will also tend to slightly increase rear toe-in under hard acceleration—which must be a good thing.

Now that we have defined bump and roll steer and very basically explained their effects on vehicle antics, it is time to discuss the measurement and removal of whatever toe change may be present.

MEASURING AND ADJUSTING BUMP STEER

My method of measuring and adjusting bump steer consists simply of swinging the wheels individually through their range of vertical travel and measuring the change of toe-in that occurs. I remove the spring and shock absorber units from the vehicle (on some cars only one end need be disconnected), place the car on ride height blocks and lock the steering rack in its center position. I then mount a flat aluminum plate rigidly to the hub flange or brake disc. The plate has horizontal lines scribed on its surface to indicate one, two and three inches of bump and droop travel. Years ago I bought two cheap dial indicators with 2" travel (1" would be OK) and made a heavy stand to hold them. The stand is adjustable for axle center height. The indicators are positioned 17" apart because I happened to have an 18" aluminum plate. I place a hydraulic jack under the lower ball joint of the wheel in question, disconnect the sway bar, adjust the dial indicator stand to the rolling radius of the wheel, and jack the wheel up until the zero line on the plate is in line with the two dial indicators. The indicators are then adjusted to the center of their travel by moving the stand toward or away from the wheel and the indicators are zeroed. Figures (93), (94) and (95) illustrate.

I then jack the wheel one inch at a time into bump and rebound taking indicator readings at each inch of travel. The difference between the indicator readings at the front and rear of the plate is change of toe-in at that position and is recorded on a work sheet. Obviously the dial indicators are a convenience, not a necessity. A micrometer caliper or a ruler can be used with equal results. The important points of this method are:

(1) It measures one wheel at a time.
(2) It is accurate and repeatable.
(3) It is portable and cheap.
(4) It works.

The same results can be achieved by leaving the toe-in measuring parallelogram in place, swinging the wheels and measuring the change of toe against the reference strings or beams.

Bump steer can also be measured with the Dunlop optical toe-in gauge by placing one gauge against the wheel to be measured, placing the other gauge on the opposite side of the car but not touching the wheel, zeroing the gauges by moving the gauge which doesn't touch a wheel until the indicator reads zero, piling a group of friends or spectators onto the car until it moves the desired distance into bump, making sure that the gauge on the wheel to be measured is still contacting the wheel and reading the change in toe. This is the quickest method of all and is invaluable for checking out the car in a hurry.

Having determined how much change of toe-in takes place during a given wheel's vertical travel and in what direction the change occurs, it will be necessary to reduce that change to an effective zero.

At the rear this is accomplished by changing the inclination of the hub carrier from the vertical by varying the relative length of the upper and lower radius rods. To gain toe-in during bump travel (or lose toe-out) move the top of the hub carrier toward the rear of the car. Some change of toe is inevitable. Minor changes are not important but any change should be in the direction of roll understeer—i.e. the wheel should gain toe-in as it moves into bump. Usually this will result in toe-out during droop travel.

Changing the length of the radius rods to minimize bump steer will effect the static suspension settings—particularly if you adjust the lower radius rod on a car with a reversed rear lower wishbone. This leads to a tedious round of readjusting everything. There is no cure for this, although you will gain a certain amount of feel for it with experience. When you have finished with one rear wheel measure the upright inclination with a bubble gauge, duplicate it on the other wheel and you will be very close. Make a permanent record of both rear uprights' inclination when you are all done and the job will take 1/10 the time when next you have to do it.

Front toe change is adjusted by changing the relative heights of the inboard and outboard track rod ends—either by moving the rack housing up and down or, preferably, by shimming the outboard rod ends at the steering arms. Shimming is practical only if the outboard joints are rod ends. In addition to offering easy bump steer adjustment, the rod end bearing is structurally preferable to the stock ball joints beloved by small race car constructors. This is always a worthwhile substitution.

There have been all kinds of clever micrometer type bump steer adjustors made—mainly on Team Lotus and Team Surtees cars. They are very clever and a convenience but I don't consider them worth the time it takes to make them. Shims are pretty quick.

In addition to moving the relative heights of the track rod ends, it is possible to change the steepness of the front toe change curve (but not its characteristics), by changing the length of the track rod. Longer track rods will soften the curve. In order to change the length of the track rod while retaining the static toe-in setting, it is necessary to change the effective length of the rack itself. Unless the rack end

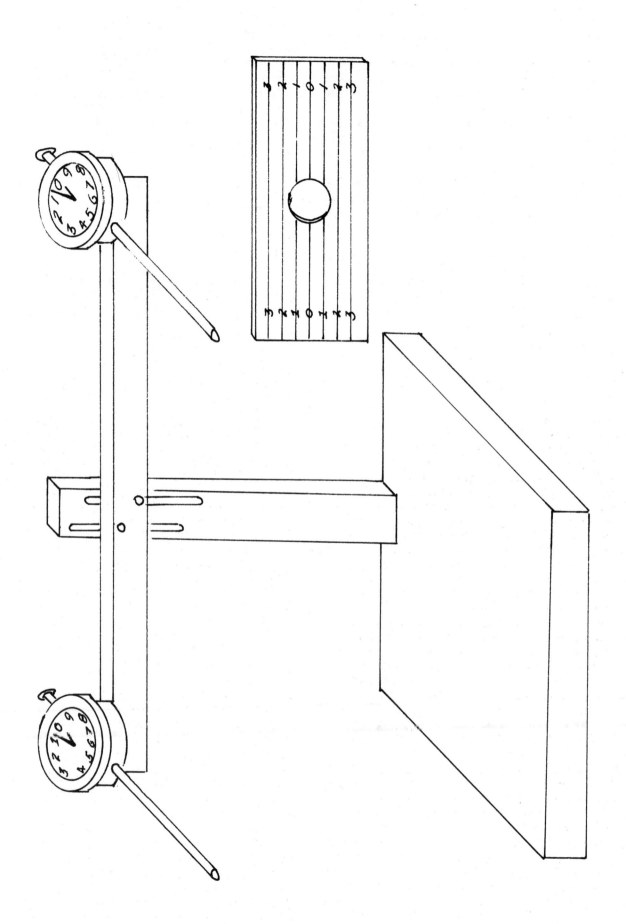

Figure (93): Bump Steer Equipment

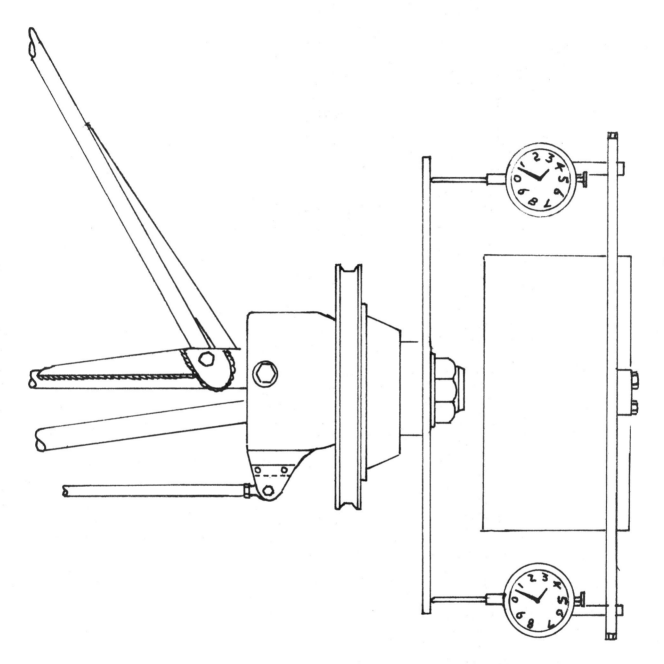

Figure (94): Bump Steer Equipment - Top View

147

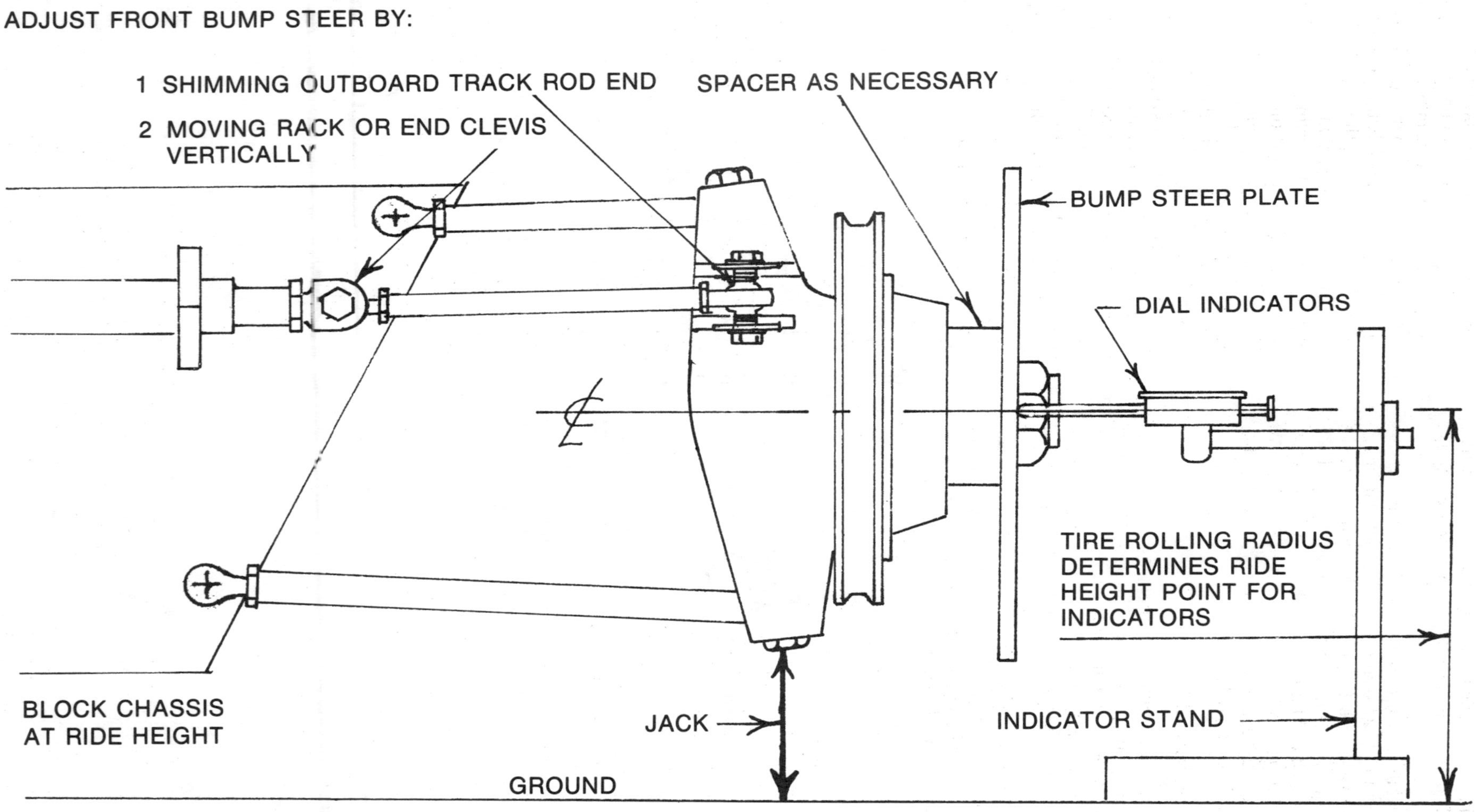

ADJUST FRONT BUMP STEER BY:

1 SHIMMING OUTBOARD TRACK ROD END

2 MOVING RACK OR END CLEVIS VERTICALLY

SPACER AS NECESSARY

BUMP STEER PLATE

DIAL INDICATORS

TIRE ROLLING RADIUS DETERMINES RIDE HEIGHT POINT FOR INDICATORS

INDICATOR STAND

JACK

GROUND

BLOCK CHASSIS AT RIDE HEIGHT

Figure (95): Bump Steer Equipment - End View

148

clevis or ball joint is threaded onto the rack this is usually impractical, and, unless the designer really screwed up it is not necessary.

Things being what they are, both front and rear toe steer curves are liable to change dramatically in the last inch of both bump and droop. As the suspension seldom reaches these positions, this is not a cause for undue worry. If the suspension does reach full bump the situation will be so dire that a little toe change won't effect the outcome. When the suspension reaches full droop—which happens surprisingly often—the wheel is unloaded.

FINISHING THE JOB

When you are all done bump steering go back and check the static alignment—if any sizable changes were necessary to bring the bump steer in it will have to be reset. Statics can be put back to specification without affecting the bump steer. Just to be sure, recheck the corner weight and re-zero the sway bars.

Now record in the permanent vehicle log what effect 1/2 turn of adjustment has on camber, castor, toe-in and rear bump steer, the effect of one turn of spring perch movement (both front and rear) on all four corner weights, the effect of one turn of upper radius rod length on rear bump steer and the effect of .031" of shim on front bump steer. Also figure out how many turns you moved each link in the course of aligning the car and applying this figure (converted to linear measure) to the installed length of each link so that you have a record of the final length of each link on the car. This will get you back to standard in a hurry in the event of damage.

The last move in recording your suspension alignment is make a quick end elevation and side view sketch showing the inclination of every link on the car and the installed height of each spring perch. If nothing else the angular data will provide data for speculation.

Before considering the job done, go back over every fastener in the suspension system, including the check nuts on the various rod end bearings. Make sure that everything is centered, tight and, if necessary, safety wired. An out-of-context tip is that it is much easier to figure out which rod ends are left handed if you install all of the left and right handed links so that the left hand bearings are on your left as you face the link.

Leave the shocks backed off until you get to the race track—they'll last longer if the car is transported with them on full soft.

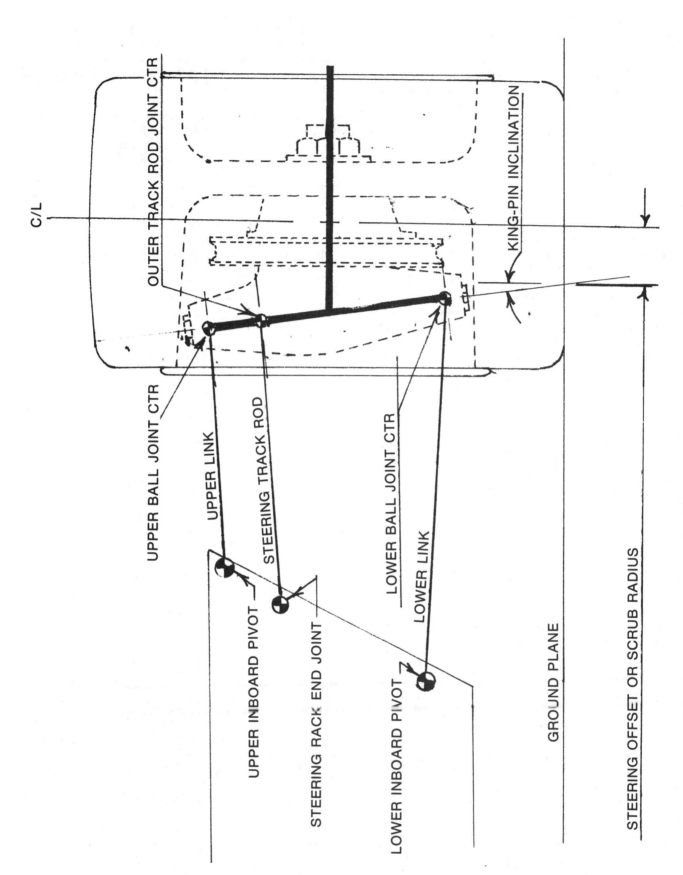

Figure (96): Front Suspension Terms & Representations Shown in End View

150

CHAPTER ELEVEN

ELECTRICS, INSTRUMENTS AND FUEL CELLS

I have a tendency to look upon anything having to do with electricity and/or electronics as a disaster waiting to happen. This is probably due to my basic inability to understand the subject. However the number of DNFs due to electrical failure of one sort or another leads me to suspect that I am not alone. In one respect—competence—I rank among the least qualified people around to make recommendations concerning the electrical system of the racing car. My rationalization for this sad state of affairs is that, having an unreasoning terror of electrical failure, I tend to be ridiculously safe. Since wire, terminal blocks and heat shrink tubing don't weigh much, my safety factors impose no significant penalty so maybe the system isn't all bad.

COMPONENTS

Smith's first law of electrical security is to use no cheap wire, switches, terminals or anything else. I buy the best aircraft certified switches (Micro Switch), the best low tension wire (Packard or, better yet, double insulated aircraft surplus), the best High Tension Wire (Autolite 7SH Silicon) and I use only aircraft certified terminals and terminal blocks.

SOLDERING

I am fully aware that the claims made for the best of the low tension solderless terminals are valid and that the aircraft industry now uses precious little solder. I am just reactionary enough to believe that a properly soldered connection is better than the solderless terminals that I can afford. Use resin cored solder and an electric soldering iron (the pistol grip Weller gun is best). The soldering iron must be both clean and well tinned. Clean it by dipping in a resin cup or rubbing on a piece of sal-ammoniac. Good terminals are supplied pre-tinned so precious little solder is required to make a good connection. A good mechanical joint is required. Excess solder not only looks nasty and increases the electrical resistance of the joint but the excessive heat necessary to deposit too much solder may well embrittle the wire leading to breakage at some later time. The right amount of heat, applied at the right place (on the back side of the terminal, not on the wire) with the right amount of solder (very little) will produce a perfect joint every time. Practice makes perfect. If you decide against soldering use only aircraft certified Sta-Kon solderless terminals—the automotive stuff is junk. In either case vinyl heat shrink tubing will not only improve the appearance of the assembly but will go a long way toward preventing short circuits.

WIRE

I use 14 gauge low tension wire for just about everything. In Los Angeles I buy really trick double insulated wire on the surplus market—(MS25471, MS27110, M.1-W-7139, MS17331, MS17332, MS17410, and MS18104). You can lay this stuff in the middle of a pretty good fire and nothing happens. In the hinterlands I use Packard wire. Autolite 7SH Silicon high tension wire has a stainless core which requires the use of stainless solder and flux available from any electrical supply house or from Sears. Prest-O-Lite, Packard and Accel also make good silicon insulated high tension wire but the Autolite is more resistant to heat (and more expensive). Use only soldered on spark plug terminals with silicon rubber boots. I used to use Rajah terminals exclusively but they are almost impossible to get on—or off—our hidden spark plugs these days and so I have switched to the standard press on terminals. It is vital to make sure that the little screw—on terminal on the end of the spark plug is tight—with pliers—not with your fingers.

I refuse to use any type of low tension wire terminal that is not positively secured. My definition of positively secured is an eye terminal held on to a stud or a bolt by a self-locking nut. I regard the popular blade and bullet type quick connect terminals as a crime against nature. Where quick connects must be used—as in wiring lights on long distance cars or brake lights on Can-Am cars, I use surplus Cannon Plugs.

WIRE RUNS

Care must be exercised in running wires from the dash to wherever they go to and come from. A little forethought and planning helps. It is desirable to have as few wires as possible (if it's not there, it can't fail) and to run the wires that we must have together in a harness as far as possible. It is also desirable to protect the wire bundle with vinyl heat shrink tubing or spaghetti and to secure it to the chassis, or to a convenient tube with adell clamps or cable ties at frequent intervals—like every six inches or so. Use a nylon or rubber grommet wherever wires pass through a bulkhead or panel. Make sure that each wire is long enough so that the terminal will not be in tension when the whole mess is installed. A short pigtail just before the terminal will remove any doubt in this matter. Once the terminals are secured (use a thin washer on each side of the terminal) I coat the assembly with silicon seal for both insulation and locking.

I tend to use terminal blocks on the rear side of the firewall bulkhead. This allows a permanent wiring installation from the dash to the firewall with easy removal and replacement of the damage prone wires at the rear of the car.

Since it takes me hours to figure out how to wire the most simple car—and I know full well that I will never be able to remember how I did it—I make a wiring diagram for each car and I color code the wires. Then I never let the diagram out of my sight until that car is no longer my responsibility. For much the same reason I use commercial vinyl number sleeves to identify the high tension leads and the distributor cap terminals.

Carrying my apprehension to perhaps ridiculous extremes, I make sure that any high tension leads which fire consecutively—such as #7 and #8 on a Ford—are isolated from each other to obviate the possibility of induction firing. I use silicon rubber boots on both the spark plug and distributor cap ends of the high tension wires and I use nylon ti-wraps on the cap and coil nipples to make very sure that the wires cannot come out. Proprietary high tension lead harness clips secured to the valve covers look good and hold the leads away from exhaust pipes, throttle linkages and such.

HEAT, VIBRATION AND QUICK CONNECTS

I firmly believe that coils, amplifiers and black boxes are destroyed by heat and vibration. Therefore they should be mounted in such a position that cooling air gets to them and they should be isolation mounted so that vibration will not shake them apart. Isolation mounts should, however, be pretty firm and will not serve as a ground. Anything that resembles a black box is certain to fail pretty frequently and should be mounted with dzus buttons or pip pins so that it can be replaced in a hurry. Better yet, one should use no black boxes.

FUEL PUMPS AND LIGHTS

Most race cars feature electric fuel pumps of one sort or another. Like coils and amplifiers, these devices like cool air and don't like vibration. It is as well to mount them as low as possible so that a positive head is present at the inlet port. They should also be as close as you can get them to the fuel source because they push a lot better than they pull. It helps to place them where you can get at them without pulling half the car apart.

All race cars now require some sort of lights—from the tail light on Formula Cars (with switch) to the full lighting system on long distance cars. Mount everything but the headlights in rubber and see if you can figure some way to do so with the headlights. If you must carry headlights around, make them useful. Provide easy aiming adjustment and take the time to set them properly. Spend some time designing the auxiliary wiring harness so that you can trouble shoot it in a hurry and replace whatever needs replacing easily.

Ground everything very well indeed. If you even suspect that a component might need a separate grounding wire of its very own, give it one.

MASTER SWITCHES AND KILL SWITCHES

All cars now require a master switch accessible from outside the car. Do not use the ubiquitous Lucas unit. It will fail. Use either an aircraft or marine "battery management switch". In fact don't use any Lucas electrical components if you can help it.

The driver must have an ignition kill switch where he can get at it in a hurry. The best place is on a horizontal steering wheel spoke so that he can reach it with his thumb while steering.

I won't mention fuses because I don't use them. If you have wired things so badly that you develop a short it is unlikely that a fuse will help. Fuses are just one more component to go wrong.

BATTERIES

Batteries are always a problem. They are also necessary—at least in road racing. I use the English Varley. If cared for and charged according to the instructions printed on the battery, the Varley is absolutely reliable. It is also small, light and plenty powerful. If charged at too great a rate it will self-destruct and you will have only yourself to blame. The Varley will start a Can-Am car about fourteen times but an external starting battery should be used whenever it is legal to do so. Use any type of plug-in device you want (welding supply house) but make the cable run as short as possible. Make sure that it is impossible to plug the starting battery in with the terminals reversed. Make equally sure that the auxiliary battery is fully charged or it will draw the onboard battery down as soon as it is plugged in. Battery terminals must be protected by some sort of nonconductive cover and the battery should be very securely mounted indeed. It should also be quickly detachable so that you can charge it in your motel room every night.

THE IGNITION SYSTEM

I will now say a very few words about the ignition system. I feel that for most pushrod engines a good coil and contact breaker system is satisfactory to about 7500 rpm. If over 7500 rpm is contemplated then a magneto should be considered. I have never found a reliable electronic ignition system. Regardless of the system chosen, the ignition cam should be trued and the individual dwell adjusted by a specialist. The ubiquitous Lucas distributor is junk and benefits greatly from a complete rework including the installation of bearings. I have my Vetex magnetos reworked by Tom Cerillo, 703 Randolph, Costa Mesa, California. I also have them rechecked every five or six operating hours.

That covers my electrical suggestions. A really neat electrical installation will not only enhance the vehicle's appearance but will add to its reliability. Many components can be bought surplus.

INSTRUMENTS

Any respectable racing car will have several instruments which the driver is expected to monitor. Most have too many. Selection and positioning was covered in Chapter Five. Since all instruments are prone to vibration damage, the instrument panel should be attached to the chassis with isolation mounts. I use manual shut-off valves on the fuel pressure line with high pressure fuel injection. I also use dash three Aeroquip line for oil and fuel pressure gauge lines even though it is both heavy and expensive.

So far as brands and face styles go I use either Smith's or Stewart Warner gauges with clock style faces. I usually use a Smith's combination oil pressure and water temperature gauge to save space and Stewart Warner for the rest to save money. The Smith's British straight pipe thread can be converted to AN by installing an AN 910-1D pipe union directly onto the gauge port. Use anti-sieze.

All new gauges should be checked for accuracy. Boiling water will test temperature gauges and an acetylene or nitrogen regulator will check out pressure gauges. Inaccurate gauges are returned to the distributor. Most gauges come with a one-year warranty which will be grudgingly honored so save the sales slip and warranty card.

Many years ago I bought a Formula Junior Cooper. It came with a Speedwell electronic tachometer. It was absolutely accurate, steady as a rock, totally dependable and neither lagged behind nor raced ahead of the engine. It required two wires to hook it up and weighed nothing. It was then and remains to this day the only satisfactory electric or electronic tach I have ever seen.

In my biased opinion there are only two tachometers worth using—the Jones Motorola mechanical/magnetic unit—which is both accurate and dependable despite its bulk—and the Smith's chronometric tach—which takes a bit of getting used to as it moves in a series of 100/200 rpm jumps and always lags a little bit behind the engine. It is smaller, lighter and cheaper than the Jones and I think that it is every bit as good. No matter what brand you decide on, have it calibrated by a good Speedometer Shop in the rotational position in which it will be mounted and use a heavy duty cable with very gentle bends. Angle drives, drive reducers and drive reversers are available at good Speedometer Shops. Mostly they come from taxi meters.

I have mixed emotions about tell-tale tachs. On the one hand the driver shouldn't over-rev the engine and, if he accidentally does, it is to his interest to tell you about it. On the other hand it is nice to know how far he over-revved the damn thing—especially if he can tell you under what load condition the over-rev occurred. I use a tell tale, but I pull it (with a magnet) 100 rpm over the red line before the car goes out so that it will not slow the needle down. I also ensure that the driver cannot re-set the tell tale.

If there were a really good rpm limiter on the market which would start to break up the ignition in a random scatter mode at a preset and adjustable rpm rather than shutting off the engine, I would use it—with a switch to render the unit inoperative in case of failure. To my knowledge there is not and so I do not.

FUEL CELLS

Fuel cells are expensive, difficult to install, remove and seal. They are very difficult to repair. They are also the biggest advance in driver safety since the hard hat. Good fuel cells are made in this country by Firestone, Goodyear, Donn Allen and Aero-Tech. Good fuel cells are made in England by Marston and Uni-Royal. Bad fuel calls are made in England by FPT. If you have a good fuel cell it will remain good until such time as it is damaged in a crash or by carelessness on your part. The only maintenance required is of the preventive variety.

The first thing to prevent is the drilling of holes in the fuel cell. This sounds ridiculous but it happens all the time. Super Mechanic is forever drilling #30 holes in the fuel cell in the course of installing brackets, adell clamps, etc. Don't let him do it! If you must drill a hole in the fuel cell container and don't have time to remove the cell, you have two choices:

(1) Remove the access plate, reach in with your hand and push the cell out of the way, install a piece of wood to protect the cell from the drill bit, drill the hole, install the rivet or whatever and tape the head. Then button up the cell and plate.

(2) With fear and trembling, using a positive stop on the drill bit, drill the hole and pray.

The next thing to prevent is chafe damage which can occur inside the fuel cell container. Theoretically the inside of the fuel cell container on your new car has been carefully cleaned and all rivet heads and sharp corners have been protected with tape. Don't you believe it! Taping of fuel cell containers is one of the nastiest jobs in racing and you cannot afford to trust either the factory or the previous owner. Remove the cells and whatever tape is installed, thoroughly clean the cavity and tape every rivet head and sheet metal seam. While you are at it make very sure that the cut-outs for cell nipples are large enough to prevent chafing the nipples and install extra protection in the form of alligator grommet and tape. Make equally certain that whatever fits into each nipple is beaded on the end and that the hose clamp that secures it is in the proper position to capture the bead.

REMOVAL AND INSTALLATION

A goodly portion of total fuel cell damage occurs during removal of the cells from their housings. This is due to two related factors—the access holes are pretty small and the people doing the job are impatient. Step one is to drain all of the fuel from the cell—otherwise an incredible mess is certain. Step two is the careful removal and labeling (so that you can get it back in again) of the foam. Step three is the removal of all of the fittings that plug into the cell and of the nut ring that holds the cell to the access plate. Now it is time to study the problem and to decide what part of the cell you really want to come out first. Tape the edges of the access hole and start fiddling and pulling. Eventually you will succeed in removing the cell without any undue force. Clean the cell and store it in a garbage can liner (the foam too) until you are ready to re-install it.

Installation is a reverse of removal. Figure out which part really wants to go in first and attack the problem logically. Brute force won't get it done. Talcum powder in copious quantities helps a lot. Once you get the entire cell inside the cavity, fiddle it around until all of the nipples are centered in their holes and there are no creases or wadded up bits of cell. Next install the foam. Never be tempted to run without the foam. A fuel cell without foam is about 50% effective in a crash. The foam must be cut away to clear one way valves and fuel outlets. A well should also be cut under the filler cap so that you can visually check the fuel level. In order to do this accurately, fill the car one gallon at a time and mark the levels in one gallon increments on a piece of wooden dowel. Fuel cell foam can be cut with a *very* sharp knife, with a hot wire or with a knife blade on a bandsaw turned up to the highest speed available. It can be cleaned by putting it through the rinse and dry cycle at your laundromat. It must be dry when it is installed.

Having succeeded in getting the cell and its foam in place within the container and having connected all of the various nipples and outlets, it is now time to attempt to install the access plate. These plates normally are installed inside the tub and form a sandwich with the meat being the fuel cell itself and the bread being the plate and the nut ring inside the cell. Goodyear and Firestone mould the nut ring integral with the cell, which is a definite advantage. In any case it is necessary to hold the nut ring in alignment with the cell, the access plate and the tub while the screws are inserted. The hot tip is to use at least four studs to align the whole mess while you are installing screws. The studs can be sawed off bolts with screwdriver slots in the unthreaded end. They should be long enough to allow you to get a good grip on them in order to pull the nut ring up into position from outside the cavity. Start all of the screws before you tighten any of them and then tighten them evenly. Marsten and FPT cells come with a "C" shaped gasket which is not necessary. I use Hylomar—sparingly—as a sealant. If you develop a leak under the head of a hold down screw (it shouldn't happen, but it does) a Stat-O-Seal will fix it. As a matter of fact, Stat-O-Seals are a good idea anyway as they also serve as a locking device.

When you have finished, fill the car all the way with fuel and check for leaks and seapages.

It is an excellent idea to provide escape holes in the bottom of the fuel cell containers for any fuel that may leak. One of the last things that we need is any quantity of fuel at all laying in the cavity. These holes should be 1/8" in diameter, loacted in the corners of the container and not covered with tape.

Keep the fuel cells full of fuel to prevent the compound from drying out.

VENTS

Everyone realizes that fuel cells must be vented. About 50% of the racers seem to install their vents in the wrong direction. As fuel is consumed, air must be able to enter the fuel cell or we will develop a vacuum inside the cell and fuel will stop feeding. This means that the very top of the cell must be vented to atmosphere. To prevent spilling fuel under acceleration with full load—or when the car is laying upside down—a one way valve must be installed. This valve should be installed so that air can enter the fuel cell but fuel cannot escape. For safety's sake it should not be mounted in

such a position that it can be torn off in an accident, but it should be mounted high.

While we are on the subject of one way valves, there are a couple of things to watch out for. We all use surplus one way valves. Most of us use the variety featuring a spring loaded swinging gate which seals with an "O" ring. Not all of the surplus "O" rings are compatible with gasoline. Take the valve apart and soak it in gas for 24 hours before you install it. Some of the springs are pretty strong. I remove them as surge will close the valve.

REPAIR

Eventually you are going to damage a fuel cell. Tape and/or epoxy isn't going to fix it. An inner tube cold patch just might work as a temporary repair—but the chances aren't good. Go to or call the nearest large general aviation airport and find out who repairs and modifies the fuel cells on the business jets and large twins. You might also look in the metropolitan yellow pages under Fuel Cells and Aircraft Repairs. When you do find a firm specializing in fuel cell repair you will probably have to snivel a lot because they are not going to want to know you. If you snivel enough they might sell you a field repair kit. Firestone might too. Aero-Tech and Allen will repair their cells. Field repair kits are great but they require reading and following the directions, the application of heat (a travel iron does nicely) and application of pressure (use your ingenuity). I carry such a kit and have never had to use it.

If all else fails, you can always repair a fuel cell (assuming that the damage is not on a corner or on a nipple) by bolting a patch on and sealing with aircraft fuel tank slushing compound. Don't get caught by the tech inspectors who would never understand.

FILLER CAPS

Fuel filler caps should be flush fitting so that they do not get torn off as you go skidding along on your head. They should also have a positive seal. The best are manufactured by Shaw and sold by Earl's Supply. They are very expensive and worth it. The worst are the flip-up "Monza" type units sold by every hot rod store. They are deadly. The second best are the screw on variety used by most everyone which seal on an "O" ring inside the cap. Spend some time lapping the threads and always use anti-sieze or you are someday going to be faced with a cap that won't come off. Be very careful not to crossthread the cap when installing it and be very sure that it is installed tight enough to grab the "O" ring or it will come off. Shaw's caps are much better.

CHAPTER TWELVE

PAINT, POLISH AND PLATING

Contrary to popular opinion, polish is no substitute for good preparation. It is, however, a valuable addition. To a great extent the final appearance of any race car is dependent upon the amount of effort put into painting, polishing and plating.

PAINT

It is necessary to be practical when it comes to painting the race car. Race cars tend to crash a lot. When they crash they have to be repainted. Even if they don't crash, they get stone chipped. This rules out lots of coats of hand rubbed lacquer. It also rules out elaborate multi-colored paint schemes. The most practical approach is no more than two colors, either polyurethane or acrylic enamel paint with a polyurethane hardener (epoxies are too difficult to touch up and virtually impossible to strip) and vinyl stick-on striping. Use the primer specified by the paint manufacturer and remember that the quality of the finished job depends largely on the preparation. Use a lot of wet or dry sandpaper and a lot of elbow grease. While a spray booth is nice, it is not necessary. A good paint job can be done virtually anywhere so long as you keep the floor saturated with water (it keeps the dust down and carries the over spray away) and it is not windy. Zoning restrictions apply and the local Fire Department is very liable to object to painting activities so it is as well to be fairly circumspect—like do it behind closed doors on a weekend.

POLISH

Polishing a race car is nobody's idea of fun—but it must be done. For plated parts and for bare alloy there is just no substitute for Simichrome. This magic paste is available at outrageous cost from motorcycle shops or at $9.00 per quart from Competition Chemicals in Davenport, Iowa. A quart will last a very busy year. A lot of elbow grease is necessary to work up the initial lustre on Cadmium plating or on bare alloy but a protective coating is deposited and subsequent jobs are much easier. The polishing must be done, however, each time the car is run.

Nothing looks worse than bare aluminum which has been allowed to corrode—except maybe magnesium in the same condition. If you can't get at it to polish it, paint it with aircraft quality zinc chromate primer. If the metal is etched first the chromate will stay on forever and it looks aerospace. Your aircraft supply house will sell metal etching chromate in Aerosol cans which makes it a one shot process on clean aluminum. The stuff works equally well on steel and mag.

There is no simple answer to the problem of keeping cast

magnesium (or spun magnesium) racing wheels looking good. There are, in fact, only two workable methods. Either have the rims machine polished (about $10.00 per wheel) and keep after them with Simichrome or paint them with a good epoxy paint in the color of your choice. If you decide to paint rather than polish, the appearance will be considerably enhanced if you polish the outside edge of the rim which involves very little work. None of the protective coatings for polished wheels work worth a damn. The best protection that I know of is carnuba based furniture or floor wax (paste) which also works well on polished tubs. It must be removed with a special remover when the time comes to re-polish.

WAX

Any good cleaner will work on painted body work. I use 409 or Fantastic because they are universally available, cheap and work well for leak checking wheels. Use a paste wax after the paint is really clean. Slipstream is the best past wax made. Classic is a close second. All of the Meguiar's products are excellent. Again much elbow grease is required.

If you can't afford good plating on suspension links, brackets and such, you have two choices—sandblast and epoxy paint or sandblast and the cheapest, nastiest flat black lacquer that you can find. The lacquer is easy to strip and repaint. The epoxy has the disadvantage that it forms a pretty flexible coating and cracks may not show through.

PLATING

If you can afford plating, don't use chrome. It is expensive; it must be baked very soon after it comes out of the bath to avoid hydrogen embrittlement and you can't weld on a chromed part without removing the chrome which is a pain. Besides, chrome will probably be outlawed in 1975 due to the danger of hydrogen embrittlement.

Cadmium plating is dirt cheap but really isn't very good except as a base for paint. It must also be baked. Cadmium requires constant polishing in order to look halfway decent and you will soon rub through the plating.

Bright nickel plating is very little more expensive than Cadmium and can be kept looking good with a rag soaked in thinner. It should also be baked. You can weld on it without stripping the part.

My favorite plating for ferrous parts is electroless or chemical nickel. While it is more expensive than bright nickel, it does not require baking. It leaves a mat silver finish similar in appearance to stainless and is really easy to keep clean.

The cost of any plating job will be drastically reduced by having it all done at once and by delivering really clean parts to the plater. Have the plater powder blast the parts before plating.

Since I don't at all enjoy polishing things and even less enjoy looking at scruffy race cars, I tend to plate every ferrous part and anodize every aluminum part on the car. It's not all that expensive ($200.00 will do a complete Formula 5000 or Can-Am car including a complete set of spares) and I feel that it actually saves money over the course of a season in that the time which would be spent polishing can be spent in more productive pursuits.

Details, such as aligning the slots in the screws holding on windshields, access plates, etc., neat plumbing, handsome wiring and safety wiring add a lot to the overall appearance of the car without taking much effort.

Spherex header paint used according to directions on sandblasted headers really works. None of the other brands do. Ignore the directions and even Spherex looks bad. Don't use a light color which will show greasy hand prints. Black is best.

Your local trim shop (or sail maker) will probably make a semi-fitted cover for your racer at a reasonable price. It will go a long way toward keeping a sharp car sharp. So will an enclosed trailer. If you intend to tow with an open trailer and a car cover, make sure that the cover fits snugly and line it with felt wherever it looks like it may touch the body or flap. If you intend to tow on an open trailer without a car cover—good luck.

Have the trim shop make an inlet cover and a pair of exhaust covers while he is at it—and use them.

Personal pride should be sufficient incentive to keep the race car looking good. Often it isn't. Every racer in the world is trying to seduce one or more prospective sponsors. From the sponsor's point of view a race car is nothing but a high speed billboard. Sponsors are not interested in scruffy billboards. This also applies to the driver, the crew and to all of the equipment. It is also well to realize that people and/or corporations with enough spare capital to consider sponsoring a race car are pretty conservative by nature. Really long hair and sandals are not appreciated in the board rooms of major corporations.

One parting comment on the appearance bit—neighborhood kids and race track spectators, cunningly recruited and sincerely appreciated have been known to work wonders.

After each practice session, and certainly after each race, the car is at best going to be covered in dust and it just may be covered in a nasty combination of dust and oil. Just as no one likes to look at a dirty car, no one likes to work on one. Dust can be blown off with an air line. A bug sprayer filled with solvent (most of us use gasoline, but we are really stupid!) will very quickly return the mess to its original pristine condition. Do not perform this act in the garage or in the paddock. Do it in the dirt and don't smoke while you're doing it.

A coin operated car wash before returning to the shop (Riverside has one in the paddock—all other circuits take note!) is the ticket after the race. Blast the water off immediately and follow up with a spray of WD-40 or the like to prevent corrosion.

Wash the tow vehicle before you get to the race track.

CHAPTER THIRTEEN

RECORDS, PAPERWORK AND ORGANIZATION

The most boring and tedious part of racing is the paperwork involved. Because it is no fun at all, it is totally ignored by about 90% of all racers. It is not ignored by the 10% of the racers who win 90% of the races.

A talk with any commercial or military aircraft engine or airframe mechanic will reveal that very stringent maintenance and modification records are kept on all individual aircraft systems. You will also learn that critical parts are both inspected and replaced according to a schedule rather than according to whim—or waiting for the part to fail. It is a long way down in a broken or non-operating aircraft. It is also a long way to the wall or the tree in a broken race car—and no parachute. Besides, DNFs satisfy neither the ego nor the bank balance.

I do not believe that total aircraft maintenance schedules are either practical or necessary for race cars. Aircraft service conditions are a lot more predictable, aircraft are much more thoroughly engineered and more history, personnel and money is available for their care. We can, however, make reasonable approximations. We'll start with log books.

LOGBOOKS

In addition to the sanctioning body's vehicle log book, three logs should be kept—one for the chassis, one for the engine or engines and one for the transaxle (which can be combined with the chassis log if desired). I keep my logs in standard shorthand pads because they are convenient and cheap. I keep the running log starting from the front of the pad. Starting from the rear I have the appropriate parts list and specification data. In that way my briefcase contains everything that I am liable to need to know about the car.

The engine log should contain approximate engine hours, cylinder leak rate readings taken after each event, a record of operating temperatures and pressures, replacement of components, condition of components when replaced, and inspection records. The log should include engine build specifications listing all clearances, critical dimensions, timing specifications, torque specifications and dyno sheets. This way you won't have to guess how long a set of pistons or valve springs has been in there—or when the last time you replaced the rod bolts was. You will know how much your cylinder leak rate has increased in the last two races. Your engine builder can give you a pretty good idea of when to check or replace what. After a couple of seasons of keeping good records you should be able to tell him.

It is virtually impossible to make even generalized recommendations about frequency of inspection and replacement since engines (and driver treatment of them) vary too much. I would not, however, advise running any highly stressed pushrod engine for more than six hours between teardowns. In professional racing I usually install a fresh engine for the last day of qualifying and, assuming that it is still healthy after the race, do a leak down check, lash the valves, check the timing and valve lift, replace the spark plugs and use it for testing and initial practice for the next event. It then comes all the way down. If it is financially feasible it is a giant help for your spare engines to be complete and ready to install—intake, pumps, pan, flywheel, clutch, engine plate and all.

The back section of my engine logs contain a whole lot of part numbers for just about every component. This not only saves time but allows you to locate parts on the telephone (all counter salesmen require part numbers in order to check stock) and further allows you to dispatch inexperienced people after the part that you need with some hope that they will return with the correct widget.

The transaxle log is almost a pleasure. The back lists all of the manufacturers' part numbers for bearings and seals and the front is a running history. The back also contains my gear and spare parts inventory. The running history merely contains hours on critical components—ring and pinion, pinion bearings, output shaft and input shaft plus backlash readings and inspection results.

Since the transaxle log tends to be short, I usually include the final drive components—hours on universal joints, drive shafts, and clutch discs plus clutch disc thickness readings.

The chassis log is the most extensive because it includes lap charts and records as well as maintenance history and a giant parts list. In the back I list every bolt, bearing, seal and circlip on the car by location, manufacturer and part number. The front is a running history of the vehicle, lap by lap and event by event. Each adjustment, every driver comment and every observation is listed as is each inspection, modification, adjustment and replacement. At the track I keep a rough log on a legal pad and a clip board so that I don't have to be neat about it. Every evening I bring the permanent log up to date and go over the day's events in detail with the driver and the mechanics. Then I draw up a work list—in detail—and go over it verbally with the crew so that everyone knows exactly what he has to do, in what order I want it done, and when it has to be finished. This ensures that everything will get done and done in time. It also allows the establishment of a valid priority schedule so that you don't spend a couple of hours polishing wheels and end up without enough time to change the ring and pinion.

Maintenance logs have one hidden advantage. Eventually the time will come to sell your racer. Complete records cannot fail to impress the prospective buyer. They will not replace a winning record—but they will contribute to establishing one.

CHECK OFF LISTS

Now comes the most difficult of all items to convince people to use—the check off list. Before any commercial or military aircraft is turned over to its pilot a detailed check off list is completed and signed off by a highly qualified crew chief—or by a group of specialized mechanics and technicians. The reasoning behind this requirement is very simple—the machine is so complex that no human being can be expected to remember every detail. The potential penalty for oversight is awesome. Hence the check off list as a written aid to human memory. The racing car is a lot less complex, but the crew is liable to be not only less qualified, but also in some stage of mental and/or physical exhaustion. The consequences of forgetting something are about the same. How often have you heard, "I thought you (or he) checked it" after the gubbin has fallen off or the car ran out of gas? It is my conviction that a reasonably detailed check off list, conscientiously used will prevent 40% of all DNFs. Carrying forgetfulness to a ridiculous extreme I know of one highly competent crew who lost a Can-Am race because, somehow, no one fueled the car before it was gridded. I know of another, also highly competent, crew who sent a Formula 5000 car into the main race with no oil in the transaxle.

The general check off list which I use religiously appears at the end of this chapter. Obviously some of the details should be changed to suit specific cars—but it works. It will only work if it is used.

The check off list must be viewed as an aid to human memory, not as an insult to the intelligence, dedication or virility of the people working on the car. Human nature being what it is, the more experienced the crew, the more trouble you will have convincing them to use it. The effort is well worthwhile and provides a really outstanding opportunity for you to develop your powers of persuasion and tact. Dale Carnegie should be in THIS business!

While speaking of "the crew" I should point out that not only would racing not be possible without the long suffering individuals who build, maintain, modify, repair and transport the cars but also that a large percentage of the worthwhile performance modifications and constructional techniques as well as virtually all of the design changes tending toward ease of maintenance and inspection are originated by mechanics and fabricators. These changes are often made after considerable opposition from designers and/or team managers. To my way of thinking this opposition is very wrong.

I feel that it is vital for the physical and spiritual well being of the racing organization, whatever its level of resources and experience, that each member of the team should know that any reasonable idea that he may come up with will be evaluated by the "man in charge" and, if it is a good idea and feasible, that it will be tried. Since the majority of bright ideas are bound to be less than brilliant and since a notable percentage of even the best inspirations inevitably fall into the "nice but not necessary" class, a certain amount of judgement and tact is called for on the part of the man in charge.

ORGANIZATION

Speaking of the man in charge, there MUST be such a person. The committee approach may work in some fields (to which I have not been exposed) but I am willing to categorically state that it does not, never has and never will work in motor racing. The ideal Team Manager is a semi-benevolent dictator willing to listen to the advice and ideas of all of the men working with him but absolutely insistent upon making and implementing his own decisions. That these decisions and the results thereof will inevitably be the subject of derision and second guessing by all and sundry is inherent in the nature of the job.

At any rate, everyone involved with the car will have his own very strong ideas on the best method of accomplishing virtually every goal. Some of these ideas will be valid. Some will even be practical. Incorporating the best and most feasible of them—and giving credit to the originator—will not only result in improved vehicle performance, or more sleep, but will also boost crew morale which has to be a good thing. I keep a list of the modifications that I, or anyone else, have thought up to do to the car. Weekly I go over the list and rearrange the priorities. Whenever a spare few minutes looms on the horizon, the list is consulted and priority #1 is started. It's amazing how many mods get done in the course of a busy season. It's even more amazing that I didn't see the need for most of them the first time I saw the car.

Each day contains 24 hours. Each week contains 7 days. Each month contains 4 and a bit weeks. Each year contains 12 months. Some totally unreasonable number of the resultant eight thousand seven hundred and sixty hours in each year can be consumed by work by the racer. Theoretically zero hours should be spent on non-productive work and the productive work should be so brilliantly conceived and scheduled that you will always be on time, get lots of sleep, eat three good meals every day, have a perfectly prepared car, be first car in line for tech, first car on the track for each practice session, win all of the races, become rich and famous and spend all of your spare time beating off prospective sponsors and lovely ladies. This is unlikely.

C. Northcote Parkinson (wonderful name and even better job title) assures us that work will inevitably expand to fill the time available for its completion. Where motor racing is concerned I emphatically disagree with the inevitable portion of the statement. I will, however, admit that there is a very strong tendency for Parkinson's law to prevail. This tendency is due only to human frailty (laziness, lack of foresight or poor planning), not to the nature of motor racing. A glance through the garage area of any professional race will reveal that a certain small percentage of the crews are always ready ahead of time—really ready. A study will further reveal that these same crews tend to spend very little time running around in circles, that they get to eat real meals, that they spend practice periods practicing, that their cars are ready to race when they arrive at the race track, that they seem to have a plan before something goes wrong and that their reaction time to the unscheduled and unexpected tends to be very good. These same crews get a reasonable amount of sleep, even though they tend to spend the evening hours working rather than partying. A study of the race results will show that these organizations tend to be very successful. The key word is organization.

The most important part of organizing a racing operation has to do with scheduling the work to be done to fit the time, personnel and resources available. This problem is not unique to racing. Experience helps, but it never becomes easy. The key is to make out a priority list on a daily (or, at the track, hourly) basis and then to stick to it. It helps to assign tasks to the people most competent to carry them out so that the only man who knows how to set up a ring and pinion is not out chasing parts or polishing wheels when he is needed at the rear of the car.

It all starts in the shop—the timeworn saying that if it isn't ready to race when it arrives at the race track, it never will be, is only too true. It is equally true that there is very little valid reason for it not to be ready when it arrives and even less for it to arrive late and still be in the tech line when practice starts. Failures of this nature are invariably traceable to hours spent in idle chatter which should have been spent in productive work—or by attempting the impossible—or by figuring that it was OK at the last race and finding out Friday night that it won't shift.

The work list should be prepared immediately after the race when the whole crew, driver included, are still together. Detailed inspection should take place upon arrival at wherever you are going to work and the worklist should be modified to suit whatever the inspection reveals. Parts should be procured NOW. Actually, they should have been on hand to start with and only their replacements should have to be obtained. Work also starts now. The time for R&R is before the next race, not after the last one.

CARE AND FEEDING OF THE DRIVER

The driver's mental attitude is crucial. This attitude will be a lot better if his car is first in line for first and all subsequent practices—especially if it is not just in line, but really ready to race. Few things put your hero off worse than to hear his rivals thundering around while his chariot is on the jackstands because you didn't do your job—or to go out and immediately return to the paddock because some stupid detail wasn't attended to. One of the few things that will put him off worse is to hit the wall on the first lap because the tires weren't pressured or the pads were installed backwards. This is, if anything, even more true of the inexperienced driver who needs all of the practice he can get in the very limited amount of time available at amateur races.

Drivers make mistakes. This is a fact of life. Drivers are called upon to make a great many decisions in the course of a lap around a race track. Often they have nothing more than intuition upon which to base their decision. There are mistakes and then there are stupid mistakes. The results can be equally disastrous. It is easy to forgive ordinary mistakes (he will make fewer of these as he gains experience). It is less easy to forgive stupid mistakes. Ranting and raving at the driver will achieve nothing worthwhile and may achieve lots that is not worthwhile. When you feel that you must have a heart to heart with your driver—or with any member of the crew—do it in private and do it quietly.

CARE AND FEEDING OF OFFICIALS

Officials can be very officious—especially if you feel that they are wrong and you are right. Again, ranting and raving is not going to get the job done. It is perfectly true that the level of competence of some of the officials appointed by some sanctioning bodies is subject to some doubt. Regardless of your opinion of their competence, their probable ancestry and/or sexual habits, you have elected to play their game on their playing field and, like it or not, you are going to play by their rules. It is up to you to be familiar with their rules and to abide by them—otherwise you don't get to play. Bad manners at registration, tech or in the pits will at best result in a long delay and, at worst, will get you thrown out. As usual, delays are best avoided by getting there early and by being ready when you get there. If the officials are on your side you are going to have a much easier time when you eventually wind up in trouble.

Even though you have four hours time between practice sessions and only one hour's work to do, do it now and rest or birdwatch later. You never know what you are going to find when you start to work. Finding out that you have to drop the pan after you have spent three hours birdwatching can ruin your whole day.

The fuel pump often has a long line (if there is a fuel pump). The time to fuel your car is immediately after the practice session or heat, not five minutes before the race.

SPARE PARTS

One last list should be mentioned—the spare parts list. Whether we are talking about a major long distance race team or a one-man Formula Ford effort, there will be a quantity of spare parts. A Formula Ford has just damn near as many parts as a Formula One car. Financial resources being what they are it is inevitable that you will frequently not own the spare part that you need. When this happens either you make it, you improvise it, you borrow it or you buy it. It is not, however, inevitable to discover that the part which you do own—and desperately need—is at home under the work bench. Hence the spare parts list.

Figuring out what spare parts you should have is not very difficult. Figuring out which of the spares that you need you can afford to have and placing a financial priority on them is something else again. A number of racing teams cease to exist each fall. Often their spares can be bought very reasonably—especially if you know someone.

Packing spare parts is the bane of the racer's existence. However there is no way out—it must be done. If you give the problem some serious thought, by expending some preseason time and a moderate amount of cash, it can be done efficiently. I recommend at least one eighteen drawer metal bin (about 43"x11"x11" with 5-1/2"x3-1/2"x11" drawers). This should be encased in a stout wooden box with a removable front to keep it from being destroyed. It will neatly contain, in labeled isolation, all of your fasteners, Aeroquip and AN fittings, jets, electrical bits, bearings, seals, shims, etc. Small parts, (nuts, washers, jets, cotter pins, etc. should be placed in 4"x8" commercial plastic bags secured by rubber bands. Plastic spark plug tubes are also handy containers for small bits. Buy a used bin if you can find one. Thus in one fell swoop you have all of the little bits and pieces which are easily lost, left behind and/or mixed up. Put handles on the wooden box and one strong man can lift it in or out of the tow vehicle and it makes a good place to put the tool box.

Another box should be made to carry all of your gears which will otherwise become hopelessly mixed up and quite probably damaged. I favor an egg-crated box with each slot carrying a gear set. Larger sections accommodate rings and pinions, bearings, shims, forks, etc.

Most other spares will fit into surplus ammunition boxes which are readily available in various sizes, waterproof and cheap. Paint them your color, number them and label the top and two adjacent sides with the contents (so that you can always read the label, almost regardless of position. Within the ammo lockers it pays to place smaller parts in cardboard cartons to prevent damage.

Whenever possible suspension spares should be carried assembled and built to dimension. The time to build up your spare hubs and uprights into assemblies is before you need them—not after the crash.

One last word on spares—if each member of the crew doesn't religiously put parts back where they belong, the best system is quickly reduced to chaos. It also helps to keep a small notebook to record parts used (so that they can be replaced) and parts which were needed but not on hand (so that it won't happen again).

What to do with the nuts, bolts and washers that you take off the car while working on it so that you can find them again when the time comes is easily and economically solved by a muffin tin which costs like nothing and provides up to twelve separate compartments. Dixie cups, cottage cheese and yogurt cartons are helpful for the bigger parts.

We all sometimes suffer from the forest and trees problem. When the car is all together and sitting on its wheels it is best to take a few hours and go over it, system by system and component by component, looking for faults. Is everything that can be removed or destroyed by vibration (coils, black boxes, instruments, oil coolers, etc.) isolated in some way? Are all electrical and hydraulic lines adequately protected from chafing, interference and off-course excursions? Electrical and plumbing runs have a way of chafing against or being interfered with by things that weren't installed or even considered when the car was wired or plumbed. Will the sway bars and suspension links clear the body, brake lines, water lines and exhaust under all conditions of wheel movement? If each member of the crew looks the completed car over in detail with the specific objective of spotting potential trouble, the chances of being embarrassed at the track are pretty slim.

CHAPTER FOURTEEN

THE END

That's it. As I stated in the beginning there is no magic to good preparation. Due to our imperfect understanding of the immutable laws of physics as applied to vehicle dynamics there is a certain black art to the science of tuning. But that is another subject. Good preparation is hours of hard work, meticulous attention to detail, a lot of planning and a certain amount of foresight. The rewards are safe race cars, relatively economical racing, personal satisfaction and, above all, winning races. That should be enough.

VEHICLE SPECIFICATION   DATE _____ EVENT _____

START	Spring	Bar	R.H.	Camb.	Cast.	Toe	Shock	Bump R.	Tire/P.	Weight
LF										
RF										
LR										
RR										
FINISH										
LF										
RF										
LR										
RR										

BUMP STEER

	LF	RF	LR	RR
3				
2				
1				
0				
1				
2				
3				
Shim				
Pin Inclination				

WING

	Ft	Rear	R'
START			
AIRFOIL SECTION			
HEIGHT			
FINISH			
AIRFOIL SECTION			
HEIGHT			

TRANS

	DIFF.	BIAS	I	II	III	IV	V
START							
FINISH							

Notes

PRE-RACE CHECK OFF LIST

I Steering

Wheel centered and secured _____
Shaft to pinion bolt in groove, nut tight _____
Rack mount bolts tight _____
Rack end clevises tight and locked _____
Rack length checked_____
Track rod bearings centered and checked for play_____
Track rod jam nuts tight _____
Rack end clevis bolts tight _____
Steering arm bolts tight _____
Steering free, lock to lock _____
Rack roller adjustment locked _____
Pinion hold down tight _____
End play checked _____

II Front Suspension

Hub bearings checked for play _____
Hub retaining bolts torqued _____
Drive pins torqued _____
Hub seals checked_____
Upper and lower ball joints checked, adjusted, locked _____
Upper and lower ball post nuts tight _____
Upper wishbone attach bolts tight_____
Lower wishbone attach bolts tight_____
Upper and lower shock bolts tight _____
Sway bar attach bolts tight _____
Sway bar link bolts tight _____
Sway bar bearings centered, jam nuts tight _____
Shocks adjusted_____Bump_____Rebound _____
Spring perches locked, threads taped_____
Front substructure attach bolts tight_____
Front wings adjusted to_____. Adjustments locked _____
All rod ends checked for play, jam nuts tight _____
Shock tops secure and locked _____
Race rubber mounted, pressure set_____
Wheel nuts tight and safetyed _____

III Front Brakes

New Pad sign on steering wheel _____
Race pads installed _____
Caliper bolts tight and wired _____
Bridge Plate bolts tight and wired_____
Discs centered_____
Discs checked for cracks and run out_____
Disc and pad slots cleaned_____
Top hat to hub flange screws tight _____
Brakes bled, bleeders tight and dry_____
Seals and unions checked under pressure _____
Master cylinder bolts tight _____
Reservoirs full, caps tight, rag in place _____

IV Cockpit

Fire extinguisher charged, mounting tight _____

Fire extinguisher flag in place _____

Safety harness bolts secure _____

Throttle cable attach to chassis and pedal secure _____

Throttle cable jam nuts secure _____

Throttle stop adjusted and locked_____

Clutch stop adjusted and locked _____

Bias bar stop nuts locked, bearing free _____

Master cylinder rods free, jam nuts locked _____

Pedal bolts secure _____

Tach cable tight and taped _____

All instrument/switch lines and wires secure and insulated _____

Shift linkage adjusted, lubed and secure _____

Mirrors adjusted and secure _____

Cockpit cleaned _____

Seat secured and locked _____

V Electrical

Battery fully charged_____volts_____

Battery connections secure and instulated _____

Battery hold down secure _____

Electric pumps functioning _____

Tail/brake lights functioning and secure _____

VI Rear Suspension

Rear substructure attach bolts secure _____

Upper radius rods in_____position _____

Lower radius rods in_____position _____

All radius rod bearings checked for play, jam nuts tight _____

All radius rod bearings centered _____

Upper and lower clevis pins centered, locked, tight _____

All radius rod bolts tight _____

Upper and lower transverse link bearings centered _____

Transverse link bearing jam nuts tight_____

Transverse link bearings checked for play_____

Transverse link bolts tight _____

Shock eye bolts tight_____

Shocks adjusted_____bump_____rebound _____

Spring perches locked, threads taped_____

Hub bearings checked for play _____

Hub retaining bolts torqued _____

Hub seals checked_____

Drive pins tight _____

Sway bar attach bolts tight _____

Sway bar link bolts tight _____

Sway bar bearings centered, jam nuts tight _____

Engine mount bolts tight _____

Bell housing bolts tight_____

Race rubber mounted, pressure set_____

Wheel nuts tight and safetyed _____

VII Rear Brakes

Race pads installed _____

Caliper bolts tight and wired _____

Bridge plate bolts tight and wired _____

Discs centered _____

Discs checked for cracks and run out _____

Disc and pad slots cleaned _____

Top hat to hub flange screws tight _____

Brakes bled, bleeders tight and dry _____

Seals and unions checked under pressure _____

Brake and clutch flex lines checked for damage and secured _____

VIII Transaxle and Clutch

Clutch free play checked _____

Clutch disengagement checked, adjustment locked _____

Ring and pinion checked _____

All plugs tight and wired _____

All unions checked for leaks _____

Cooler mounts secure and checked for cracks _____

Universal joints checked (drive shafts) _____

Output shaft bolts tight _____

Drive shaft checked for twist _____

Drive shaft spline collars tight _____

Shift linkage U-joints checked _____

Shift linkage pins and locks checked _____

All gears engaging _____

IX Engine

Oil level checked, cap tight _____

Water level checked (engine running), cap wired _____

Race plugs installed (no new plugs) _____

Plug wires tight and clear of headers _____

High Tension leads tight in cap and coil _____

Valves lashed _____

Water pump belt and pullies checked _____

Oil pump belt and pullies checked _____

Fuel pump belt and pullies checked _____

All fuel-oil lines and unions checked _____

Water hoses and clamps checked _____

Radiator/oil cooler cores and ducts clean _____

Exhaust checked for cracks _____

Header bolts tight and wired, gasket checked _____

Collector bolts loose and locked _____

Valve covers tight and wired _____

Throttle linkage checked and lubed _____

Throttle return springs checked _____

Fuel cam lubed _____

Fuel mixture set _____

Race fuel on board _____

Fuel fillers secure _____

Engine fired, leak checked, oil and fuel pressure OK _____

X Body and Rear Wing

All Dzus buttons and body pins locked _____
Rear wing mounts checked _____
Rear wing bearings centered and locked _____
Engine air intake cleaned _____
Catch tanks emptied _____

XI Grid Check

Tire pressure checked _____
Tire valves tight, valve caps installed _____
Wheel safeties in place _____
Tires cleaned _____
Mixture set _____
Fire extinguisher safety removed _____
Master switch ON _____
Body Dzuses and pins in place _____
Safety harness tight and locked _____
Tear off visors in place _____

XII In Pit

Spare dry rubber, aired _____
Rain rubber, aired _____
Jacks _____
Wheel removal tools, spare wing nuts _____
Air tank and gauge _____
Oil, water, fuel and funnels _____
Tape _____
Signal boards _____
Spare visors _____
Tool box _____
Fire extinguisher _____
Spare front wings and tube _____
Spare nose _____
Rags _____

	Date	Date	Date	Date
Transaxle Build				
Clutch arm clevis spacing checked				
Clutch arm clevis pin cotter pin in place				
Throw out bearing OK				
Input shaft bearing and seal OK, circlip in place				
Input shaft bearing carrier bolts locked				
Oil pump inspected				
Oil pump screen cleaned				
Oil pump drive and driven gear circlips in place				
Pinion bearing(s) inspected				
Pinion bearing carrier bolts locked				
Ring and pinion backlash				
Carrier pre-load				
Pinion Spacer ring and pinion depth marking				
Input and output shafts magnafluxed				
Output shaft bearings and seals inspected				
Output shaft circlips in plac				
Shift forks inspected and aligned				
All gearbox bearings inspected				
Fifth gear thrust ring checked				
Shift rails aligned				
Detents checked and locked				
Shift linkage bearings/circlips inspected				
Shift linkage universal joints checked				
Shift linkage adjusted and locked				
All gears tried				
Side covers torqued				
Oil added front				
Oil added rear				
Dranin, filler and screen plugs wired				
Reverse lock out functioning and plug wired				

SOURCE	TITLE
Earl's Supply Co. 14611 Hawthorne Blvd. Lawndale, Calif. 90260	Earl's Supply Co. Catalog - $1.00
Standard Pressed Steel Co. Precision Fastener Division Aerospace Fastener Sales Jenkintown, PA. 19046 and Santa Ana, Calif. 92700	"SPS Bolts for the Aerospace Industry" and "SPS Reference Guide to Self Locking Nuts"
Machine Design Reader Service Dept. Penton Building Cleveland, Ohio 44113	"Machine Design Fastening and Joining Reference Issue" Volume 41 No. 21 $2.00 plus postage
ARP Inc. 531 Spectrum Circle Oxnard, CA 93030	THE engine and drive line fastener people 1997 Catalog
Earl's Performance Products 189 West Victoria Street Long Beach, Calif. 90805	THE high performance plumbing people, Earl's also stocks AN BOlts, Dzuses, plate nuts etc. Earl's performance Products Catalog
Coast Fabrication Inc. 17748 Sampson Lane Huntington Beach, CA 92647	THE source for AN and NAS and specialized hardware in general Coast Fabrication Catalog
Helicoil, Inc. Insert Products Div. Danbury, Conn. 06810	Bulletin 800-A - Helicoil Standard Insert and Helicoil Screw-Lock Insert
Dzus Fastener Co. 425 Union Blvd. West Islip, N.Y. 11795	Dzus Fastener Catalog and Installation Manual
B.F. Goodrich Co. Aerospace and Defense Prods. 500 South Main St. Akron, Ohio 44318	Catalog #8-7542NS - Rivnuts
Waldes Kohinoor, Inc. 47-16 Austel Place Long Island City, N.Y. 11101	Waldes Tru- Arc Retaining Ring Technical Manual
Loctite Corp. Newington Corp. 705 N. Mountain Road Newington, Conn. 06111	Loctite Technical Bulletins

Table Two — Useful Catalogs and Publications — PLUMBING

SOURCE	TITLE
Aeroquip Corporation Jackson, Michigan 49201 and Burbank, Calif. 91502	Catalog #105 - Aircraft Catalog Catalog #106 - Teflon Hose, Fittings and Assemblies Aircraft Service Bulletin ASB-61-601 - Lightweight engine Hose
Earl's Performance Products 189 West Victoria Street Long Beach, Calif. 90805	THE high performance plumbing people Earl's Performance Products Catalog
Earl's Supply Co. 14611 Hawthorne Blvd. Lawndale, Calif. 90260	Earl's Supply Co. Catalog - $1.00
Parker Seal Co. Culver City, Calif. 90230 and Cleveland, Ohio 44100	Catalog #5700 - "O" Ring Handbook

Table Three—Useful Catalogs and Publications - Riveting and Welding

SOURCE	TITLE
Allstate Welding Equipment Distributor	Allstate Instruction Manual and Catalog
Eutectic Welding Alloys 40-40 172nd St. Flushing, N.Y. or Eutectic Distributor	Maintenance Welding Data Book
Cherry Rivet Division Townsend Company Santa Ana, Calif.	"Cherry Rivets" and "Cherry Tool Catalog"
USM Corp. Fastener Division Shelton, Conn. 06484	"Flush Break Pop Rivet Catalog" "Closed End Pop Rivet Catalog" "Blind Rivetting Handbook"
Avdell Corp. 10 Henry St. Teterboro, N.J. 07605	"Avex Rivet Catalog"

SOURCE	TITLE
Baker Precision Bearings Grundy Ave. Long Beach, Calif.	Knowledgeable rod end and spherical bearing distributor. Catalog
Aurora Bearing Company 970 So. Lake St. Aurora, Illinois 60506	First quality rod end and spherical bearings with excellent technical advice. Catalog
Coast Fabrication Inc. 17748 Sampson Lane Huntington Beach, CA 92647	Very Hi-Tech rod end and spherical bearings from exotic materials. Catalog
Thompson Industries,Inc. Manhasset, N.Y.	Thompson Nnylined Bearings
Marlin- Rockwell Co. Div. of TRW, Inc. Jamestown, N.Y. 14701	MRC Bearings Catalog #60
INA Bearing Distributor	INA Catalog E301–Needle Bearings and Needle Cages
The Timken Bearing Co. Canton, Ohio	Catalog #670–Master Design Catalog and Timkin Design Manual and Engineering Journal
Chicago Rawhide Co. 900 N. State St. Elgin, Illinois 60120	Chicago Rawhide Co. Catalog #457017

Table Six—Useful Catalogs and Publications - Gearbox and Final Drive

SOURCE	TITLE
Lisle Corp. 807 Main St. Clarinda, Iowa 51632	Lisle Magnetic Plugs, Catalog P 71
The Apex Machine and Tool Company P.O. Box 952 Dayton, Ohio 45401	Apex Catalog #48—Universal Joints and Assemblies
Dana Parts Co. P.O. Box 321 Toledo, Ohio 43601	Spicer Universal Joint Parts Catalog #J300P
Automotive Parts Division Borg-Warner Corporation Franklin Park, Illinois	Current Car and Truck Universal joint Catalog
Rockwell Standard Corp. Local Distributor	Rockwell Standard Universal Joint Layout and Selection Data Book
Carl A. Haas Automotive Imports 1732 First St. Highland Park, Illinois 60035	Hewland Transaxle Manual and Parts List
B.R.I.T.S. 28921 Arnold Drive - F6 Sonoma, Calif. 95476	Excellent source for Hewland, X-Trac and Staffs Gears and transaxle parts - AP distributors and general racing candy store. Catalog

Table Eight - The Candy Stores

A lot has changed since I wrote PREPARE TO WIN. All of the information is still valid and little has been learned about race car *preparation* in the ensuing 22 years. The sources for obtaining the parts that we need *have* however changed. Racing has grown to the point where it now supports a number of very well stocked candy stores manned by very knowledgeable people. My favorites in alphabetical order:

Armadillo Racing Enterprises
1783 N.E. Bently Drive
Bremerton, WA 98311

B.R.I.T.S.
28921 Arnold Drive - F6
Sonoma, CA 95476

Earl's Sevi-Shop #3
302 Gasoline Alley
Indianapolis,IN 46222

Essex Parts Services Inc.
2530 Industrial Park Blvd.
Cumming, GA 30131

Frey Racing
1911 Plymouth Street
Mountain View, CA 94043

Pegasus Auto Racing Supplies
2475 South 179th Street
New Berlin, WI 53146

Transatlantic Racing Services Ltd.
5730 Chattahoochee Ind. Park
Cumming, GA 30131

We also have a comprehensive source book/product directory:

RACE PAGES - Youngson Publishing Company
P.O. Box 8127
La Jolla, CA 92038
(619) 459-2304

Table Nine—Books That Cost Money But Are Worth Buying

PUBLISHER/AUTHOR	TITLE AND COMMENTS
Macmillan C.A. Overbey	"Aircraft and Missile Design and Maintenance Handbook" The bible—covers just about everything that we need to know about fastening, joining, sheet metal work, hydraulics and electrics.
Aero Publishers, Inc. Available at any aircraft supply house	"Standard Aircraft Handbook" Don't be without this pocket sized compilation of how to do almost anything.
L. Pazmany P.O. Box 1051 San Diego, Calif. 92110	"Light Aircraft Construction for Amateur Builders" Specifically how to build Mr. Pazmany's airplane, but loaded with useful shortcuts in sheet metal technique. Contains the best words ever written on fibreglass.
Dover Publications, Inc. New York Ira A. Abbot	"Theory of Wing Sections" The wing profiles listed are no longer useful to us, but the theory is.
Dover Publications, Inc. F. R. Shanley	"Weight-Strength Analysis of Aircraft Structure" Useful only if you want to design your own vehicle. If you do, it is invaluable.
McGraw-Hill Book Company David J. Peery	"Aircraft Structures" The bible of structures. Again useful only if you want to design or understand design.
Aviation Maintenance Foundation Box 547 Berhoud, Colorado 80513	"Airframe and Powerplant Mechanics Airframe Handbook" How to do it in great detail. Buy it!
John Wiley and Sons, Inc. Colin Carmiahcel, Editor	"Kent's Mechanical Engineers' Handbook" The basic Mechanical Engineering reference. You should own either this work or "Machinery's Handbook".
Robert Bentley, Inc. Costin and Phipps	"Racing and Sports Car Chassis Design" Very, very basic, but still the best in print.
Robert Bentley, Inc. Terry and Baker	"Racing Car Design and Development" Disappointing but well worth reading. Probably not worth buying.
Superintendent of Documents U.S. Government Printing Office Washington, D.C. 20402	FAA AC No. 43.13-1A. Acceptable Methods, Techniques and Practices - Aircraft Inspection and Repair - 1972. $3.70 Postpaid.

AIRCRAFT QUALITY FASTENERS:
  Earl's Supply, 14611 Hawthorne Blvd., Lawndale, Calif.
  Local Van Deusen Aircraft Supply House
  Local Albany Products Supply House
  Local Aircraft Supply House
  Local SPS Distributor
  Local Surplus Outlets

PLUMBING EQUIPMENT:
  Same as fastener sources, plus
  Local Aeroquip Distributor
  Local Caterpillar Distributor (believe it or not!)

BRAKES AND BRAKING SYSTEMS:
  Girling
    Contact nearest branch of Lucas Electrical Systems.
    If all else fails, write Mr. P. Anthony Cross
        Girling Ltd.
        200 Manchester Ave.
        Detroit, Michigan

  Lockheed
    Automotive Products, Ltd.—Competitions Dept.
    Leamington Spa, Warwickshire, England
        or
    Scott Instruments Co.
    3734 West Slausen
    Los Angeles, California
  Airheart
    All American Racers, Inc.
    2334 South Broadway
    Santa Ana, California
  Ferodo
    ELSCO, Inc.
    1843 East Adams St.
    Jacksonville, Florida
        or
    Haas Auto Imports
        or
    Scott Instruments
  Mintex
    Haas Auto Imports

CLUTCHES:
  Borg and Beck
    Automotive Products, Ltd.
        or
    Haas Auto Imports
        or
    Scott Instruments

THROTTLE CABLES:
  Meyer Engineering Co.
  Speedway, Indiana   (317) 291-8838
    These people make ACCO cables to order quickly and
  reasonably. They are the best cables available.
        or
  Local boat dealer for Morse "Red Jacket" cables.

SAFETY HARNESSES AND FIRE SYSTEMS:
  Simpson Safety Equipment Co.
  22638 South Normandie Ave.
  Torrance, Calif. 90502

LUCAS INJECTION PARTS (AND IGNITION):
  Lucas Electrical Services
  30 Van Nostrand Ave.
  Englewood, N.J. 07631

LUCAS IGNITION PARTS AND TESTING SERVICES
(INCLUDING OPUS):
  Lucas Electrical Services
  Walnut Street
  Compton, California

MELMAG WHEELS:
  Chuck Jones Racing
  Ohms Way
  Costa Mesa, California

BANANA WINGS:
  Jim Busby
  Costa Mesa, California   (714) 497-1092

KONI SHOCK ABSORBERS:
  Kensington Products, Inc.
  150 Green Street
  Hackensack, N.J.

ROAD SPRINGS:
  Rockwell International Corp.
  Mechanical Spring Division
  500 East Ottowa St.
  Logansport, Indiana

GOOD QUALITY SMALL SPRINGS:
  Local Associated Spring Distributor

"O" RINGS, STAT-O-SEALS:
  Local Parker Seal Co. Distributor

ROD END AND SPHERICAL BEARINGS:
  NMB Corp.
  9730 Independence Ave.
  Chatsworth, California
        or
  Troutman, Ltd.
  3198 L Airport Loop Drive
  Costa Mesa, Calif. 92626

TAPERED ROLLER BEARINGS:
  Local Timken Distributor

BALL BEARINGS:
  Local MRC Distributor

NEEDLE BEARINGS:
  Local INA Distributor
  Local Torrington Distributor

FLUSH FUEL CAPS:
  Shaw Aero Devices
  Industrial Road
  East Hampton Airport
  East Hampton, Long Island, New York

DRIVE SHAFTS, CONSTANT VELOCITY, PLUS HEWLAND
DOG RING REGRINDING:
  Traction Products, Inc.
  Weismann R&D Division
  686 West 17th St.
  Costa Mesa, Calif. 92627

HEWLAND PARTS:
  Haas Automotive Imports

WEBSTER GEARS FOR HEWLAND TRANSAXLES:
  Webster Racing Enterprises
  244 Shore Line Highway
  Mill Valley, California

WEISMANN DIFFERENTIALS AND TRANSAXLES:
  Traction Products, Inc.

Order Form

Carroll Smith Consulting Inc.
1236 Via Landeta
Palos Verdes Estates, CA 90274   Date _____

Enclosed please find my check for $_____ . Please send,
postpaid:
_____ Copies of DRIVE TO WIN @ $24.95 ea. ($27.00 in California)
_____ Copies of PREPARE TO WIN @ $19.95 ea. ($21.60 in California)
_____ Copies of TUNE TO WIN @ $19.95 ea. ($21.60 in California)
_____ Copies of ENGINEER TO WIN @ $19.95 ea. ($21.60 in California)
_____ Copies of SCREW TO WIN @ $19.95 ea. ($21.60 in California)

Ship to: _____
Address _____
City and State _____ Zip _____

Order Form

Carroll Smith Consulting Inc.
1236 Via Landeta
Palos Verdes Estates, CA 90274   Date _____

Enclosed please find my check for $_____ . Please send,
postpaid:
_____ Copies of DRIVE TO WIN @ $24.95 ea. ($27.00 in California)
_____ Copies of PREPARE TO WIN @ $19.95 ea. ($21.60 in California)
_____ Copies of TUNE TO WIN @ $19.95 ea. ($21.60 in California)
_____ Copies of ENGINEER TO WIN @ $19.95 ea. ($21.60 in California)
_____ Copies of SCREW TO WIN @ $19.95 ea. ($21.60 in California)

Ship to: _____
Address _____
City and State _____ Zip _____

Order Form

Carroll Smith Consulting Inc.
1236 Via Landeta
Palos Verdes Estates, CA 90274   Date _____

Enclosed please find my check for $_____ . Please send,
postpaid:
_____ Copies of DRIVE TO WIN @ $24.95 ea. ($27.00 in California)
_____ Copies of PREPARE TO WIN @ $19.95 ea. ($21.60 in California)
_____ Copies of TUNE TO WIN @ $19.95 ea. ($21.60 in California)
_____ Copies of ENGINEER TO WIN @ $19.95 ea. ($21.60 in California)
_____ Copies of SCREW TO WIN @ $19.95 ea. ($21.60 in California)

Ship to: _____
Address _____
City and State _____ Zip _____